PRAISE FOR STREET-LEVEL SUPERSTAR:

'Will has finally written his masterpiece. Glad I could be of service'

Lawrence

'This book will make you laugh and cry – Lawrence is a monument to the power of Pop. The best and the worst of it. Essential reading'

Jarvis Cocker

'In a music world awash with fakes, straights and careerists on the make, Lawrence is that rare creature – an artist committed to realising his vision no matter how many humiliations and bad rolls of the dice he's had to endure. Lawrence is the one true poet of austerity Britain and Will Hodgkinson's wonderful book captures the essence and strangeness of the man'

Bobby Gillespie

'I can't tell you how good this book is'

John Niven

'*Street-Level Superstar* has the same sense of discipline and whim as Andy Warhol's *From A to B and Back Again*, with a hint of the entirely personal philosophy of Huysman's *À Rebours*. A fantastic, singular book'

Mat Osman

'There's success and there's failure but Lawrence's destiny was to be something uniquely in-between. A fascinating tale beautifully told'

Brett Anderson

'A litany of perceived slights, unrequited lust, milky tea and liquorice quests. Celibacy, control-freakery, glitter and grit. Lawrence is elusive and obsessive. The enigmatic auto-didact. This funny and often impossible tale of the romantic who always fails in love is grandiose, unflinching and low-rent. His world of vagrant glamour exists in the rare place where fame and destitution meet. It is champagne taste and beer money. *Street-Level Superstar* is a masterclass in self-sabotage from a connoisseur of 20th-century pop'

Adelle Stripe

'If you admire Lawrence for his timeless songs and sublime lyrics, his embrace of the absurd and all-sacrificing dedication to his art – you'll love this book. If you've dismissed him as a self-deluded, self-sabotaging fuck-up of niche interest – you'll love this book. If you're fascinated by the legions of anecdotes mythologising Lawrence's eccentricities, control-freakery and failed attempts at pop stardom – you'll love this book. If you want to read a hilarious, infuriating and ultimately insightful and touching account of what it is like to spend a year in Lawrence's company – you'll love this book. I've felt all of the above and I loved this book'

Miki Berenyi

'Lawrence is Britain's greatest enthusiast for the arcane and unloved, who can find magic in suburban sweet shops, high-end book shops, or Chas and Dave B-sides'

Bob Stanley

'[An] excellent book . . . worthy of your full attention. If you love *Anvil*, if you love Paul Simpson's *Revolutionary Spirit*, if you love Copey's *Head On*, this is a worthy addition to your library of mythologising music's messier corners. Superb'

Joel Morris

'Will Hodgkinson has written a brilliant and affectionate book about a year in the life of the mysterious pop legend Lawrence. As he accompanies him on a series of walks across various urban hinterlands, searching for records, liquorice and other clues about how the man under the blue vinyl visor became who he is today. This beautifully told zig-zag wandering biography is an utter joy from start to finish'

Caroline Catz

'This is a terrific book; I didn't want it to finish. Loved it, loved it, loved it!'

Nige Tassell

'Completely brilliant. Really unusual and original. It tells you something very specific about the nature of fame and the pursuit of fame. It's fantastic'

Mark Ellen

STREET-LEVEL
SUPERSTAR

STREET-LEVEL SUPERSTAR

A YEAR WITH LAWRENCE
BY WILL HODGKINSON

NINE
EIGHT
BOOKS

NINE
EIGHT
BOOKS

NEB 029

First published in the UK in 2024 by Nine Eight Books
An imprint of Black & White Publishing Group
A Bonnier Books UK company
4th Floor, Victoria House, Bloomsbury Square, London, WC1B 4DA
Owned by Bonnier Books, Sveavägen 56, Stockholm, Sweden

🅧 @nineeightbooks

⊡ @nineeightbooks

Hardback ISBN: 978-1-7851-2022-0
eBook ISBN: 978-1-7851-2021-3

A CIP catalogue record for this book is available from the British Library.

Publishing director: Pete Selby
Editor: James Lilford

Cover design by Alex Kirby and Paul Kelly
Typeset by IDSUK (Data Connection) Ltd
Printed and bound in Great Britain by Clays Ltd, Elcograf S.p.A

3 5 7 9 10 8 6 4

Nine Eight Books is an imprint of Bonnier Books UK
www.bonnierbooks.co.uk

Stars must be killers, always striking first and last. They have to be so totally obsessed and paranoid about this year's vision of themselves that it's beyond obsession – it's reality, logical and natural. There's no remorse when they kill, no regrets when they pimp and no shame when they whore. And it's really a fair exchange: the world needs them and they need the world.

Andrew Loog Oldham, *Stoned*

As soon as I opened my eyes I started wondering, by force of habit, whether I had anything to look forward to today.

Knut Hamsun, *Hunger*

CONTENTS

CHAPTER ONE

TEMPLE FORTUNE

'Golders Green,' said Lawrence, 'is the worst place in the world when you need to go for a pee.'

We stepped out of the Underground station for the north London suburb, which since the 1950s has been home to the city's Orthodox and Hasidic Jewish community, to find the public conveniences closed, forlorn, blocked out by a dirty-grey, wire-mesh fence.

'This is the only neighbourhood in London where you can't find a lonely bush or tree to relieve yourself against,' Lawrence declared, shuffling his narrow, surprisingly fast-moving little frame from concourse to high street. The black curtains of hair on either side of his baseball cap flapped gently in the wind. 'You do not want to be caught peeing behind a bush in Golders Green. In certain areas of south London you can do that, and I could write a guide book to weeing in the open, but here you must be respectful.'

Lawrence first came to the area a few years previously. He had taken up long walks in the suburbs, with no map and no purpose in mind, as a way of clearing his head, finding solutions to problems and, most importantly, coming up with ideas for songs. Perhaps Golders

Green would provide him with the inspiration for that elusive hit he had been aiming for since 1980, the hit that would transform his life and envelop him in a glorious bubble of money and fame. He had been wandering about Muswell Hill one day when he saw a sign for North Finchley. Knowing nothing about the place beyond the fact that the teenage punk band Eater came from there, he went to carry out an investigation.

'I thought, *Let's have a look around, see what kind of a place Eater grew up in.* As it turns out, Finchley is a very suburban area. That led me to Finchley Central and from there I ended up here. I fell in love.'

There was so much for Lawrence to love in Golders Green: a self-contained community; an atmosphere of order and the reigning-in of chaos; the mysticism of a belief system in which God is embedded into all things; a strict dress code; complex rules regarding food; a group of people steeped far deeper in tradition and ritual than wider society allows. For someone who has never connected to the internet, whose one concession to the modern age is a grey rectangle of a phone that can make and receive calls and not much else, whose food issues restrict him to crackers, cups of tea and varieties of liquorice, all this proved not just appealing but profound. Then Lawrence discovered a residential enclave at the heart of Golders Green called Temple Fortune.

'Can you believe it? Temple Fortune sounds like a Felt song. The first album had "Fortune" and also "Templeroy". I was walking down the high street when I saw it, written on a poster outside a bank in felt tip, but the bank was no more and the poster was unofficial and I was left thinking: *Is it real?* I carried on a little bit and saw an actual sign, proving it is indeed an actual place. How did it come about? Why is it called that? It's where I should have lived when I first moved to London from Birmingham. If only I'd known, things would have been so different.'

The first Felt album, *Crumbling the Antiseptic Beauty*, came out in 1982, three years after Lawrence fashioned a plan from his teenage bedroom in the Birmingham village of Water Orton: Felt would release ten albums and ten singles in ten years while following a tight musical and visual aesthetic. This was to be an art band, with black-and-white photographs of Lawrence and his co-conspirators looking moody and deep, forming the perfect accompaniment to hazy, dream-like music dominated by the flowing guitar of Maurice Deebank, a retiring virtuoso Lawrence discovered in the village who he saw as his passport to glory.

'I had been going around telling everyone I was the guy who liked guitar music but didn't like hard rock,' said Lawrence as he walked with increasing haste through Golders Green. 'Maurice turned up at my house one day, so I said, "Can you tune my guitar?" And he went, "Er, yeah," as if to say "Of course I can." For me, it was an impossible task, but he did it in a few seconds and instantly I was overwhelmed. He started strumming to check it was in tune and I went: "What the hell is that?" "Calm down, it's only 'Mr Tambourine Man'." That was the point I knew this was the guy for me. In a small village of a couple of thousand people, right on my doorstep, was a genius. I was very lucky.'

Given Felt was Lawrence's vision, and that he was someone who dealt foremost in words and ideas, it is surprising that more than half of *Crumbling the Antiseptic Beauty* is instrumental. Deebank's melodic twists and turns accompany Lawrence's rudimentary but sturdy rhythm guitar, not much bass and drums that are never accompanied by cymbals or hi-hats because of Lawrence enforcing an outlawing of all accompanying percussion, known in the trade as metalwork.

'I realised that the moment I started a band,' he said of his metalwork ban, 'I kept hearing this horrible hissing sound on records and thought: *Wouldn't it be great if we could create music without that awful noise?* I had such trouble heading down this path, with engineers and so on going, "What do you mean, no hi-hat?" As it turns out, Peter Gabriel didn't like them either.'

He took a moment to stop and stare into the rain.

'If only I'd known.'

The vocals are buried so deep in the mix that it is hard to decipher the words, but on 'Fortune', Lawrence sings something about breaking his back, feeling like it's all too much. With Felt, nothing is clear.

'I thought about what Johnny Rotten said: be influenced by me but don't copy me,' said Lawrence, hobbling past a kosher wine shop and the Carmelli bagel bakery in search of that elusive bush to relieve himself behind. 'We were going to be the new underground. There was a small avenue to head down and you saw it work with Echo & the Bunnymen and Orange Juice: go on John Peel, be on the cover of the *NME*. On top of that, I wanted to be a mysterious pop star, a famous figure who wasn't seen all that much. I would never go on the *Six O'Clock News* or anything like that. Not that I ever had the chance to put it to the test, but all I can say is: I wouldn't do it if they asked me.'

The unattainability seeped into the music. '"Fortune" is about suicide, the feeling that life is too much to bear. With "Templeroy", I had a sheet of lyrics and I was singing odd things from it. Shielding from reality – that's what I was trying to do. When I think about it now, Felt was about hiding. He's singing, but you can't quite hear

4

him. You can see him, but you can't quite get to him. The sound has an ambient quality, like there is depth you can't grasp onto. At the same time Felt were going to be my band of brothers, like in a buddy movie, *Thunderbolt and Lightfoot* for example. But it never happened because Felt were the kind of people where, when someone left the room, everybody would be going, "Did you see the state of his shoes?"'

He reflected on this awhile.

'And I was the worst of the lot.'

We pushed our way through the rain.

'I'm a lonesome figure.'

The dream of stardom began in February 1977, when Lawrence went into the newsagent's and saw a copy of the *New Musical Express* with Television on the front cover. It was the photograph of the New York band led by the cadaverous Tom Verlaine and the movie star-handsome Richard Lloyd that grabbed him, and he was impressed by the fact that the cover story related not to an interview, but a review by Nick Kent of Television's debut album, *Marquee Moon*. By May, Lawrence had enough money to buy *Marquee Moon* for himself and he was entranced by its musical complexity, poetic mystery and brittle energy. He knew he had to do something similar and, in Maurice Deebank, he had the maestro to make it happen.

'Maurice didn't know Television, didn't hear Television, didn't like Television, wasn't bothered about Television. He thought punk was ridiculous and he didn't care for the subtleties of the fashions I was interested in. He was a classical guy, and I thought: *This is fortunate because the way he plays guitar sounds like my favourite group.* But there were tensions at the heart of Felt from the very beginning.'

For Lawrence, details were of neurotic importance. One press shot was made up of the four band members' footwear, all thin-soled, lattice-topped Dr Martens-style shoes from a fashionable '80s shop called Robot, which Lawrence managed to talk his less sartorially obsessed band members into shelling out on. Check shirts from the second-hand American imports shop Flip on the King's Road and pegged trousers from Kensington Market were also mandatory. There was a ban on guitars in a sunburst finish and a ruling on white plectrums only. 'And guess what Maurice's first guitar was? That's right, a sunburst finish. So we got it sprayed black. It was the first rule and Maurice adhered to it, but the arguments started soon after.'

As Lawrence saw it, there is an essential training period to being in a band and it must be adhered to with rigorous discipline. 'I can only equate it to an army structure. If you do your basic training and you learn how to shoot your gun, you win the war. If you don't bother with basic training and you don't know how to use your gun, it will jam and you will get a bullet in the head. Unfortunately, the rules were broken early on and these people, these musicians, didn't want to toe the line. They didn't want to be told what to wear. They didn't want to be told they're not allowed to drink. It was incredibly frustrating. Bit by bit, your dream is dismantled by other people and you realise you are on your own. Again.'

I remembered another early photograph of Felt from December 1980. Lawrence is staring into the camera with clenched-teeth intensity, an art band pin-up in his striped shirt, flecked woollen sports jacket fitting perfectly onto narrow shoulders, short hair scuffed with just a touch of bohemian unruliness, and brown eyes shining with the frustration of someone who can see the pot of gold at the end of the rainbow, but has no way of getting there. The band's burly drummer Tony Race looks, in his Fred Perry shirt and suspicious expression, like he's about to challenge the photographer to a fight. Maurice Deebank's weathered leather jacket and vacant stare almost fits the bill, but his spiky mullet hairstyle definitely does not. Then there is bassist Nick Gilbert, a Birmingham everyman pulling a comical face at his old school friend, as if to drag him down from whatever lofty perch he's tried to clamber onto.

'That photo tells you the whole story of the early days,' said Lawrence sadly. 'The guy who had been my friend since I was seven was goofing around to make me laugh, because he knew I wanted to look cool and distant and his goal was to jinx that. But I'm taking no notice at all. I'm already preparing for the catwalk. They were regular guys from Birmingham – one had an apprenticeship at British Leyland, the other at Dunlop – and there was no way they were going to be in the band for long. I would say to them, "We're going to do a photo session for the *NME*. Let's get ready." But they didn't even want to make the trip down to London. It was the beginning of the downfall.'

Lawrence couldn't talk about the past any more. Not because he didn't want to dwell on it, but because there was a pressing need at hand and it was dominating everything. 'The only time I'm focused on reality,' he announced, 'is when I'm desperate for a wee. Forget about meditation. We only live in the moment when we're on the verge of wetting ourselves.'

We had to find a place where Lawrence could urinate without offending the community he had developed such a respect for, so we kept going along the high street in the rain until ending up on an unlovely litter-strewn strip of the North Circular. There was a yellow and brown patch of scrubby earth underneath a flyover, out of view from everyone except people zipping by in cars and lorries, who might have been able to spot, if they strained their eyes through the diesel smog, a narrow figure in a clear visor baseball cap with a Gap Kids rainbow balaclava stretched over it. Then it was back to Golders Green.

Our current problem was that Lawrence, with his button eyes shining out of a face with papery skin, a narrow downward curve of a mouth and cheeks hollowed to the point of emaciation, had a tendency to inspire suspicion. Paul Kelly, who spent seven years making a film about him called *Lawrence of Belgravia*, remembered the day he told Lawrence to wait by his car while he went off to get something from the flat. 'By the time I got back, four police were surrounding him and he had his hands on the bonnet. It is a regular occurrence.'

That suspicion extended to the Orthodox Jewish community Lawrence was hoping would take him to its collective bosom. 'It has been happening for years. I wrote a poem about walking these streets with the line: "I'm the same as you. Why won't you talk to me?". It's quite sad that I can't make friends in Golders Green, but perhaps they think I could be trouble. "He might ask us for a spare room. He looks a bit homeless." I go up to the men in the big hats and say: "Gentlemen, hello."'

He threw his arms wide open.

'And I get nothing back.'

Years before he started his regular walks through north London's Orthodox enclave, Lawrence wrote a tribute to the traditions of the Jewish faith called 'Useless Foreskin' by the Rabbis of Tomorrow. 'I gave it to Vic Godard of Subway Sect. At a gig of his, Vic came up to me and said, "We should do a song together," which was a dream come true, one of the biggest moments of my life, because it doesn't get better than Vic Godard as far as I'm concerned. I sent him the lyrics to 'Useless Foreskin'. And he said no! He said it wasn't his style.'

Vic Godard formed Subway Sect with his friend Rob Symmons at the age of nineteen, after Malcolm McLaren spotted them at a Ramones concert at the Roundhouse in July 1976 and said they looked like a band. From then on, from playing with the Sex Pistols, the Clash and Siouxsie and the Banshees at the 100 Club for the September 1976 punk special, to rejecting punk fashion in favour of utilitarian grey, to writing sharp songs inspired by a love of French literature and film, Vic Godard provided Lawrence with a template on what a pop visionary could be.

'Number One Subway Sect Fan in Birmingham was my official title,' Lawrence announced, although I suspected it was a title awarded by himself. 'Rob Lloyd of the Prefects was into them, but they shared a stage with Subway Sect, so it wasn't the same. I was a pure fan.'

Lawrence gestured at a man in traditional Hasidic dress: long black coat, baggy black trousers, curled forelocks reaching down to a snowy beard, and a large round fur hat topped off with a clear plastic sheath to protect it from the rain.

'Details like that are just brilliant,' he said of the rain covering. 'When I first started coming here, I wanted to know where to buy the clothes because I couldn't find any shops on Oxford Street that sold this gear, so I went up to a man and said, "Where did you get that hat? It's lovely." Turns out there is a hat shop in a back street in Stamford Hill. The man measured my head, told me the size of hat I needed, and announced he could do it for £125, but unfortunately, they were all in black and I wanted a light shade of grey. That was when I realised: there are rules here that must be followed.'

Felt was set up with the idea of doing your best within strict confines. As per Lawrence's ideal, there was a structure to the day, a dress code, self-discipline and a sense of ritual. 'Even though I'm very liberal in outlook, there have to be parameters, which is what the Jewish community here realised. These things apply to make you a better person.'

On one side of Golders Green Road was a superstore called Accessory World, which catered to the clothing needs of the traditional Orthodox woman: long check skirts, quality jumpers, the very best wigs. On the other was a pink-fronted boutique called Bitz of Glitz, which had in its window bright-pink headbands and headscarves in colourful symmetrical prints.

'Accessory World has it all for girls and women, while Bitz of Glitz is there for a little bit of *jeuje* on the weekends,' Lawrence explained. 'The women must shave their heads, and I don't want to say anything negative about this community, but I have to admit I'm not into that, and it worries me. If I became Orthodox, I fear I would cause disruption from the beginning, which I don't want to do at all. I might say: "Let's stop with these wigs. Let's move into the modern age, at least when it comes to hair."

'Inevitably, it wouldn't go down well because my wife would reply: "But my dad and granddad say I have to wear this wig."

'"I'm telling you not to."

'"I don't care what you tell me. I'm leaving and going back to Mum's. And you can forget about coming to temple this evening."

Once again, I would be ostracised, my marriage in tatters. That's why I'm always on the outside, looking in.'

The alienation began with punk rock in 1977, when Lawrence was fifteen, although a defining crisis happened nine years previously. He was born on a council estate in Edgbaston, an area of Birmingham with a botanical garden at its borders, and the way he described it sixty-one years later made it seem like a concrete Eden. Growing up near the centre on Bristol Road, a main artery for the city immortalised in 'Bristol Road Leads to Dachau' by the Birmingham punks the Prefects, Lawrence spent his infant years watching city kids getting the bus home from school, dreaming of the day he would be among their number. He achieved that dream aged five, but two years later tragedy struck. A boy called Derek got stabbed in the back, right on the estate. Lawrence was standing around with the other kids when Derek trotted past in a pastel blue polo neck, blood running down his back.

'Derek was fine, actually,' remembered Lawrence. 'The real tragedy was that my mom saw it as the final straw as far as living in the city went. We were like, "Oh dear, Derek's been stabbed," but we didn't care so much that we wanted to move. No longer could we grow up alongside these horrible children, who were our friends, and we had to move right to the edge of Birmingham, almost in Warwickshire. We went from a council estate in the city centre, which I loved, to an old railway cottage in a tiny village, which my parents thought was safe, but was in fact surrounded by the two of the biggest estates in Britain: Chelmsley Wood and Castle Vale. I was very angry with my mom. I was seven.'

Not long after the family moved, the violence of the countryside made itself apparent in the most visceral way imaginable. Lawrence returned from junior school to see his sister Beverly, older by a year, sitting at the kitchen table in a nightie, the dull white of Calamine lotion patched onto angry red cuts and swollen purple bruises all over her body. Two policewomen were at the table with her. She had come out of school that afternoon with her friend Carla to find a man sitting on a bench on the green next to the school, an unfamiliar red sports car parked nearby. Once they were away from the school gates, he tried to grab the two girls. Carla ran into the village but Beverly, panicking, ran in the direction of a series of fields called the Stiles and was chased across six of them, clambering through hedges and brambles. He never caught her.

'My sister was eight. My mom moved us to this suburb, 9 miles out of the centre, because she wanted to get us out of trouble, and the first thing that happened is my sister is almost killed by a paedophile. It summed it up for me. It is so much more dangerous in the countryside.'

Watching *A Clockwork Orange* a few years later didn't help, not least because of a scene where Alex and his Droogs attack a writer in his country house. 'That was certainly terrifying, although my fear of the countryside is really to do with the supernatural. Wild animals live in the jungle, ghosts and spirits live in the countryside and they cause untold trauma for people with a vivid imagination.'

Once the family were settled into the routine of rural life, Lawrence's imagination went into hyperdrive. There was a farm at the edge of Water Orton and a bridge was built over the nearby motorway so the farmer could get his cows across it, the downside being it connected the village with the notorious Chelmsley Wood Estate. That meant Lawrence suffered regular visions of marauders pouring over the bridge to rape, pillage and burn Water Orton to the ground.

'I now had a lot of time on my hands, which meant boredom became the real killer because I kept thinking up horrific scenarios. There was a day when the skinheads from the estate invaded, a great big gang of them, probably only twenty or so, but in my mind it seemed like hundreds. It only happened once, but from then on I was thinking, *This is going to occur all the time.* It was a terrifying world over that cow bridge, which is why I've spent years being angry with my parents for taking us out of the city and into the suburbs. But the only thing I can say is: I wouldn't have met Maurice Deebank if we hadn't moved. Should I still be angry with Mother? I'm not sure I should.'

Lawrence found salvation in pop music. He was twelve when in 1972 he saw T. Rex perform 'Metal Guru' on *Top of the Pops* and it changed something inside him. 'From then on, I was T. Rex mad. I think I was actually in love with Marc Bolan. It was the moment I knew what I wanted to do with my life.'

Still, dreams of pop stardom were an awkward fit with the realities of early '70s life on the outskirts of Birmingham; of growing up with an older sister, a significantly younger brother called Sam, a father who worked on the markets and a mother who came from the Joan Collins school of big-haired glamour but, lacking Collins' resources, had a job on her hands in keeping the whole operation going.

'I despised our home. It was dirty and horrible, and my mom couldn't keep on top of it. The railway cottage was ramshackle and unkempt, one of three in a row on a piece of waste ground, the worst house in the village. My room was particularly horrible, probably because I had to share it with my brother. She got halfway round with the wallpaper and just stopped, so my side of the room was left with lining paper. Obviously, I could have done it myself, but you don't do anything in your room until you leave home, do you? Annoyingly, my parents were happy there because it was cheaper than a council house. The rent was seven pounds a week.'

Beyond writing FELT on a wall (having come up with the band name in his mid-teens before there was a band to go with it), Lawrence didn't bother making any home improvements. He simply expected his mother to do them and was duly outraged when she failed to meet his exacting standards.

'I would go over to Nick Gilbert's house to listen to records and his parents had everything tip-top, which struck me straight away: this is how I'm going to live. What I didn't take into account is that if Nick Gilbert made us a cup of tea, he would clean up after we finished, which I would never dream of doing. As far as I was concerned, washing clothes, making the food . . . that was a mother's job. If my mom asked me to make an effort, I would go, "You wanted me. I didn't ask to be born." I was one of them, so it couldn't have been easy for her. She did have dreams of doing up the house and making it nice, but three kids and a dog stopped everything.'

Not just any dog, but a vicious bull-terrier called Lucy, who Lawrence's father got after joining the English Bull Terrier Club. Bull's Eye, malevolent companion to Bill Sykes in *Oliver Twist*, was a bull-terrier, but otherwise the sullen breed was an unknown in Lawrence's world. 'Nobody in Birmingham had seen one before and I was so embarrassed. People would ask me, "Is it a pig?". It attacked everyone, which is just wrong. The neighbour threatened to shoot it. After my parents got divorced, we came home one day and Mom was on the sofa, chain-smoking. We said, "Where's Lucy?"

'"Oh, I put her down."

'We all went, "YES!"'

At least it didn't affect Lawrence's popularity. 'I had a free pass at school with the older kids because my sister was a year above me and she was really cool, totally different to me: very confident, top of the pecking order. She enabled me to be recognised at school and I was okay thanks to her. Then she got pregnant and married at sixteen. Lost potential for sure.'

It struck him deep. There is a song on the final Felt album, 1989's *Me and a Monkey on the Moon*, called 'She Deals In Crosses'. 'To you it seemed so simple / Yours was just another life,' sings Lawrence in a lamenting, off-key tone against mournful country-rock backing; 'When you left school / You became a mother and a wife.' The chorus, what there is of it, consists of Lawrence asking: 'Hey sister, what are you doing with yourself?'

We walked through the rain into an empty park, where the swings swayed bleakly in the wind and rivulets of water coursed down the silvery contours of an uninviting slide. Rainy days in Lawrence's childhood meant a trip to the library, where he discovered the way words could be put together to create not just rhythmic drive and poetic impact, but also the evocation of other worlds.

'I knew I was good at words because I had been writing poetry since I was eight,' said Lawrence as we stuck to the concrete path in the hope of keeping his Yogi footwear − round-toed suede lace-up shoes made by the same people behind a mod-tinged '90s streetwear label he liked called The Duffer of St George − free of mud. 'God knows why, but I joined the library at seven and was reading books all the time. I wanted to be a poet. Songs seemed like such a hard thing to do and poetry was an easier route to take. Then punk happened.'

It was both the eureka moment and the derailing force in Lawrence's life. In January 1977, he walked into class for registration and saw a girl reading a copy of the weekly music paper *Sounds*. 'I snatched it off her, like you would at that time – well, like I would – and went, "What's this?" I would never normally read a newspaper because they were inky and it would get on my fingers, but there was something about punk in there that caught my attention. Next week, I bought the *NME* for the first time and there was a little article on Generation X, not even a whole page, and it said: "We don't drink, we don't take drugs." I thought, *Ooh, that's good*. It wasn't actually true, but it was a novel attitude. From then on, I would buy the *NME* or *Sounds* every week.'

Before punk, Lawrence was a high-street kid with an interest in books and poems, a protective elder sister and a healthy crowd of friends. After punk, he knew the order of his life would be upset for ever. Beverly, married with a kid, was no longer in the bedroom next door, sharing stories of wild nights out, so at fifteen he went to the Birmingham punk club Barbarella's on his own, where he knew nobody and had no idea of how to talk to the older, unusually dressed people surrounding him. A few months earlier, in March 1977, he went to see Iggy Pop at the Birmingham Hippodrome, where, playing keyboards at the side of stage, was David Bowie.

'That made things even more confusing,' said Lawrence, staring glass-eyed into the mist. 'The support was the Vibrators, a bandwagon-jumping punk band who didn't get much respect, and yet they had the sound I liked: fast and angry. I didn't like Iggy Pop, with all that writhing about. Then there was David Bowie, who should have been amazing but, by an incredible misfortune, it was the only time he didn't dress well. He was wearing jeans, a

16

checked shirt and horrible mountain boots: no glamour at all, just a man playing keyboards at the side of the stage, and I thought, *Okay, he's having a break from dressing well. He's doing it on purpose.* In the year when he needed to look great, when punk happened and he could have used the moment to show these guys how it is done, he went the other way. A year later, he came back and looked brilliant in extra-wide trousers, which we called Bowie bags, and a Henley shirt with three buttons. Just my luck I had to see him in 1977, his year off from fashion.'

Not that punk itself offered any easy answers. Lawrence didn't have a leather jacket, he didn't wear a safety pin through his ear, he didn't rip his T-shirts or scrawl anarchy signs on them. And he was so small that even if he did find the right clothes, it would have been impossible to get them in his size.

'I had been in sartorial heaven and now I was thrown into hell,' he cried. 'I was known at school as the high street kid who knew how to look good in affordable items, and suddenly it was a case of *Where the hell do I get these clothes from*? I knew there was a shop on the King's Road [Malcolm McLaren and Vivienne Westwood's Seditionaries, the Ground Zero of punk fashion], but there was no way I could get there. Here comes this amazing fashion and I'm lost . . . totally lost. I couldn't get the look. But what look did I want anyway?'

There must have been punks in Birmingham, I suggested, to look to for inspiration. 'Only a handful, but they were amazing, the elite. They all hung out at Barbarella's, which as far as I was concerned, was the best club in the world. John Taylor was around, long before he ended up in Duran Duran, but he didn't look like John Taylor back then. He looked even worse than me.'

Actually, there was someone he knew at Barbarella's, another future member of Duran Duran, in fact. A year above Lawrence at Park Hall Comprehensive was the band's drummer, Roger Taylor, whose best friend was a boy called Jonathan Hodgson. Jonathan had been to the house in Water Orton a few times because his doctor father's receptionist, one Pat Potts, lived next door and Jonathan got dropped off at Lawrence's whenever his father needed to attend to important matters at Miss Potts' house. That's where, on fireworks night, Jonathan found himself eating baked potatoes and standing by the bonfire next to a legendary figure of the school.

'Lawrence's sister Beverly was in the same year as me and I was madly in love with her,' remembered Jonathan, who formed a post-punk band with Roger Taylor called the Scent Organs. 'It was impossible to talk to her because she went out with the bad boys, not wimpy middle-class student types like me. And I think she found the fact that I was so tongue-tied around her vaguely amusing. I have a strong memory of her in white flared jeans, an orange T-shirt and long black hair: a hippie version of Marie Osmond. Lawrence, with his thatch of chestnut hair, looked a lot like Donny Osmond. They were the Osmonds of Park Hall.'

This proved a problem a few years later, when Lawrence would see Jonathan and Roger Taylor at punk gigs and naturally wanted to be their friend but wasn't allowed. 'It wasn't that we didn't like him,' claimed Jonathan. 'It was more a case of, "Oh, it's that kid from school." For one thing, he was a year below us. He was so shy that it was difficult to talk to him, and on top of that, he didn't look like a punk. We dyed our hair and wore ripped T-shirts, but he dressed like he was going to a supper club: very suave, in a smart shirt and a nice jacket with lapels.'

'It was a brown zip-up jacket, actually,' Lawrence countered. 'He's getting mixed up with the early days of Felt. Still, it's true. I couldn't get it right.' Staring at the swings as they made a sad insistent squeak, taking a handkerchief from his oversized coat pocket to give his narrow, dripping nose a wipe, Lawrence confessed it was not something he was proud of, but it was not until 1978 that he found his way. Help came from an Army & Navy store in Birmingham, where surplus clothing from Britain's military, nursing staff and other uniformed personnel gave him the chance to adapt the fashions of punk to his own neat sensibility.

'I did get some lovely grey trousers in there.'

Finally, the rain stopped, the wind became less of an enemy to coiffured hairstyles, and a vibrant burst of sunlight cracked the clouds and bathed us, to borrow a phrase from a famous Felt song, in a golden glow. The ideal time then to enter Temple Fortune, Lawrence's Shangri-La of north London.

'Get ready for this,' said Lawrence as we walked down a narrow alleyway with crisp packets and blue plastic bags lying sodden in puddles on the concrete. He claimed the rain had brought out the rubbish, and if it was summer, he would be clearing it up and putting it in a bin as a free service to the community. 'I like this alley because it leads to one of those *The Lion, the Witch and the Wardrobe* situations: another world.'

Temple Fortune, so named because the Knights Templar took ownership of the land sometime around 1243, is a smart if unremarkable chunk of wealthy suburbia: box hedges, semi-detached mock Tudor homes, little mopeds with rain coverings occupying paved driveways. A blue 1960s Triumph Herald sat by the kerb on a wide residential road, dwarfed by a minivan on one side and a black SUV on the other. The feeling was of a comfortable, rather than a flash or ostentatious, neighbourhood, an old-fashioned place. Its quietness, lack of people and unobtrusive order brought a sense of 1950s calm.

'It is a bit like a horror movie,' said Lawrence in a reverential tone as we paced along the empty street and tried to peer through living-room windows for clues about the lives inside. A car belonging to the Shomrim, a neighbourhood watch-style police organisation, drove past slowly – very slowly.

'Where is everyone?' wondered Lawrence, lilting about like a bendy straw in the wind. 'Probably at the edge of their curtains, looking at me. For a while, I was coming here every day. I would walk around, talking to myself like some crazy old gent, dreaming that if I won the Euro Millions – £72 million, I think it was – I would buy four houses in the London suburbs: north, east, south and west. And the first one would be right here in Temple Fortune.'

The sadness was that Lawrence had nobody to bring to his favourite place in the world. Nobody but me, that is. 'I'd love to show this to my girlfriend. But then I remember: I don't have a girlfriend. I will never have a girlfriend. And even if I did, if I brought her here, she would start doing all the things that drive me mad.'

Stopping for a moment under a large beech tree to escape the glare of the sun, Lawrence acted out a possible scenario.

'"What do you want to walk here for?"' he began, playing the part of his imaginary girlfriend.

'"Because I like it."'

'"At least let's go somewhere interesting, like Kew Gardens."'

'"But I do find it interesting."'

'"You're looking at streets and houses. Are you mad? Besides, my foot aches. I've got the wrong shoes on. Why didn't you tell me we were walking for 10 miles?"

'"I did tell you. If you hate it so much, why don't you go home?"

'"Alright then, I will. And don't bother calling me ever again."'

The answer to Lawrence's inability to co-exist peacefully with his fellow men and women lay in building his own world. Before enlisting Maurice Deebank for Felt on a permanent basis, he worked out how to write, record and release a noise-laden 45 called 'Index' from his bedroom in Water Orton. He sent two copies to John Peel, but the BBC Radio 1 DJ never played it, so Lawrence wrote a letter to Peel, demanding he send the copies back.

'It was the nastiest, most vindictive letter I have ever received,' John Peel later stated. Nonetheless – given that Lawrence cited the late Peel, alongside Rough Trade (who never got behind Felt) and Mark E. Smith (who did, inviting them to play with the Fall in Manchester, Liverpool and London in July 1980), on his future band Mozart Estate's 2022 tribute to the alternative music world, 'Record Store Day' – it seems the impact and importance of Peel never left him. Nonetheless, 'Index' made it to single of the week in the music paper *Sounds*, and a deal with Cherry Red Records duly followed.

'At the beginning, I thought: *Here we are, up and running*,' said Lawrence as we headed back towards Golders Green. 'I realise now that I kept getting it wrong. Mark E. Smith came up to me after one gig and said, "You have a good rock drummer there." But I couldn't get past the fact that he had curly hair, so I fired him.'

I asked Lawrence what he had against people with curly hair.

'I love curly hair,' he assured me. 'Just not on drummers in Felt.'

A bigger mistake was a generational one. All the alternative British bands of Lawrence's generation, the white ones at least, wanted to be like the Velvet Underground, with everyone from the Weather Prophets to Primal Scream to the Jesus and Mary Chain wearing leather trousers and Ray-Bans, combining sweet childlike melody with fuzzed-out noise, and singing about rain, candy and other things that could be interpreted as both druggy and innocent at the same time. But there was only one Velvet Underground.

'We all got it wrong,' said Lawrence. 'We got sucked into this idea that being like the Velvet Underground was a free pass to credibility. We thought it was okay to be rough and tumble because the Velvet Underground were, but it was a misapprehension. They were a one-off.'

Nonetheless, for a boy from suburban Birmingham, the in-house band of Andy Warhol's mid-'60s Factory seemed like a portal to a more glamorous, exciting, arty world. 'In 1980, Andy Warhol's memoir *Popism* came out, there was Jean Stein's *Edie* [the classic oral history on Edie Sedgwick, troubled rich kid and Warhol superstar], and all of a sudden you could get an insight into what happened at the Factory. Then, in 1983, along came *Up-Tight: The Velvet Underground Story* by Victor Bockris and it summed up everything about Felt. We were uptight. It was: top button done up, never have your shirt hanging out of your trousers, shoes must be shiny at all times. I didn't realise it at the time, but it was staring at me from the cover of this book: uptight.'

In the early days of Felt, Lawrence had a job at Birmingham Repertory Theatre. It afforded him the luxury of moving out of Water Orton and into his own flat in the city, which he kept in a state of hysterically good order. 'It was a fantastic time. I was the cellar man. "Hey, cellar man!" they went, when they wanted me to do something. I got the beer to the bars, putting the crates in a dumb waiter, and packed everything into the day: got up early, worked on a song for half an hour, went to work, thought about the song all day before finishing it at night. But if you want to make it big, you can't have a day job and that's the dilemma, because work is good for the soul. To be without purpose is the worst thing I can think of.'

The rain started up again. Now it was cold as well as wet and we hadn't eaten anything all day. You wondered how this frail man did it: hauling barrels of beer up from the cellar of Birmingham Rep in his late teens, leading Felt, Denim, Go-Kart Mozart and Mozart Estate through young adulthood and middle age, wandering the suburban streets for hours on end in his early sixties, never seeming to eat a thing. Finally, he relented and allowed us to stop for a cup of tea at a bakery on the high street, where he reflected on the eroding effects of time on people, civilisation, principles. There was a line in 'Problems' by the Sex Pistols that summed up the vulgarity of modern life for Lawrence: 'Eat your heart out on a plastic tray'.

'Today there is no more, "Get your best cutlery out",' he said with Colonel Blimpish disapproval as we sat down at a table, only after he'd instructed the man behind the counter on precisely how much milk to put into his Styrofoam tea cup. 'All that has finished. John Lydon saw it happening, but then he went on *I'm a Celebrity . . . Get Me Out Of Here!*. And Lou Reed got a mullet in the '80s. There was no inkling of what was around the corner and it was crushing. Age has an adverse effect on most people, but perhaps those particularly bad decisions come with the complacency wealth and fame brings, because I'm sixty-one and I think, *Wow, it has never happened to me*. I never had a hit record, which meant I never stopped caring.'

That's when Lawrence spotted something nasty in the fridge, sitting alongside the pickled herring and the cream cheese.

'The modern world is catching up with these places,' he muttered darkly, gesturing with a subtle nod of his plastic visor at the fridge. 'I've just spotted an individual portion of spaghetti Bolognese.'

Lawrence stared out of the window, at the men ambling by, the women picking children up from school, the teenagers coming out of a library and shrieking happily as they ran into the rain. He leaned over the Formica table, as if to reveal a secret with dire implications for humanity.

'Changes are afoot.'

He looked from left to right, then leaned in even closer.

'I'm not happy about it.'

CHAPTER TWO

ON THE ROAD

'I've got a great idea for your book.'

There had been plenty of great ideas for the book already and most of them involved the word 'no'.

'No dust jacket,' he insisted, when the idea of a book was first mooted. 'We have to print the title directly onto the board.'*

The publisher had no problem with that. It would keep costs down.

'No talking to the other people in Felt. I'd rather you didn't mention them at all, actually. We don't want a list of boring names, do we?'

What about Maurice Deebank, the Jimi Hendrix of Water Orton? Or Martin Duffy, the sixteen-year-old boy wonder who joined in 1985 after answering an advert Lawrence posted up in the Birmingham branch of Virgin Records, which posed the question: 'Do You Want To Be A Rock 'n' Roll Star?' Duffy's swirling, seesawing organ transformed the sound of Felt, adding harmonic richness and a kaleidoscope lens of candy-coloured '60s psychedelia, which moved the band away from the atmospheric mysteriousness

---

* A year later, after demanding a matt finish that didn't exist in any known universe, Lawrence came up with the ideal solution: a dust jacket.

of the early albums and towards the groovy song-based immediacy of the later ones.

'Even if you do go behind my back and contact Deebank, good luck getting him to talk about me. As for Duffy, he's dead.'

Also, there could be no use of the word 'just'.

Why not?

'I just don't like it!'

Under no circumstances could I use Lawrence's surname, or even acknowledge that he has one (he doesn't). There would be no descriptive passages about walking and talking. It was fine to talk about walking. It was fine to walk about, talking. Just not at the same time.

So, I was wondering what his latest idea for the book would be as he stood on an empty street in Ramsgate, in an acrylic jumper emblazoned with the Lidl brand logo under an oversized maroon zip-up leather jacket, a Styrofoam tea cup in one hand and a 1970s multi-use WH Smith bag in the other.

'No anecdotes.'

I couldn't think of anything to come back with on this one.

'I was reading your last book yesterday and someone – the bloke from Mud, I think it was – went off on an anecdote about an adventure they had back in the '70s,' he said in his gentle, unsettlingly forceful way. 'And I thought: I'm not into this. I don't want to read: "Felt were doing seventy down the motorway when the van careered out of control and headed straight in front of the lorry roaring towards them in the other direction. Lawrence grabbed the wheel and saved everyone from a hideous death."'

This was not an anecdote to be recounted, chiefly because it never happened, but what about this one? In 1986, Felt, having become one of the hottest bands around, were about to play a concert at a venue called Bay 63 under the Westway flyover in west London, where six A&R representatives from Britain's biggest record labels were to turn up to check out the great hope of alternative music. Felt had signed recently to Creation and the label's founder Alan McGee was looking to forge links with major labels to inject some cash into his ailing independent operation. The hot-to-trot Felt were the band to make that happen.

The afternoon before the concert Lawrence called his friend Douglas Hart, who left his native East Kilbride in Scotland as a teenager to become the bassist in the Jesus and Mary Chain, and told him he wanted to take LSD.

'I said, "Aren't you playing tonight?"' remembered Hart. 'For me, it was a push doing acid in a pub, let alone before a concert, but Lawrence insisted he would be fine. Then he took it shortly before he went on stage.'

Washing down the innocuous-looking portal to another world with a glass of Coca-Cola, Lawrence's idea was that, since Felt were so static and never said anything, he would turn the concert into a mind-expanding journey. He had read interviews with people who said that being on stage was like an out-of-body experience, but he had never felt it himself, probably because the small audiences Felt played to tended to clap politely rather than enter a state of mass delirium. Perhaps, if he were a little less uptight on account of being on acid, the crowd might respond accordingly and flip their collective bowl cut.

Half an hour later, Lawrence walked onto the stage, stared at the roomful of people standing before him, and said: 'Why are you all looking at me?' Sometime during the second song, the back wall of the venue started to melt away. He told the lighting engineer to turn the lights down until the whole place was cast in blackness. Then he refused to play a note until everyone turned around to face the back of the room. When they didn't comply, he told them to ask for a refund. 'Go talk to that guy over there,' he said, pointing to Jeff Barrett, a gig promoter soon to form the Heavenly Records label, who was busy slamming the lid on his metal money box and getting out of there as quickly as possible.

Could we tell that anecdote?

'No!'

* * *

Lawrence was in Ramsgate for the first concert of 2023 by Mozart Estate, which emerged out of Go-Kart Mozart, which Lawrence intended as the world's first B-sides band. Mozart Estate's debut album, *Pop-Up! Ker-Ching! and the Possibilities of Modern Shopping*, had come out a few weeks previously in the first week of January, marking its position as the album to provide the soundtrack to the year ahead. The catchy melodies and bright arrangements – filled with brutal observations on homeless drug addicts sleeping in department store doorways, how the barcode has transformed our lives, the ongoing struggle of living on a tenner a day and the general reality of getting from one day to the other under societal breakdown – inspired the best reviews Lawrence had ever received. One song with a particularly lovely chorus really sounded like it had radio hit potential. It was called 'I Wanna Murder You'.

'We did a BBC 6 Music session and they said, "Maybe you shouldn't tell people that you want to murder someone, because someone was murdered in London earlier tonight and the listeners might not like it",' said Lawrence. 'But people are murdered every day in London, killed in knife attacks all the time. You can't stop playing songs like this because of that.'

Things were falling into place with Mozart Estate. Lawrence had found three sharp, enthusiastic, youngish musicians, alongside a cheery tough nut of a bass player of his own age called Rusty Stone, and together they formed the one thing he had been dreaming of since the early days of Felt: a band that doesn't drink.

'They're all in recovery, which means we have no beer or wine on the rider and you don't end up with someone talking nonsense after the gig. It is remarkable that it has happened – finally.'

Lawrence even wrote a postcard to his agent to complain about Mozart Estate getting the old Go-Kart Mozart rider. 'It was sandwiches and cider and shit. I had to tell him we only want chocolate, Cadburys Dairy Milk ideally, alongside raw cashew nuts, pistachios and confectionery. No tea because nobody can make it to my specifications, and the band want 0 per cent beer. A can of Coke for me, not a great big bottle you can't take anywhere. It's very simple – the simplest rider in the UK, I reckon.'

I asked Lawrence if liquorice was on there, knowing he had a fondness for it. 'Are you mad?' he snapped. 'Can you imagine them sending someone out to find my liquorice? Not a chance. I'm one of the foremost liquorice experts ever to have walked the face of the earth. I've tried every type of liquorice known to humanity. For example, there is a liquorice sweet I like, which you can only buy in Poundland. They're called King Kong Kubes, and guess what? You can't even get them at Poundland any more. I'm going to have to do some research into King Kong Kubes because currently, they're not to be found anywhere in the UK.'

While rappers had for the past three decades waxed on about the glories of high-end consumer products like Courvoisier brandy and the Mercedes-Benz 500SL, Lawrence, in keeping with the more straitened realities of British life in the 2020s, opted to celebrate the country's most successful bargain outlet. A song on *Pop-Up! Ker-Ching!* called 'Poundland' illustrated, to an advertising jingle-ready melody, a few of the things available in the shop, like plastic Christmas trees and bandages for water on the knee. Lawrence sang in chirpy Cockney tones about being addicted to a place where things are almost free, and at these prices you may as well buy not two but three, somehow managing to both celebrate and denigrate a popular chain where so much is on offer for so little that it is close to worthless. But the King Kong Kubes krisis was hitting his love of the budget store hard.

'It is a surefire sign Poundland is going down the drain.'

Lawrence announced that later in the year he planned to take me on one of his regular wanderings through Beckenham, which he went to not only in hope of soaking up former resident David Bowie's energy, but also because it was there he found a sweet shop that sold Drop Fruit Duos, a German/Dutch creation pairing liquorice with wine gums in a chewy lozenge.

'It is the only shop in Britain which stocks them,' he claimed. 'The man in the shop is horrible, and I have no idea why he decided to go into this line of work because he is extremely ill-suited to customer relations. But he does have Drop Fruit Duos and I appear to be the only person who likes them. I encountered them first in Cologne, when I asked a guy there to take me to a supermarket.

"That's what we ate when we were two years old," the guy told me. I had to explain to him that, in Britain, they're considered a delicacy, and expensive too: £2.50 for a quarter.'

Concerts – planned over a year-long tour in which the band would, if at all possible, drive up to the date and back home again on the same night – were selling out. As we stood outside the Ramsgate Music Hall, which despite its grand name was a 140-capacity windowless room on the high street with a bar up some clanking metal stairs on the first floor and a venue below, a man and woman came up to say they travelled all the way from Manchester to be at the concert tonight. That was nice. Yet problems remained. Disappointments continued. Record shops were not stocking the album, or at least not as many as Lawrence hoped.

'I don't understand it,' he said, as a drop of rain turned the white paper of his cigarette a muddy grey. 'We've got a red-hot record, yet something is wrong. We have a website – when I say "we", I mean the label, of course – and so many people are writing in to say that they can't buy our record in their town. I'm trying to please people. I want fans to visit their local record shops and have a relationship with the guys inside, but I wonder if these people are scared of going in and asking, because the shops don't even have it. It used to be that you got a review in the *NME* and it was in the shops the next day. I don't think it works that way any more.'

Pop-Up! Ker-Ching! had an arresting cover too, with the title written in friendly shades of red and brown and the song titles appearing on a supermarket receipt attached to the corner by a paper-clip. The fingertips of a feminine hand, topped by bright red acrylic nails, held a lipstick from which a curving line of red ejaculated. It was the work of Lora Findlay, an artist and illustrator whose crisp, stylish, pop art designs had been shining out from Lawrence's albums for over two decades.

'Actually, I designed the writing, the nails, and the lipstick,' corrected Lawrence, holding up a copy of the album. He pointed to the thin smeary line of ejaculate and said, 'Lora did that bit.'

Lawrence resolved to come up with the most commercial single of all time by the end of the year and do as much as possible before he got there because *Pop-Up! Ker-Ching!* was not the hit he hoped for. 'For some reason, we seem to go under the radar,' he said, worrying the pavement with a patch of Yogi shoe. 'What can you do? You must arrange a year of activity that will be guaranteed to change your fortunes.'

We walked into the Ramsgate Music Hall and down to the basement where a small room at the back served as a backstage area, with various gig posters and set lists tacked onto the wall with peeling Sellotape. Sitting on a small black sofa was Charlie Hannah, Mozart Estate's genial, blond-haired keyboard player, and his friend Xav Clarke, the band's wild-haired guitarist. In their brightly coloured shirts and cut-off denim shorts, they looked like a couple of surfer boys who'd washed up at Ramsgate by mistake. Behind them, rummaging through a bank of guitar cases, stands and effects pedals, was Rusty Stone; a stocky sixty-one-year-old bassist who spent decades in countless bands, playing everywhere from weddings to concert halls. The drummer, a man called Tom Pitts, had wandered off somewhere.

'You'll meet Tom soon,' said Lawrence. 'I like him because he doesn't say much. If I ask him to do something, he goes, "Yes, boss".'

The band also had a new driver because the old one died. 'That's a good start, isn't it? He was only fifty-five. He went home to see his parents in Italy and died in his bed. He was a big fan of mine, the driver of our dreams, or my dreams anyway, because he would do any crazy journey I wanted, which a normal driver would refuse to do. I would say, "We're driving back from Glasgow all through the night". And he would do it.'

In the early days of Felt, Lawrence would want to stay out all night after the gig, but it was different now. Now he wanted to get home as soon as possible, not least because the nervous energy he expended before and during the set left him totally bereft, depleted, empty inside. 'These days I'm about to go on stage and I'll think, *I've forgotten every single lyric. What am I going to do?* Then you go on and somehow it all comes back. It was so different with Felt. Back then I was excited, full of life, not worried about anything, no stage fright whatsoever. I was leading the charge. The rest of Felt were Birmingham people, a bit dour, and I would be going, "This is it, the beginning of all our adventures. We are taking over the world."'

The first inkling that all would not be as he imagined came when Lawrence realised his goal of being a total tyrant, taking inspiration from his fellow West Midlander Kevin Rowland who, in the early days of Dexys Midnight Runners made the band head off on 6 a.m. jogging sessions, would be harder than he thought. In 1982, Felt landed some dates in the Netherlands and Lawrence, thinking of things an art band would do on their European tour, told his comrades they were to spend the days visiting art galleries, discussing pioneering works of literature, pondering philosophical quandaries and ensuring their stage outfits radiated simplicity and elegance to the discerning eyes of their fashionable overseas fans. 'And they went, "What you on about?" They got completely plastered on the ferry over, and when the ferry started rocking, the bass player threw up in the bin. We got to Holland, and the only place they wanted to go was the pub next door to the hotel. For Brummies, as it is for most musicians, actually, going on tour is a drinking holiday.'

Getting the right bunch of people with whom to launch the greatest art band of all time proved a challenge in the first place. One of the biggest decisions Lawrence faced was whether to choose, say, a bass player because he had great taste in clothes, or because he could actually play bass.

'In the end, I had to opt for the latter option. But it wasn't easy.'

Neither were his attempts to enforce a total ban on drinking, make everyone wear a uniform, only use rectangular guitar cases, submit to bag checks (as in, bags must be checked by Lawrence to see if they conformed to his stylistic standards) and, in what proved his most ambitious ruling yet, only drive cool vintage cars.

'That was the really difficult one,' accepted Lawrence, who had cadged a lift in Rusty Stone's car to get to the Ramsgate gig. 'I don't know anything about cars, but I felt strongly that people in Felt should only be driving ones which looked like they belonged in a classic movie. Being tyrannical on tour was the dream and God knows I tried, but they didn't like it. Didn't like it at all. And, unfortunately, I didn't have the money to buy their loyalty.'

At first, Lawrence did at least follow his own rules. Fed up with Felt's bass player holding the rest of the band to ransom because he was the only one with wheels, Lawrence learned to drive and invested in a car himself: a 1961 blue-and-white Morris Oxford Estate with an old-fashioned oversized steering wheel and a blue leather interior. With a hatchback to pile the band's gear in, it was the £50 car of his dreams. It would have been ideal but for one minor detail.

'It broke down on every single journey we went on. I was so proud of that Morris Estate that there is a publicity photo somewhere of me sitting on the bonnet. And it would have been the ultimate car for Felt except for the fact that it never went. I had to ring my neighbour and ask him to charge it up using his jump leads each time I wanted to use it. He got sick of that in the end.'

The situation left Lawrence with no choice but to renege on his own dictates and buy an extremely ugly Vauxhall Viva Estate for £300, which did at least have the advantage of working. 'It went everywhere, all over the country, until I left it in Brighton one day and realised the parking tickets it accrued were far more than the value of the car. They towed it away and that was the end of that.'

The one aspect of touring Lawrence could control was his own luggage, which was stark enough to make the stingiest budget airline's baggage allowance look positively decadent. Just as he avoided the accoutrements of modern communication in the name of minimalism, eschewing the internet, smartphones and all digital technology, so on tour he took a single carrier bag and that was it.

'I never once had a case in all the time we went on tour. It's how I've always been. When I was young, I wanted to live in a matchbox. I had a little rubber naked man who I kept in one. I remember feeling quite jealous of him, actually.'

Packing for holidays was not an issue because, apart from one fateful trip to Paignton in Devon, Lawrence's family was known in Water Orton as the family who never went away. Instead, they treated themselves to day trips once a year; the locations included Doncaster, Aintree and Ascot. 'We only sussed it years later, but it was always a town with a racetrack. My dad would say, "Right, get in the car. We're off to Cheltenham" and as soon as he got there, he went to Mom: "See you in a couple of hours." That was the last we saw of him. He was completely addicted to gambling.'

The tragedy of the tour disappointments was that, having hardly left England before, Lawrence set so much store by his first big European adventure. There had been a school day trip to Boulogne when he was eleven. 'We went there and back in one day, believe it or not. I had a white jumper, nylon polo neck, checked mini-flares in grey and white, and I said, "I don't care what the weather's like. I'm wearing this because I look good." And, of course, it was pouring with rain and freezing, and I ended up having to get a green plastic mac off a girl. I would never take notice of the weather because the most important thing, always, was to look good, but it made for a lonely pursuit in young adulthood because the rest of Felt couldn't care less.'

Did Lawrence even enjoy doing concerts, the ultimate purpose of being on tour? A song called 'I Don't Know Which Way to Turn', from Felt's album *Ignite the Seven Cannons*, suggested not. 'When I'm up there on the stage / I just hide my eyes and pray that soon enough the show will end,' he sings, asking himself, 'Why do I go through this hell?' The song ends with the conclusion that performing a concert is the same as life: he can't wait for it to end. It is incredibly depressing.

The answer lay in finding a girl to share his passions with and it actually did happen once, in Barcelona in 1984. 'It was one of the greatest nights of my life. She was beautiful and – get this – she was called Angels. Can you believe it? After the show, she picked me up on her little Vespa and showed me the Gaudí Park, the culture of the Basque region, and the artistic triumphs of Barcelona. At first, I was bringing my culture of Birmingham to Spain, trying to rush it and get back to her flat as quickly as possible, but she seduced me by making a great night of it.'

One of the things that most impressed Lawrence about Angels was the way she didn't have a kitchen in her tiny flat in the centre of the city. Instead, she would go out and eat at a café or bring street food back and have it at home. Yet it was food that caused the relationship's downfall. A wonderful memory of a magical night after a Felt concert in Barcelona soured rapidly when the couple mistook their holiday romance for a lasting relationship and Angels came to visit Lawrence in Birmingham, where they spent a few awkward evenings in his flat together. Then he made a second trip to Barcelona, in one final attempt at salvaging the relationship. Angels even took Lawrence to a restaurant.

'She was going, "Eat something!"

'I said, "I want one of them thin steaks on a plate, nothing else. I don't like Spanish chips."

'"Let me introduce you to Spanish food."

'"No!"

'The final straw was when she wheeled out her big line, "How could I fall for someone who hates their mother?" To her, it was unnatural, because mothers are sacred in Spain. It's why they're all called Maria.'

What happened with Angels was not untypical of Lawrence's relationships in the Felt days. 'At the very beginning of being with a girlfriend, I would project this longing and go, "Gosh, I love her." Days and weeks later, it would dissipate, which meant I would start at the top of the mountain and slide down into the bog at a phenomenal rate. I never had the good fortune to meet the perfect somebody, which is a shame as I wasn't particularly hard to get on with. I wanted a normal life of going to the pictures, going out for meals, nothing outrageous. I saw other people in art galleries, or characters in films even more so, and went, "Wow, they look really close. Why can't I have that?" Me and Angels, this beautiful girl, went on a ferry trip to the island of Formentera and completely ran out of things to say. That's when it all went wrong.'

It was time for Mozart Estate to do the soundcheck on the foot-high stage of the Ramsgate Music Hall. Tom Pitts, a silent figure with a helmet of nut-brown hair and something of the stoic about him, had to make do with a side drum and a snare. Xav Clarke was advising Charlie Hannah, as he practised the high notes for 'Record Store Day'. 'Save yourself, save the voice.' Sitting through the tedium of the soundcheck, I found my mind drifting towards a reflection on Lawrence's dietary habits. He had never eaten an olive. He was terrified of cheese. You could not help but wonder how he got through the rigours of touring.

'My mother took me to the doctor's and went, "This boy won't eat and he despises vegetables,"' he said, once the soundcheck was over and he headed onto the street for a cigarette. 'The doctor said, "Does he eat fruit? Yes? Well, he's alright then." And I do, but it's very hard to find fruit in England. You can't buy a tangerine. You open it and it's all dried out. Still, you can't live on nothing. There is a strange woman who started a cult called Living On Light, and they really did live on nothing but light. Then they went on a pilgrimage to the Scottish Highlands and they all died.'

Lawrence decided to drink some water and eat a dry satsuma, which concerned Rusty Stone, who had been sorting through various cables in the corner of the backstage room. 'It has been a while since he had any vitamin C and I'm not sure his system can handle it,' said Rusty as he put the guitars back in their cases with casual efficiency. 'I am a bit worried something unpleasant might happen on stage as a result.'

Nothing unpleasant happened on stage. In fact, the concert was a smashing success. 'Hey man, we're nearly as good as the real Mozart,' said Lawrence, wearing a Felt sweatshirt emblazoned with two identical black-and-white photographs of the saucer-eyed '60s model Penelope Tree.

'Sometimes I get the impression that I'm talking into a very deep well and nobody understands a word of what I'm saying,' he announced, before the small but enthusiastic crowd shouted out the words to 'When You're Depressed', giving particular oomph to the line 'Seven years since I've had sex' – I think in truth it had been more like twenty-seven – and joined in the chorus of 'I Wanna Murder You'.

'Wow, man, sounding good,' he said of himself after a cheerful Go-Kart Mozart song called 'Summer is Here'. Of an old song called 'Plead With the Man', that featured a line about a man coming round with the gear, he claimed: 'It's about plumbers, and workmen in general.' At the end of the set, he gave each band member a little pat on the shoulder as they marched in single file towards the dressing room.

When Lawrence went to the bar to sign his name on the merchandise ten minutes later, a chisel-jawed, crop-haired man who had been singing along the whole time was at the front of the queue. He was a twenty-seven-year-old builder from the American Midwest called Evan, and he had saved up the money to come to the UK with the purpose of seeing Lawrence in the flesh.

'I was listening to some music, I can't tell you where it was, and on the sidebar was Martin Duffy's face,' he said of how he discovered his unlikely hero. 'It was *Forever Breathes the Lonely Word* by Felt and I was immediately enraptured. Later on, "The Stagnant Pool" showed up on my recommended feed. You know how there is AI to drive you towards music it thinks you will like? That happened with me and Felt.'

It was strange to think artificial intelligence would drive someone, anyone, towards Lawrence, a man who couldn't do anything technological beyond tying his own shoelaces – and he couldn't even do that until he was twelve. 'From there, I got into Go-Kart Mozart and became obsessed about him,' Evan continued. 'Probably my favourite Lawrence album is *Denim On Ice*, and it is crazy to think Denim went on tour with Pulp yet there is hardly any photographic evidence whatsoever. I guess it adds to his mystique and everything. I was a baby when *Denim On Ice* came out and now here I am.'

Another man told Lawrence that he sent him a copy of Jim Carroll's teenage New York drug memoir *The Basketball Diaries*, back in the early days of Felt. 'I remember that,' said Lawrence, nodding. 'I've still got it. Very good book.'

He was at the merchandise stand for an hour or so, taking the time to offer a straightforward type of charm to every person he met. 'In the punk rock days, if I saw someone on the street, I would be very scared to approach them,' he explained afterwards. 'For that reason, I like to be approachable. We spent half an hour following Bananarama around Liverpool once and we were too scared to say hello.'

When I was fourteen, I saw Jim Reid of the Jesus and Mary Chain with his girlfriend on the Underground. By an incredible piece of luck, I had a copy of the Mary Chain's single 'Some Candy Talking' in my bag, so I asked Reid to sign it. He sighed, raised his eyes upwards, said, 'Giz it here then', and scrawled a massive JIM using the Bic Biro I handed over. It was years later that I realised he almost definitely went home and phoned his mum immediately to tell her that a fan stopped him on the Tube and he was now there-fore officially famous.

'Jim and William Reid, the Brothers Grimm,' remembered Law-rence of the mop-haired duo from East Kilbride. 'Were they mis-erable on purpose? If they were simply shy, they couched it in a terrible way. Once you have done your gig, you have to welcome in the fans and friends, but Jim and William would slam the door of the dressing room and have a massive fight.'

A few days after the Ramsgate concert, Lawrence and I found ourselves once again walking through the rain, this time in Green-wich Park in south-east London, with its famous observatory and its mums and dads jogging along with all-terrain baby buggies. That's where he pointed out another issue related to the touring life: toilet usage.

'You may have noticed how I went to the cubicle in there,' he said after we found a public toilet, only for me to have to swipe my card to let Lawrence in since the barriers only took contact-less payments. This type of so-called convenience made life very inconvenient for people like Lawrence. 'I would never use one of those . . . what do you call them . . . toilet sinks?'

Urinals?

'Yeah, those things on the wall. There must be something about boys who don't pee in public, because I can't even stand next to someone using a urinal unless I'm absolutely bursting. I remember going to the dogs with my dad, and he would take me to the toilet and I could never do it. Then, as you get older, you don't want your friends to see you either. The problem you encounter in a band is that there is always one person who wants to reveal themselves pretty quickly, to show everyone what they've got. I remember a bass player running out of the shower in a towel, which he then whipped off in front of everyone. Me, I'm a private toilet person. A psychologist would probably be able to explain it.'

As we walked out of Greenwich Park, onto the flat expanse of Blackheath Common, which was used to bury the bodies of plague victims back in the days of the Black Death, Lawrence remembered seeing a photograph by Ray Stevenson of the Sex Pistols in a hotel room in Paris, 1976. Steve Jones is naked, grinning at the camera, while John Lydon stands in a corner, uptight, buttoned up. 'Johnny Rotten couldn't be more trussed and bondaged, and next to him is this guy who is totally free. It sums up the Sex Pistols and it sums up me. I was Johnny Rotten. Various members of Felt were Steve Jones.'

Maurice Deebank once claimed he kept leaving Felt because the other members teased him relentlessly. 'That is something he came up with later, because I don't think it's true,' countered Lawrence. 'Maybe the bass player was a piss-taker, but that's how he was with everyone and, besides, Maurice was six foot one and could have belted this kid if he wanted to. What happened to Maurice was nothing compared to the way most bands rip into each other. I have seen bands soundchecking when some guy goes, "Don't fucking play that chord. What are you, dumb or something?" We never had that going on.'

In the early days, with no agent and no manager, Felt took whatever gigs came their way. There was one concert in Champagne, deep in the French countryside, where a hygiene issue in the house forced Lawrence into spending the night in a barn, where he had a sleepless few hours on the hay bales, petrified by the creaks, squeaks and howls of nature. They performed at a shopping centre in Amsterdam before a handful of senior citizens who came along to see what the noise was. They spent four days in Oslo, despite having only one show booked – at the Rats Club, which had an illustration of a happy rat on the wall. There was so much free time in Oslo that Lawrence even managed to get his bandmates to do something they would never normally do: visit a museum.

'The Edvard Munch museum was in town and Maurice Deebank was walking around, passing these incredible paintings, going, "I could paint better than that when I was three." I was having my photo taken in front of Munch pictures and there is the guitarist, my so-called partner, just not getting it. So much passion and pain and no one to share it with.'

Felt's appearance on a 1982 Cherry Red compilation called *Pillows & Prayers* really helped in the touring stakes. It only cost 99p, which meant plenty of school kids discovered the band, which then meant more people wanting to come and see them in concert. One girl phoned the Cherry Red offices and asked if Felt would come and play her local scout hut in Wokingham.

'That girl used to write to me all the time,' said Lawrence. 'We would chit-chat and I told her I was really cold in my flat in Birmingham, so she sent me one of those silver blankets they give to you on mountaintops, for when you're dying. I had never seen one before.'

As for fans becoming groupies, it only happened once, and even then, not really – to Lawrence's eternal regret. A young fan wrote to say she was coming to Birmingham to visit the university and he felt compelled to offer her his place in Moseley.

'I didn't want her to come and stay, but she was hinting big time. I learned to never do that again,' said Lawrence, as we left Black-heath to get the train back into the centre of London. 'I should have said, "There are lots of hotels in the city centre that can accommodate you very well", because we ran out of things to say almost immediately and I had a whole evening where I had to put the telly on, listen to records . . . any diversionary tactic I could find. It was a businessman's flat in Moseley, with two beds that came down from the wall, so I got her into one of them and I went in the other.

'You imagine a scene where a beautiful girl jumps off the train and comes towards you, like Julie Christie in *Billy Liar*, but that wasn't the case at all. It taught me that you mustn't get too close to fans. You must be pleasant, you must say, "Oh yes, I do remember that time in Aylesbury in 1985", but that's where it ends. Ideally, I'd have a bodyguard to end the conversation for me. Guess where this girl came from?'

'Where?'

'Cockermouth.'

Lawrence stared into the rain.

CHAPTER THREE

PRIMITIVE PAINTERS

Lawrence called to say his artistic immortalisation was on the horizon. For the past year, a sculptor called Corin Johnson had been working on an enormous marble sculpture of Lawrence's head, and now it was imperative we find a place to present it to the world before the year was out. There was a possibility of getting it into the Gallery of Everything, a high-end exhibition space popular with wealthy, sophisticated people, which specialised in low-end outsider art by poor, unsophisticated people. It was on Marylebone High Street, so Lawrence suggested we go there and check it out.

I was on my way when Lawrence called to announce he couldn't find it.

'There is no point in giving you directions,' I told him with no little peevishness. 'You'll only go the wrong way. You'll have to ask someone.'

A week previously, he had turned up to my office half an hour late for a Zoom talk before an online audience for *The Idler*, the magazine my brother Tom started three decades previously. The magazine had given Lawrence his first-ever cover story, the interview was a big hit with the readers, and now Tom wanted to capitalise on its success by getting Lawrence to do an online talk for the subscribers. But, by its very nature, an online talk requires punctuality in order for it to work. The excuse this time was that the traffic was murder, and there were nodding heads of sympathy from the various figures represented in little squares on the screen as Lawrence regaled his tales of entrapment by unmoving London traffic. It was only after he left that I realised he had walked to the office from his flat a mile away.

For that reason, I couldn't be bothered to provide him with a personal navigation service, because it would only mean he would be wandering about in circles before arriving to accuse me of giving him the worst directions ever. Incredibly, as it transpired, Lawrence actually arrived at the Gallery of Everything before me. He was on the pavement, shuffling about, pulling on a cigarette, talking to an affable shaggy bear of a man who turned out to be Corin Johnson.

'We can't go in there,' announced Lawrence. 'It is full of people.'

There was a talk on. It was about a woman called Hermione Burton who, having had no artistic training, took to painting portraits of herself, mostly naked, after developing various debilitating health conditions. 'One hates to use the word "authentic. . .'" began a compact fellow in horn-rimmed glasses, a neat beard and a bobble hat, in an introduction to this late outsider artist's untutored but characterful, rather poignant paintings. 'Most of you here will have, if not a few letters at the end of your names, then at the very least the highest levels of education money can buy,' he continued, and after that he lost me. I squeezed my way into the small room and sat through the talk about a woman whose work had been found in a charity shop in Bedford for a few quid and which was now selling for a few thousand. Lawrence remained outside.

When it was over, Lawrence and Corin told the man in the bobble hat, who turned out to be the Gallery of Everything's owner, about the head and their plans for it. Lawrence said he wanted it to be displayed in the centre of the room, on its own, like a sacred relic or a body in a mausoleum. Visitors, stunned into silence and contemplation by the beauty of the work and the grace of its subject, would pass by slowly, circling around the bust before leaving to make way for the enormous queue of people waiting solemnly outside. Rather like the lying-in-state ceremony of 2022, when thousands of loyal subjects paid their respects to the late Queen by passing her coffin in Westminster Hall, this would be an opportunity for Lawrence's loyal acolytes to honour their lord and master, who, though not dead as such, was at least not available for selfies.

'The problem,' said the man in detached stentorian tones as he stood with his back right up against me, arms crossed, in a way to suggest that I didn't actually exist or, if I did, shouldn't, 'is how to make actual money from the bloody thing. Nothing makes money in art except from the big stuff and that's how you keep the whole operation going. We need to think about what we could sell.'

The man went on to say he had so much going on in his brilliant brain, with countless exhibitions and all kinds of people wanting to work with him, that he couldn't possibly think about an exhibition on Lawrence right now.

Corin Johnson threw in that he did have other work to be included: pastel-coloured figurines of the devil from childhood to old age, which he had been making with Nick Cave; a wooden statue of Grace Jones. 'Lawrence is an important cult star,' he added. 'Maybe he could do a performance in the shop.'

'Oh yes, that would be good,' pondered the man, eyebrows raising. 'I grew up around here and now the place has been taken over by these awful new-money people. I'd love to piss them off with a really loud concert.'

'I couldn't do that,' interjected Lawrence. 'I'd be too nervous.'

Other suggestions were made: merchandise for sale, miniature versions of the head, candles of the head, which, given Lawrence's waxy pallor and ever-present air of disintegration, could work rather well. He was looking increasingly uncomfortable about the whole thing, especially after the gallery owner, who dropped that he bought Denim's first album back in the '90s, suggested a group show featuring a variety of underground stars with artistic leanings.

'We can't just include the last thing we found down the back of the sofa,' Lawrence snapped. 'You're the curator. You tell us what you want.'

Corin went back to his idea of including Nick Cave heads, wooden heads, something he did for Grace Jones some time back . . .

That's when Lawrence flipped.

'No!' he yelped, jumping up and down on the pavement like Rumpelstiltskin. If he had driven his foot through the ground in rage, to create a chasm into which he disappeared, never to be seen again, I wouldn't have been surprised. 'It's my head or nothing!'

The man shrugged, said, 'I'll let you know,' and strutted back into the gallery.

The head was a summation of Lawrence's dream of transcending life through art, something articulated in Felt's greatest song, one of the greatest songs of all time in fact. 'Primitive Painters' came out in 1985, halfway through the band's career, and it captured everything that preoccupied Lawrence: the dream of being more than you can ever be; the voyeuristic torment of seeing beautiful people from a distance and feeling their lives must be so much richer than your own; a narcissistic abundance of self-hatred at the heart of it all, with the song's chorus, raised to churchy grandeur thanks to a soaring vocal spot from Liz Fraser of the Cocteau Twins featuring the words: 'You should see my trail of disgrace / It's enough to scare the whole human race'.

The music was Maurice Deebank's finest moment, with the E minor guitar chords in the introduction leading to a swelling strum creating that aural monolith beloved of music journalists in the 1980s and '90s: a cathedral of sound. 'Primitive Painters' is hopeful and despairing at the same time. It reached number one in the UK independent charts, a rare moment of success for Felt.

'"Primitive Painters" came from an inability to enjoy myself,' said Lawrence. It was the day after the disastrous Gallery of Everything pitch and he had come to my house in Peckham because it was a short bus ride to Corin Johnson's studio in Camberwell. In the meantime, I made myself a cup of tea, but not one for Lawrence: he said he would rather buy one from the café. 'I was sure that once I joined a band and got into the music world, my life would explode. I would be at wonderful parties, surrounded by interesting people, accompanied by beautiful girlfriends. The shock of that not happening inspired the song.'

'Primitive Painters' begins with Lawrence wishing his life could be as strange as a conspiracy, but tragically he is trapped in reality as it unfolds from moment to moment. It isn't like that for mythical creatures. Dragons blow fire, angels fly, spirits wither in the air. He is just himself, neither here, there, nor anywhere.

'We're nothing more than humans,' said Lawrence, as my son Otto wandered into the kitchen from his converted shed of a bedroom at the bottom of the garden and shook out a bowl of Rice Krispies. 'The human being is inert and stuck. We can't do anything like a dragon or an angel can. I'd like to. Wish I could.'

On the bus, where we sat at the back of the top deck, Lawrence tried to make himself heard over the shrieks of kids rapping into their phones as he explained how 'Primitive Painters' concerned the romantic ideal. 'It came from seeing good-looking couples in the art gallery because I would long for other people's relationships, definitely. *Why can't I meet someone with the same record collection?* It is a dumb thing, really, but I didn't realise at the time that my ideal partner was a female version of me. I was trying to go out with myself.'

Years later, he did come close, in a platonic fashion at least. In 2018, the Canadian director Douglas Arrowsmith made a video for 'When You're Depressed' that featured Lawrence variously walking past an amusement arcade in Margate, sitting on a broken armchair in a junkyard, and singing on stage in some of his favourite clothes: gold and silver bomber jackets, a leather biker jacket studded on the back with the word 'KILL', a blue, red and yellow knitted tank top, all of them accessorised with his signature blue and white baseball cap, oversized shades and curtains of jet black hair. Except it wasn't Lawrence. It was a girl.

'She had a great name too: Liberty Dye. It was my idea to create a teenage, female version of me and frankly, the results were fantastic. Liberty was very shy, unfortunately. Can't say I got to know her very well.'

We stopped for another cup of tea in a smart little café on Camberwell Church Street, where Lawrence instructed the man behind the counter to pour away half of the water to make space for all the milk he would be adding to it until Lawrence told him to stop. 'Corin will offer you a cup of tea, but whatever you do, don't accept it,' he warned in ominous tones as he stirred his milky brew. 'He makes the worst tea known to humanity. He boils it in a metal bucket. Then he brews it in the same plastic tub he uses to soak his brushes in turpentine.'

What does he serve the tea in, I asked, a paint pot?

Corin's studio was down a cobbled road round the back of Camberwell Church Street, a mews lined with old garages and stables taken over by artists. A friendly black-and-white sheepdog hopped out of a studio and bounded towards us. 'Hello, Charlie,' said Lawrence, giving the dog a few hearty pats. 'Hello, boy.' He picked up a stick and chucked it down the mews. Charlie raced after it with effervescent happiness before leading us to the lair of his master.

Inside the studio, every inch of the white-painted brick walls, and most of the floor space, groaned with an anarchic melange of creation: white plaster heads, paintings of Jesus, the devil figurines Corin made with Nick Cave, a dusty stack of records with Alan Stivell's Renaissance of the Celtic Harp at the front, wooden shelves bending under the weight of classical busts and religious figurines, chisels, drills, hacksaws and brushes sitting on everything from wooden stools to towering stacks of paint pots. Corin's assistant, a pretty woman with tousled hair called Alice, was polishing a devilish green figure by a desk. At the centre of the room was a work of solemn beauty: a giant, peach-coloured bust of Lawrence.

Lawrence's monkish, aquiline face was shrouded by a cowl-like hoodie and baseball cap. Large sunglasses perching on top of a modest nose brought a touch of distance, like the figure was locked into some kind interior monologue that could never be fully revealed or understood. There was sadness – the culmination of all the sadnesses the world had ever known from one end of it to the other, in fact – but also a silent strength, like the figure could withstand any manner of suffering and remain unbroken to continue onwards for all eternity. The name was carved in Roman letters on the base. The essence, the soul of the man, was captured within that marble.

'Nick Cave plays the arenas so you would expect a marble bust of him,' said Corin, as Lawrence wandered about the studio with Charlie jumping about at his heels. 'For that reason, it is nice to make one of Lawrence instead. He's had his ups and downs, he has stuck to his guns, and I find it more heroic than doing a statue of an admiral. It is the reality of his life which made me want to do the head.'

'I like that,' said Lawrence, nodding ever so slightly. 'It's not like everyone gets a head when they reach my age, is it?'

Corin grew up in Sutton Coldfield, not far from Water Orton. After leaving school, he worked in demolition before doing a YTS scheme with a wood carver called Rachel Shorter, and meeting the sculptor Faith Tolkien, daughter-in-law of the author of *The Lord of the Rings,* which led to studying fine art at City and Guilds in south London. Along the way, he got into music, in particular anything with a tinge of vulnerability. Nick Drake was a favourite, as were Lawrence's records with Felt.

'I think there is a similarity between Nick Drake and Lawrence. Something about their softness and sensitivity, which may or may not have something to do with the place they grew up in,' said Corin as he offered us a cup of tea, which I declined (politely) and we toured the studio, passing a wooden statue of a black-and-white collie with no back legs, gazing up with loving obedience at a red-headed woman. 'I had never heard anyone come out and say the things Lawrence did on those Felt records. The lyrics are so bare, even though they're often hard to make out, like "I don't know whether I want to live or die". And he was so elusive. I couldn't find out much, but every now and then I would see photos of him in a hoodie and that's when I realised: he was like a monk in a cowl, or a Madonna in a headdress. He has a devotional air.'

Corin set off on his mission to create the Lawrence bust by going to see Go-Kart Mozart in a working men's club in Hackney called the Moth Club. 'You have to walk through the audience to get to the stage,' Lawrence remembered, 'and I thought *How am I going to do it?* I was really nervous. That's when Corin offered to walk me through, like Muhammad Ali coming into the ring with his bodyguard. Once I learned he was from Sutton Coldfield, it all came together. Corin, the Swell Maps, Julian Cope, Nick Drake, Tolkien, Shakespeare, Felt . . . We're all from the same part of the Midlands.'

As to where the Lawrence bust would find a home, it seemed that, right now, everything was hanging on the whims of the man from the Gallery of Everything. 'We had a guy from Belgium who came over specially to see if it would work for his gallery,' said Corin. 'He took one look at it, said "No" and walked out. We'd better hope that guy from the Gallery of Everything goes for it.'

* * *

In the earliest days of Felt, the achievement of artistic glory didn't seem difficult at all. Lawrence was seventeen when, wishing to take part in the revolutionary idea that you could do it yourself, whatever 'it' was, he resolved to record and release 'Index'.

'I knew people had started making their own records, but I didn't know how they went about it. What's a recording studio? What's a pressing plant? I saw an advert at the back of *Melody Maker*: "Make your own record. We will do everything for you." And I thought, *That sounds good, because it's a bit complicated for me.* I sent off my cassette.'

And they sent you back 500 copies?

'No, they sent a letter that went: "Are you sure you want to release this?"'

'"Yeah, why?"'

'"Because it's on a cassette and it sounds awful. Usually you make it on something called a master tape." I did it in my bedroom with a practice amplifier and a cassette recorder, although I did buy the most expensive cassette in the shop: a Memorex. Occasionally, I leaned over and mumbled something into the little microphone on the recorder. It was the idea of making a record that counted. Then a friend drove me to Cambridge to pick them up.'

Putting out 'Index' fitted in with other dreams of being in a band, most of them culled from reading the music papers. Lawrence was getting the coach for day trips to London, which consisted of visiting the Rough Trade record shop off Portobello Road, going to a shoe shop called Robot on the King's Road for his favourite Doc Martens with wafer-thin soles, and ending up at Malcolm McLaren and Vivienne Westwood's shop, which had formerly been SEX, and then Seditionaries, but in 1979 transformed into World's End, reflecting the whimsy of Westwood's pirate-themed fashion sensibility of the time with a slanted wooden floor, like a galleon at sea, and an oversized thirteen-hour clock going backwards.

'I stood outside. I was too scared to go in.'

We left Corin's studio in Camberwell to get the bus to a shop on the outskirts of Greenwich, where Lawrence went for all his ancient mobile phone-related needs. On the way, we passed a library, which brought memories of an important figure in Lawrence's creative development: Sue the Librarian. Along with being the resident health food-eating hippie, with hair that went down to her waist, oversized glasses in plastic frames and a weakness for hypo-allergenic skin creams, Sue the Librarian was the keeper of Water Orton's literary treasures.

'When I was seven, I got out *The Lord of the Rings*, all three big books, and Sue the Librarian said to me, "You're the only boy your age I would let these books out to",' he declaimed, to the apparent disinterest of the pensioners gazing at the misted windows on the bottom deck of the bus. 'Even then I was inclined towards something challenging so I got these massive books. I didn't actually read them, of course. Couldn't understand a word.'

It made me think of a line from Felt's 'Sunlight Bathed the Golden Glow', on which Lawrence sings, over Maurice Deebank's chiming guitar, 'You're reading from *A Season in Hell* but you don't know what it's about.' I guessed it was about him, searching for the books that would define him, even if the meaning within them was lost.

'That was based on my friend Jon,' he corrected. 'Jon called himself a poet, but he was trying too hard and it infuriated me. Jon was gay. Gay Jon, we called him. He looked like Vincent Price.'

Sue the Librarian proved an important ally in enriching the young Lawrence's blossoming mind, leading him not only to pretend to read books he didn't understand, but also to ones he did. Then a neighbour from two doors down called Roger lent Lawrence his copy of *A Clockwork Orange*.

'You know *Alfie*?' asked Lawrence, referring to the quintessential Swinging London movie starring Michael Caine as a promiscuous man about town. 'If you imagine a lorry driver in *Alfie*, that was Roger. He was a strong guy, looked hard, younger than my mother, didn't speak much, and as a long-distance lorry driver he went off and came back again in a way that made him interesting, so him giving me his copy of *A Clockwork Orange* was a major event. He was a big character in my life from the ages of ten to fourteen.'

From there came *Diary of a Rock 'n' Roll Star* by Ian Hunter and *The Warlock of Love* by Marc Bolan; the first an impressively downbeat account of the realities of touring the US in the early '70s by the singer of Mott the Hoople, the second a pastorally inclined poetry collection by the glam superstar of T. Rex. 'The idea of pop stars writing books really did it for me. Ian Hunter gave you tips on dealing with groupies, which wasn't something I had to watch out for at the time but was good to know for future reference, and then you had Marc Bolan writing amazing poetry about enchanted forests and so on. We saw the different avenues that life as a pop star could lead us down.'

When he was eight, Lawrence resolved to write a book himself, announcing to a friend they were going to work on it together. 'My friend went, "Oh, right" and we went back home and got ready to do it. I remember it so well. We began with "The wooden carved box lay on the table." We couldn't think of what to write after that one line, so we put THE END and went off to do something else.'

Among Lawrence's other early achievements, he pointed out – after we got off the bus at Blackheath and passed a Span housing estate, box-like modernist developments from the 1950s and '60s – were his prototype designs for social housing. Arguably the foundations were laid down by Eric Lyons, an architect who, in 1957, formed Span Developments Limited, a company that aimed to bring modern housing to middle-class, middle-income people and thereby 'span' the gap between the council estates and one-off homes that remained the preserve of the wealthy. But perhaps Lawrence's part in their history has not been duly recognised.

'Why do I like housing? Why not nature? It is simple: because I fell in love with houses from a young age,' Lawrence declared after calling on me to appreciate the beauty of a square block of a house with a red door and four windows arranged neatly around it. 'When I got a Lego set for Christmas, I was inclined to build houses. Now I look at these housing developments and go: that looks exactly like the Lego house I built aged five. Without knowing it, I designed social housing.'

He was also a poet.

The Tortoise

I've asked a great many people
But nobody seems to know
Why the tortoise walks so very, very slow
Perhaps it's the little legs
Perhaps it's the weight of its shell
Perhaps it's got no stamina
I really cannot tell
So next time you see a tortoise

Go up and say hello
And ask it for me
Why do you walk so slow?

Lawrence, seven and a half

'It was an amazing feat,' Lawrence proclaimed as we trooped through the rain, down a street filled with vape outlets, betting shops and shuttered, abandoned pubs. 'It just came out. I didn't have a tortoise. I didn't even like animals. I think I was inspired poetically by the slowness of their movement. I sent it in to a competition in one of my sister's pop magazines and won a record token for one pound. Unfortunately, it took me two years to finish the next one, probably because I had set the bar so high with the first.'

There may have been another reason for this junior writer's block: horror. Alongside the ever-present threat of the skinhead marauders storming the barricades of Water Orton, a decision by Lawrence's parents to allow their middle child to stay up late on Friday night exposed him to all manner of scary movies and sent his imagination into overdrive. The 1970s began in the shadow of the Manson murders, and in their wake came *The Texas Chainsaw Massacre* and *The Last House on the Left* – seamy, grit-encrusted depictions of crazed hillbillies or cultish hippies massacring innocents in all manner of gruesome ways. Throw in Satanic visions like *The Omen* and *The Exorcist* and you can see the effect it would have on a porous, fragile mind.

'I knew about horror anyway because we lived among trees and woods, where there were owls and foxes and, oh lord, bats,' said Lawrence, revealing an association with the natural world and all things sinister. 'It was around the age of ten that I became fixated with the devil. To be honest with you, it hasn't really stopped.

Although it is good to live in the city because you are less likely to be tormented by phantasmagorical spirits, horror still haunts me on a daily basis.'

Lawrence was the first person I met who believed in ghosts and also had a mobile phone. But he only had an old Nokia phone, so perhaps there was a correlation. He interrupted his tales of terror to pay a visit to the phone shop, which, judging by the time, distance and speed we had been walking, was somewhere in Woolwich, way beyond the outer reaches of Greenwich. Someone gave Lawrence a battery for his ancient Nokia that was superior to the one he presently had, so he wanted to see about getting it installed. The man in the shop explained, with impressive patience, that putting a new battery into an old phone was a case of the tail wagging the dog; better to think about replacing the handset with something made within the last twenty years. Lawrence's phone had 128 megabytes. Most new phones had at least four gigabytes. One gigabyte was comparable to a thousand megabytes.

'I've heard of that,' said Lawrence. 'The more megabytes you have, the better it is. Good to know, isn't it?'

Dazzled by phone speak, we left and went along our way.

Lawrence became fixated with the idea that, of all the people in the world, the devil was coming specifically for him. 'Why me?' he cried, upset at the memory. 'I would forget about it during the day, but at night I would go, "Maybe it's tonight he's coming, if not the devil himself, then at the very least one of his vampire underlings." I made a big stick with a point on it, a stake to use the official word, in case I had to plunge it into a vampire's heart at four in the morning. Each night, the same thought occurred to me: the devil is really real.'

It didn't help that *The Exorcist* became one of the biggest films of the 1970s, the fictional story of demonic possession traumatising an entire generation with its visions of spinning heads, projectile vomiting and the sound of a young girl telling a man of the cloth that his mother sucks cocks in hell. Lawrence was too young to actually see the film, but he made the fatal mistake of reading the book aged eleven and, fooled by rumours running through the school that it was not fiction at all but a true life account, he became morbidly obsessed with *The Exorcist*.

'The common thread here is that nothing was real; it was all inside my head. We lived in a boring suburb where you didn't even have to lock the door, yet I was convinced that the devil, vampires and skinhead marauders were coming for me.'

It inspired his second poetic work of note.

The Vampire
Dead in its coffin
A corpse lies down
Buried beneath the bracken
Is a vampire.
Face deathly pale
Eyes red as fire
Lips reveal the canine teeth
Full of desire.

A new problem occurred the moment Lawrence exorcised his demons into rhyming verse. Accepting that his two completed works were miniature masterpieces, he knew everything he wrote had to be of an equal standard, otherwise it was downhill from there.

'It was problematic. I was going to be the tip-top poet of the village who wrote infrequently but brilliantly, so it had to be class.' So class, in fact, that he followed the pattern of so many would-be geniuses by producing nothing whatsoever, thereby ensuring what he *might* have written was up there with Coleridge and Byron. Nonetheless it seemed like Lawrence could have a future in words, not least after discovering that Mr Blank, the English teacher at junior school, had achieved the remarkable feat of getting a book actually published. *The Great Gem of Rikkenberg* by Gerald Blank is a Hobbit-like fantasy that came out in 1971.

"*The Great Gem of Rikkenberg*, hooray! They're always following a ring or a stone in those books, aren't they? Mr Blank read us *The Hobbit* and then he said, "I've written a book as well. It is a real book, and it is going to get published." Well, I for one was impressed. That was incredible to me. In the reading class, once a week I think, he read it to us. Then it came out!'

Knowing his mother would not agree to buy it for him because hardbacks were expensive, Lawrence asked Mr Blank if *The Great Gem of Rikkenberg* would be available in paperback. 'That's when he revealed to me some inside info I carried around with me for the rest of my life. Mr Blank said: "It depends on how many copies the hardback sells." As an eight-year-old, this blew me away. And guess what? It didn't become a paperback. After *The Great Gem of Rikkenberg*, Mr Blank wrote a follow-up, *The White Gem*, which didn't even get published. None of that should take away from the fact that, as far as I was concerned, this was a success story. Mr Blank was a hero in my eyes, paperback writer or not.'

Lawrence loved school.

'I never wanted to play truant,' he said, lurching up a residential street on the edges of Greenwich in search of more block-like homes similar to the ones he designed on the Lego set of his childhood. 'I enjoyed the rough and tumble. I had a gang of mates and my attitude was that I might as well make the most of this while I was there because when I left, I was going to be a pop star.'

It came as a bit of a surprise. Lawrence was such a wayward character, so singular, so far from the model of the ideal citizen, I had assumed he would have rebelled against school, perhaps even priding himself on an inability to coexist peacefully within the educational herd. To picture him sitting in classes for maths, science, French and English, listening, asking questions, studying diligently, doing his homework, generally making teachers, parents and other adults proud, was not an image I had previously held.

'Was I good at lessons?' he asked, glaring at me as if I had asked if he would like an olive. 'What are you talking about? I was terrible! I was useless! I was the only boy in our year who didn't choose any science subjects when we got to thirteen! You had to do physics, biology or chemistry, or ordinary science if you were a bit thick. With the mind I had I thought, *Why do you have to do any?* I tried not picking one to see what happened and got out of the whole lot. I was the only person in my year who didn't take a science. On top of that, I enjoyed getting the cane. It was a badge of honour.'

It helped that Lawrence's sister Beverly's first husband, the one she married and had a kid with at sixteen, was a delinquent of legend called Gary McDonagh. Beverly's best friend, Beverley, also had a weakness for bad boys, so much so that, in 1986, she was convicted of accomplice to murder after her boyfriend, one Philip

Portington of Stapleford, was convicted of stabbing a man to death in Greece.

'Gary McDonagh was a year older than my sister and two years older than me. One day, him and Billy Leckie – great name, Billy Leckie – left school early, went to the Midland Red bus station in the centre of town and stole a double-decker bus. Billy Leckie was driving it, Gary was the conductor, and they were singing, "We're All Going on a Summer Holiday". That turned out to be their big mistake because everyone could hear them, so they only got to go round the block a few times before they were caught. Everyone at school was talking about it.'

Gary and Billy also went on to figure in a defining event of Lawrence's life: the time he lost his virginity, or rather, didn't. He was thirteen.

'I really liked this girl. Karen was her name. One night, when everyone was paired off on the grass, we nearly had sex. But I couldn't get it up, didn't know what to do, and she wasn't too sure about the whole thing either. So afterwards I said to her, "Shall we just say we did it?" Had we known about the fuss it would cause, we would never have gone down that path, because nobody in my year had done it and the whole thing blew up. Everyone was coming up to us, going, "What's it like?" Them two, the guys on the bus, said, "Is it true that you've done it?" I lied, of course, and they said to each other, "He's done it and we haven't." It was an important lesson, that day, because they gave me all this respect for something I didn't do. I still feel bad about it, actually.'

After leaving school at fifteen, Lawrence worked towards finding his own form and expression, which fell somewhere between the immediacy of punk and the elaborate fantasias of Marc Bolan.

There was inspiration from 'How Much Longer?' by Alternative TV, on which the former bank clerk-turned-fanzine writer Mark Perry asked of his fellow punks, 'How much longer will people wear / Nazi armbands and dye their hair?' On the other side came the deep sea of meaninglessness contained within a line like 'Prophet pumped the car star / Deeper only sweeter loves everyone', from 'Rock On' by T. Rex. By Felt's third album, 1984's *The Strange Idols Pattern and Other Short Stories*, a layered production from John Leckie, helped bring a new level of professionalism not only to Maurice Deebank's flowing river of guitar, but also to Lawrence's ability to match romanticism with realism. 'I was feeling desperate / Unable to decide / Between a life of misery / Or awful suicide,' he sang with deceptive good cheer on 'Dismantled King is Off the Throne'.

'I wanted to come alive, because I thought by then I would *be* alive,' said Lawrence of that 1984 period when Felt were making music reflecting both brutal reality and the haziest fever dream. 'I was living in Moseley, and if you want to know what Moseley is like, imagine Notting Hill in the 1970s: a counterculture neighbourhood, very bohemian. It felt like everything should have been falling into place in my life, but it wasn't.'

In 1982, Lawrence heard 'River Man' by Nick Drake and it blew his mind; the idea that a song could have a melody astonishing enough to make you cry, aligned to lyrics as mysterious as they are impactful. Around the same time, Bob Dylan's 'I Threw It All Away', from *Nashville Skyline*, showed him it was possible to write a love song with subtlety and originality. Maurice Deebank was coming up with graceful, classically inspired pieces like 'Crucifix Heaven' and 'Sempiternal Darkness', Leckie was helping Felt find the balance between the weird and the friendly, and Lawrence forged a unique sound thanks to a simple discovery: a knob on an amplifier. Serious musicians liked valve amplifiers, but Lawrence, in his dedication to avoidance of authenticity, favoured the HH 100-watt transistor amp with its lack of an organic valve throbbing away inside. One day, Lawrence noticed a knob at the top of the HH, asked 'What's that?' and flicked it.

'That was it, the sound of the band,' Lawrence remembered. 'It was brittle, treble-heavy, like nothing else out there. Aligned to Maurice's classical style, which he wanted to bring into rock, it was perfect.'

So perfect, in fact, that Lawrence sent a tape to Tom Verlaine of Television in the hope of hiring him as a producer. Verlaine replied to say he couldn't possibly work with this band because the songs had no beginning, middle or end, no light or shade, no arrangements, just Deebank cramming as many notes as possible into three minutes or so. Deebank never allowed for a guitar-free introduction or a break in the middle. He wouldn't stop. And Lawrence didn't try to make him stop because he thought it was great. They were the perfect pairing. If only Maurice Deebank wouldn't keep leaving the band.

'He did that every now and then,' Lawrence confirmed. 'We tried to make it on our own, three of us doing "Penelope Tree" in 1983, where I played all the guitars, but I could only manage the odd single, so I would cry, "I need him!". I went round to Maurice's house and begged him to return. I wasn't proud. "Please come back to us, Maurice. We can't do it without you." He had young-man sulks, always about something I had done that he didn't like. He didn't like to be told what to wear. He didn't like my attempts at instituting a set of rules. Eventually I thought, *I've had enough of this. I'll get someone else.*'

After an *NME* review of *The Strange Idols Pattern* dismissed Felt for writing the same song over and over, Lawrence decided the sound needed expanding. So he posted a notice in the Birmingham branch of Virgin Records and Felt embarked on the next phase of their artistic journey.

'Martin Duffy turns up with a crazy Italian keyboard and I go, *Wow, this could change everything.* By coincidence, I had been getting into the Hammond organ, buying Jimmy Smith and Jack McDuff records from this amazing shop in Birmingham called the Discery, and then along comes a guy with an organ. *Oh yeah, this will do!* On top of that, Martin Duffy was mild-mannered and amenable, coming into a fully formed band he thought were already big, so we didn't have the kind of problems we had with Maurice. He played me a beautiful piano song he had written called "Ferdinand Magellan" and I said, "We're in business".'

Maurice Deebank heard about the new arrangement – when he was in a nightclub – and decided he might get back on board after all. There began the birth of Felt's finest moment, but also an illustration of the impossibility of translating the visions in your head into reality. 1985's *Ignite the Seven Cannons* is the only Felt album to feature both Deebank and Duffy, and in keeping with its status as a pioneering dream-pop masterpiece, it was produced by Robin Guthrie of the Cocteau Twins, fans of Felt who had invited them to come on tour.

'We all crammed into a little splitter van and the Cocteau Twins paid for the hotels and everything,' said Lawrence as we got on the bus back to Peckham. 'It was all going so well that I said to Robin Guthrie, "Can you produce our album?" He said yes, but only if I signed a piece of paper to say I was not allowed into the control room for the mixing. I had to abide by his rules. Big mistake.'

Guthrie duly booked eleven days in a residential studio on the outskirts of Edinburgh. Liz Fraser, who as the singer of the Cocteau Twins had a voice celestial enough to make a committed atheist fall down on their knees and herald the Second Coming, was in the room upstairs, writing Cocteau Twins' lyrics. 'We were in the middle of recording "Primitive Painters" when Robin Guthrie said, "Hang on, I'll get Liz to sing on this." He called her down, played her a chunk, she did the lot in half an hour, and went back upstairs.'

With Lawrence banned from the studio for the three days it took Guthrie to mix the record, he had nothing to do but take the bus into the city and wander around before listening to what Guthrie had come up with in the evening. 'I didn't like it from the word go. I didn't like the mixes. By the time we got to "Primitive Painters", he was going, "This is the single, no argument! And I'll have to mix it again in London." I said yes, but also that he couldn't ban me this time, which is why "Primitive Painters" sounds so good and the other tracks don't. We went to a studio in Camden in London run by Barry Blue, who had massive hits in the '70s with Lynsey de Paul like "Sugar Me", so you knew it was going to be good. The rest of the album sounds like a Cocteau Twins record – all because I wasn't there.'

Lawrence was also subjected to a vicious mauling by a crazed Alsatian during the making of the record. 'I think Robin Guthrie knew about the dog, but he didn't tell me. This dog was terrorising the local community, but for some reason the rest of the band and the villagers in general knew to stand still when he went crazy. I freaked out, of course, and suffered horribly as a result, but the worst of it was that everyone, all the locals, were happy I got attacked because now they had an excuse to put the dog down. The police came and said I had to go to court and say it attacked me and there was no way I was going to do that. The man who owned the Alsatian was a sad figure – maybe a lone farmer, maybe a tramp. It was a real one-man-and-his-dog situation, and I couldn't face being the one responsible for having his beloved killer dog put down. Of course, if I had been allowed in the mix in the first place, we would have ended up with a better album and I wouldn't have ended up in hospital.'

Lawrence's phone went.

It was Corin.

The Gallery of Everything didn't want the head.

CHAPTER FOUR

ONE DAY IN SOHO

We met at a coffee shop near Lawrence's house, the unfortunately named Fix on Whitecross Street, at the heart of a busy market filled with stalls entirely useless to my unknown pop star friend because they dealt primarily with food, and he didn't like food. We were not planning to talk about anything in particular. Instead, we were going to experience a typical day in the life of Lawrence, and at the top of the agenda was a visit to Fopp Records in Shaftesbury Avenue, because they finally had copies of *Pop-Up! Ker-Ching! and the Possibilities of Modern Shopping* in stock. It was released two months previously.

'I don't think young people know the realities of being a pop star these days, so it will be useful for them to find out,' said Lawrence, after instructing an Italian girl with long brown hair and oversized Chloé glasses – who told us her dreams of being a highly artistic photographer and was working at the coffee shop until they became a reality – on how much hot water to pour out to make way for the excess of milk entering his tea in a disposable cup. 'I want to educate the kids on what happens when you make a record.'

Lawrence shuffled out onto the street so he could smoke a cigarette, drink his milky tea by one of the little metal tables, which he dragged out from a shadowy section of the pavement next to the window and into a narrow strip of sunlight, and get ready for the day. Market stallholders lugging crates of vegetables gave a casual nod and an 'Alright, Lawrence?'. 'Morning Lawrence,' chirped an official-looking woman with a clipboard who turned out to be in charge of collecting the stallholders' rates. A lot of people seemed to know him.

'And not a single one of them knows what I do,' he said softly. 'The younger ones think I've retired. I suppose the people working in the café might know because they like to take photographs of me. For everyone else, I'm the local character.'

We had to pop up to Lawrence's flat because he had two sackfuls of coins that he wanted to feed into a machine at his local branch of NatWest, which would then be converted. It would go straight into his account, and out again in the form of crisp new ten- and twenty-pound notes.

'There should be about forty quid there in brown money: pennies and 2p coins. I'll use it to buy myself something nice,' he said, opening the clanking metal door of his council block and pressing the button of the narrow metal lift, which was big enough for three people at a push and had a combination of mirror and strip lighting to ensure the creation of an environment highly unsympathetic to one's vanity. 'It's mad, isn't it? The Mozart Estate single "Relative Poverty" got into some vinyl singles chart and the label got all excited, but I didn't even care because it wouldn't translate into money. Getting into the charts is meaningless these days. It's all about adverts now.'

The metal doors wheezed open onto his floor, where the flat next door had a sign commanding people not to post any circulars or junk mail. Lawrence's own deep-blue door had a reinforced glass window at head height. Inside the flat, on the right was a narrow corridor with wooden record bins, as you would find in an actual record shop. Straight ahead were sturdy wooden shelves of books from floor to ceiling. The best covers were on display: a glum-looking woman on Jeremy Sandford's *Cathy Come Home*, the 1966 play about a young couple falling into homelessness and poverty, which made enough of an impact to inspire the creation of the homelessness charity Shelter; John Baxter's *Ken Russell: An Appalling Talent*, a biography of the wayward film director featuring a photograph of Russell on the cross, sticking out his tongue; and *The Early Pohl*, a collection of short stories by the American science fiction writer Frederik Pohl, which featured an image of a man on an Edwardian-style telephone with a pencil for a head.

Elsewhere, there were true life accounts by and about junkies (Bill Clegg's *Portrait of an Addict as a Young Man*, Alexander Masters' *Stuart: A Life Backwards*), '60s kitchen-sink classics (*Poor Cow* and *Up the Junction* by Nell Dunn), lots of Kerouac, Bukowski, Burroughs and Selby Jr, and a shelf dedicated to biographies by relatives of murderers and the murdered (*The Devil's Daughter* by Christine Hart, daughter of the Moors Murderer Ian Brady, *And I Don't Want to Live This Life* by Deborah Spungen, mother of Sid Vicious's girlfriend, Nancy Spungen). The books were arranged with a conflicting view to aesthetics and content. Addicts and down-and-outs had their own section, but a section for Penguin paperbacks with orange spines meant the jazz great Charles Mingus found himself sharing company with Edna O'Brien and Shelagh Delaney. In literature as in life, Lawrence was making a brave if ultimately doomed attempt to impose order on chaos.

Wooden cabinets, which he opened using a metal shoe horn because he couldn't bear the prospect of handles, lined a wall of what would normally be described as a bedroom, although this one had no bed in it. Inside one cupboard was his extensive archive of a life in pop, while on the opposite wall was a glass cabinet for his clothes so that they, like the books in the hallway, could be on display. 'I've had enough of second-hand clothes unless they're dead stock, never worn,' he announced, rifling through his latest purchases. 'These days I'm in the market for the very best branded items.'

Among them were some swimming shorts emblazoned with the Lidl logo. 'These are really rare, extremely limited edition,' he declared, holding them up to the light pouring in from a window looking out onto the city. 'Every year, Lidl have a day when special items are available and they sell out immediately, so I go to the suburbs to get them. You know if you go on holiday, to Spain or something? That's when you wear the swimming trunks. And look at this . . .'

Lawrence unsheathed a baseball jacket and T-shirt featuring the logo of Greggs, Britain's premier low-cost pastries outlet. 'I got them in Primark when they did a special Greggs collection. They're only available in the suburbs.' He also had a pair of Greggs underpants decorated with little sausage rolls, which made me wonder if there would come a day when Lawrence would be fully kitted out in clothing emblazoned with the official Greggs logo.

'Next time we play London, I'm going to do it.'

Even the pants?

He looked a little affronted at the suggestion that he might not. 'Of course. The fans would expect nothing less. Although I bet you that if you started going out with someone, after a while they would go, "You're not putting those pants on." Girls don't like that sort of thing, I've noticed.'

Lawrence had a lot of designer clothes, including a hoodie in yellow and red shades similar to the rhubarb and custard chewy sweets that were popular with '70s kids. It cost him £210. 'Sometimes I buy that, sometimes I buy shirts for seven pounds, and the result is that I look a bit like a tramp, even though I'm often in really expensive clothes. Westwood Chav, I call it.'

He pulled out a checked Ralph Lauren polo shirt which he found in TK Maxx for a few quid. 'Feel the quality of that,' he commanded, taking out the sharply folded shirt from the cupboard, which as far as I could tell was made of some standard-issue cotton mesh. 'Feel it! Isn't it amazing?'

There was hardly any furniture in the flat, although Lawrence was planning to get a carpet as soon as he found a new decorator. The renovation had been going on for ten years and there was still a long way to go, not least because a large blurry grey mark stained one of the walls in the living room – the result, he said, of water seeping through the window frame. The only way to deal with the seepage was by replacing the window entirely and that could only be done with scaffolding, because Lawrence's flat was on one of the highest floors of the building.

'Guy Chadwick is in the window replacement business these days,' said Lawrence, citing the former singer of the House of Love, the band that replaced Felt in the affections of Creation Records' Alan McGee when they were touted briefly in the late '80s as the great hope of indie. 'Perhaps I could talk the council into getting him round for a quote.'

There was no kitchen, just a microwave and a sink. In the living room was a foldaway surgeon's bed from the 1940s, alongside Lawrence's big investment: a Ligne Roset armchair that he had made in Paris and had to wait six months for. Unusually flush one month due to a foray into male modelling, he shelled out £1,600 for it.

'To sit in a really beautiful chair, playing music or playing my guitar – it is my one luxury,' he said, although it looked like a luxury he was yet to indulge in given the Ligne Roset chair was still in its plastic packaging. 'Apart from that, I'm into denial.'

One recent alteration was the culmination of a long-held dream for Lawrence. Over the years, journalists who came to the flat for interviews invariably reported on his response to their request to use the toilet: he drew them a map to the nearest public convenience. But even if he could keep the journalists out, there remained the danger that friends or workmen might use the toilet without asking. Now he had come up with what he believed to be the ideal solution.

'Have you noticed anything different about this toilet?' he said, gesturing towards the unremarkable white porcelain bowl and accompanying cistern, before resting his hands on his hips in proud anticipation. I confessed I hadn't.

'I've had the door taken off. Nobody but me can use it ever again.'

I took a moment to reflect on this.

'Haven't you opened yourself up to the possibility,' I asked, 'that someone will just use it anyway, not caring about whether there is a door on the toilet or not?'

What little colour remained in his face drained entirely. He stared at the toilet in silent horror.

'I hadn't thought of that.'

On one of the walls of the living room was a series of Post-it notes, there to remind Lawrence of the various things he needed reminding of. There were his names for future girl bands. Bin Bags was one. Victoria Boots, inspired by a trip to Boots in Victoria, was another. 'Listen to new records for an hour every morning' was a motivational note to self he posted up there. In the main, the flat was functional, with a minimum of clutter and everything behind doors so it wasn't doing his head in. He was in the process of hiring a handyman to cut any cables to an absolute minimum, so they weren't lying about the place, snaking up the walls and generally getting into his brain, jabbing at his synapses and sending him spiralling into a vortex of chaos. The commitment to minimalism began when he was a child, watching gangster movies and thinking about how appealing the prison cells looked, especially ones in top jails like Rikers Island and Alcatraz. He even looked into getting a concrete slab bed built into the wall but it proved prohibitively expensive. It was a monastic life, albeit one surrounded by the things that made him come alive.

'Books are the house bricks of my world. Records are the slate roof. Clothes are the soft furnishings.'

It was a world he occupied alone. 'That's because I never met the one person who could have been a partner in this life,' he said as we took hold of the remarkably heavy plastic bags filled with coins and lugged them out of the flat and into the lift. 'Instead, I met people who were jealous of what I was doing, because I was 100 per cent consumed and that left no room for a relationship, which is sad. For them it was a betrayal, like I was in love with another woman, but it was my music I was in love with. I would say, "We're never going to live together", and at the time there was one clear example of the kind of living I wouldn't have minded trying. Woody Allen lived across Central Park from Mia Farrow, him in one townhouse, her in the other, and I would say, "There's someone who lives in this way, and it works really well . . ." Obviously it didn't work out so well, but my idea was that we could live in a block together, like Kenneth Williams and his mum. No one I met wanted to go along with this scenario unfortunately and now there hasn't been anyone for decades. I had a really nice girlfriend who I liked a lot, a French girl, and when she walked out the door, I said, "I'll never be in a relationship ever again." I never have. I like my own company. The sex part, you forget about it after a while. And I wasn't, what do you call it, testosterone-heavy. I was a two-minute wonder. They're not missing much.'

It was time to go to the bank, a ten-minute walk away, next to Barbican Underground station, and we could only go to this branch because going to any other simply wasn't worth it. 'Honestly, I get so much hassle,' he puffed, as we shuffled along the underpass connecting the Barbican Centre with its Tube stop. 'They take one look at me and I'm out, but at this branch of NatWest they know me so it's okay. It is important for fans to know that even at this point in my life, I still need to cash in my pennies. This is the kind of thing I have to do just to get by.'

Lawrence didn't possess a bank card. He couldn't go to a cash machine and take out money. Instead, he had a cheque book, so he could enter his local branch and get money out from his account that way. 'I'm a cash man,' he announced. 'A gangster gets a big wad out, held together with a tie pin, and everyone stands back in amazement. A lady opens her purse, the cash pours out, and everyone goes, "Ooh, she's doing well, isn't she?" You know where you are with cash. These days, you can have a card even if you don't own a pair of shoes, but you'll get into so much trouble if you keep swiping everywhere. Cash gives you hope – even a lack of it. I find it heartening, in a way, to realise you only have 2p left, because it can't go any lower. It can only go up from there.'

We had to hope so, as we poured Lawrence's big bags of brown money into NatWest's coin-eating machine and he ended up with £40.50. Not a bad result. After getting the money in note form from the cashier, Lawrence put it into an envelope and explained that he liked to compartmentalise his cash: some for the ever-increasing gas and electricity bills his little flat was bombarded with, some for looking good, some for buying records. He was thinking of blowing the £40.50 at a record fair held once a year at an old working men's club in Stoke Newington where, for the past two years, he had been allowed to have a tiny slither of a friend's stall. 'I'll sell records I've bought that I don't like, or stuff people have given me that I don't want. I'm not selling any old iron. I'm selling rare records I thought were good but turned out to be bad.'

Sometimes he bought two copies of an album – 'just in case' – and now he was having to sell his duplicates. Caroline Catz, an actress, film director and friend of ours who had recently found herself appointed as parking monitor for Mozart Estate when they did a gig at a venue near her home, bought Sandie Shaw's 1969 album *Reviewing the Situation* off Lawrence at the record fair. Tacked onto its sleeve was a series of Post-it notes:

I bought two copies of this reissue so that I could sell one to you!! I want to share this masterpiece of the late '60s – and for once the bonus material is essential and on a separate disc so as not to spoil the flow of the main LP.

This, like Scott 4, *was a huge flop! They are similar bedfellows. Sandie redesigns Lionel Bart's clever classic for an underground crowd and tears open Dylan's 'Lay Lady Lay'. Even 'Sympathy for the Devil' is transformed with very serious surgery. She does not falter once. The original is ultra rare – never to be seen at a record fair so this is your only opportunity to own a copy. Do NOT pass it by. If you buy it and don't like it you'd better go to hospital coz there is something seriously wrong with you!!!*

Lawrence £25

Lawrence's shopping obsessions, I reflected as we got on a bus heading down Tottenham Court Road, spilled over into his creative life. Below a window of Heal's, the quality furniture store that for the past 200 years had been furnishing the homes of the British upper middle classes, was a figure in a sleeping bag, curled up caterpillar-like against the wall. On the other side of the shop window was a wood-framed bed on sale for £1,200. The scenario had been depicted on a song on *Pop-Up! Ker-Ching!* called 'Lookin' Through Glass', in which a homeless man is separated by a thin sheet of glass from the most basic of comforts: a bed.

'Not having money for so long, you can't stop going to the shops,' said Lawrence, staring at the figure from the top deck. 'When I had no money at all, I would go to Selfridges and look at the expensive men's clothes. Now that I've got a little bit of money, I'll go to Lidl and Aldi, and it made me realise: shopping is all anybody does. It's a fixation. We're in a shopping world. People will do it on a Sunday, then panic because it's early closing. "Lookin' Through Glass" is a true story. I saw a man living in the doorway of Heal's, just like the one down there. He's down on the floor, in the dark and the damp, and he's thinking, *If I could only have a bed.*

And the chorus is about someone who has so much money, there's nothing left to buy.'

We stepped off the bus and went into a vast, empty branch of Benetton on Oxford Street, where the children's section had an item of clothing Lawrence had taken a shine to: a white sweater with a cherry inlay, on sale for £75. And the moment we walked in, the security guard went from bored and sullen to suspicious and engaged. We light-footed it down the wide shiny stairs, under lights so bright you felt they were interrogating you, and the young sales assistant down there gave us a nervous hello and asked if we needed any help. Lawrence sped over to the cherry jumpers and picked one up, as the sales assistant edged ever closer without getting so near that it would constitute harassment. The security guard had no such qualms. He stood a foot behind us, arms crossed, scowling.

This kind of thing simply didn't happen to most people, which made me realise how much I took for granted the freedom of being seen as a potential customer, of sales assistants being pleasant and welcoming, of the biggest problem being someone trying to sell you something you don't want. For Lawrence, it was a different experience entirely. Together we were objects of suspicion, shoplifters, troublemakers, another pair of inner-city undesirables, unlikely to make an honest purchase, bad for Benetton's image as a place of health, vitality and brightly coloured leisurewear. It wasn't nice. I wanted to get out as quickly as possible.

'The look he gave me,' said Lawrence of the security guard once we did what everyone in Benetton wanted and went elsewhere, padding with extra rapidity away from the scene of the non-existent crime. 'I wanted to say hello and let him know I'm okay, but you know what they're thinking. "He's trouble. Got to keep my eye on this guy." They take one look at me and assume I'm going to lift something. Not that I would. Well, I would if I could, but I'd be too nervous of getting caught.'

It was time to visit Fopp, where a thin man in a tie, a V-neck sweater, glasses and a name tag that said Mark arrived to announce some incredible news: a thief had been targeting Lawrence's entire output. The first thing he, she or they got their mitts on were the Felt album reissues, all ten of them, swiped in one go. Then they set their sights on a copy of *Lawrence of Belgravia* in the DVD department. Next, they tackled the Go-Kart Mozart albums – all on vinyl, of course – and finally, the day it arrived in the shop, the thief lifted the new Mozart Estate album. This was a particular feat of daring, given the handful of copies were on display on the counter top right next to the staff.

'The Lawrence Thief of Covent Garden,' said Lawrence in a reverential hush as Mark gave him a handful of Mozart Estate albums to sign. 'Can you believe it? I've got my own special criminal. Don't they know about my poverty-stricken situation? You would think these fans would want to help me, rather than make matters worse. Having said that, I bet Coldplay don't have their own dedicated robbers.'

'I nicked a calendar once,' said Mark. 'I got twelve months.'

'Conditional discharge?' Lawrence enquired, before getting the joke. 'The Lawrence thief must be a boy, or a man. A girl wouldn't do that.'

'Yeah, they do,' Mark corrected.

I pictured the Lawrence Thief. They would be a slight figure, furtive and apologetic, slinking around Fopp dressed in black, most likely with an overgrown fringe shading their eyes. They spent so many years garnering such little attention that lifting the products of their obsession without anybody noticing would prove an easy task. They lived alone, or maybe with a parent or two, and if they had a job, it would be in the civil service or a library: somewhere safe, regular. We hung around for an extra half an hour in the hope of luring the thief in with the ultimate bait: Lawrence himself. But they never revealed themselves. They were too clever for that.

It was lunchtime. We found a seat on the pavement outside an old-fashioned café on Wardour Street called Bar Bruno, where Lawrence asked to use the toilet and the waitress, despite calling us both darling and saying she would ensure his tea was sweet just like her, told him it was out of order, they were cleaning it. An invisible force field had appeared over the doorway and could not be penetrated.

'That happens in the West End all the time and it isn't fair,' he said glumly. 'I suppose they think I'm going to shoot up or something. The awful thing is I only ever want to go to the toilet, just like anybody else. It certainly increases your feelings of alienation.'

The alienation found its parallel in *Taxi Driver*, the first film to really speak to Lawrence. Martin Scorsese's 1976 movie – about a mentally unstable Vietnam vet working as a taxi driver and swearing to clean up a bankrupt city that Scorsese presented as a sweltering, overpopulated hell – had a central figure he could relate to. Travis Bickle thinks of Cybill Shepherd's presidential campaign volunteer as an angel, unreal, untouched by the filth around her. He doesn't know how to exist in normal life. He deals with the chaos in his head by writing everything down. Travis Bickle is adrift in the city, with a front-row seat to it all, yet totally apart.

A man passed us on the street and did a double take, giving Lawrence what he interpreted as a dirty stare.

'What are you looking at?' Lawrence snarled, raising his fists like a boxer. 'Come on then.'

He leaned over the table and, in a confiding tone, declared: 'You'll notice I only said that after he turned his back. I would never dare do it if he could see.'

Lawrence first saw *Taxi Driver* in 1980, around the time he formed Felt. It made him realise that films were as important as records in shaping one's view of the world, in making sense of it all. 'It is still my favourite film today. Just at the point I was getting interested in writing songs, here was an ordinary guy in psychic trauma who was confused and everything was upside down. And he didn't know how to behave. He tried hard to get a girlfriend, yet he didn't understand that taking her to a graphic porn movie wasn't the thing to do. He was after a goddess like Cybill Shepherd, and then along comes Jodie Foster as a twelve-year-old prostitute. He doesn't want to have sex with her. He wants to be her friend.

'I also loved the fact that Paul Schrader, *Taxi Driver*'s scriptwriter, was so desperate to write something outstanding that he was living in his car due to his dedication to it. Harvey Keitel is the pimp, and the scene between him and De Niro made me cry simply because I had never seen acting so intense before. It is uncompromising.'

A big-shouldered six-footer in turned-up Levis and Dr Martens, a bomber jacket and a little woollen hat perched far enough on the back of his head to make space for a quiff protruding from the front stopped before us. 'So sorry I couldn't be at your last gig,' he said. 'Heard it was great.'

'Yeah, it was,' confirmed Lawrence. Then, after the man went on his way: 'He looked good, didn't he? Like he was from the 1980s. Must be his thing.'

'*Goldmine Trash*, what an album,' said a sandy-haired man who had been pacing about on the other wide of the street with a furrowed brow, before rushing over and making his statement.

'Amazing concert in Tufnell Park, Lawrence,' said a dark-eyed woman with an Italian accent, making a bowing, praying gesture of respect. 'Any chance I could have a photograph?'

Following his usual guidelines as regards to selfies, Lawrence rejected the offer. But in order to make sure this respectful acolyte did not go away feeling bad, from his WH Smith reusable carrier bag he dug out a clean white card bearing the legend: YES I MET LAWRENCE.

'That's better than a photograph,' he said, handing over the card. 'It'll be worth quite a bit one day.'

After 'Primitive Painters', it looked like Felt might actually make it big and become a proper, famous band, up there with Echo & the Bunnymen and the Psychedelic Furs. Mike Alway, the man who signed Felt to Cherry Red, had left to start Blanco Y Negro, an indie-style label that was actually a subsidiary of the massive Warner Brothers. 'But he took everyone else apart from us. They didn't want us. We were the only band left behind.'

Meanwhile, a voluble Scot with a love of '60s garage punk and a £1,000 bank loan got in touch with Lawrence to suggest Felt sign to a label he started in 1983, sending him 45s by bands with names like Biff Bang Pow! and Revolving Paint Dream in an attempt to lure him. At the time, Lawrence wanted Felt to move away from the lengthy guitar solos and the atmospheric instrumentals, and towards the economy and precision of great songwriting, which is the kind of thing Alan McGee's Creation Records were dealing in. An indie pin-up called Pete Astor was the label's high hope: his band, the Loft, had released a 1984 single called 'Why Does the Rain', which had a Byrdsy, melancholic jangle aligned to a jagged, contemporary energy, heralding a new '60s-influenced '80s underground sound. Lawrence decided to check it all out by taking McGee up on an offer to visit a little club he was running on Tottenham Court Road called The Living Room.

'I said to Gay Jon – you remember Gay Jon – "Let's go and see this guy who keeps sending me these records." We went down and the Jasmine Minks were playing: great name, awful band. Pete Astor's band the Loft was supporting: awful name, great band. The next time I came to London, I stayed with Pete at his house in Crouch End and he played me *Friends* by the Beach Boys, who I thought I didn't like and, wow, it was amazing. Straight away I was interested in these people. Pete Astor was going to be a big star and he had it all: the looks, the songs, the image. But he made a massive mistake: he split the band up at the wrong time. He wanted total control, and when he got total control, it wasn't as good.'

Creation delivered what Lawrence had been looking for since his early teens: a scene, built on friendship, a touch of ambition, and a shared taste in cool, interesting things. Lawrence marked Felt's new direction in May 1986 with 'Ballad of the Band', a two-and-a-half-minute, melody-rich kiss-off to Maurice Deebank that presented Felt as a major act, talking about how it all went wrong, even though hardly anyone had heard of them yet. The inspiration was 1973's 'Ballad of Mott the Hoople', which documented the struggles Ian Hunter's proto-glam rockers had gone through before Bowie's 'All the Young Dudes' saved their career.

'"Ballad of the Band" was a conceit,' said Lawrence as he sipped his milky tea. 'You can't have a ballad when you haven't done anything yet, so I thought: *Let's do a song like we are already a part of history.'*

A headline slot at the Clarendon Ballroom in Hammersmith in 1986, supported by Pete Astor's new band the Weather Prophets and the Jesus and Mary Chain's stand-up drummer Bobby Gillespie's band Primal Scream, cemented the camaraderie – to the extent that Lawrence didn't even mind when Alan McGee set his sights on making Pete Astor the first star of Creation, Bobby Gillespie the second, and Lawrence the third. He believed in McGee from day one.

'We all had good lyrics, good melodies, but what really impressed me is that Alan kept saying, "We're going to be famous. We're going to change the music business." Not, *"You're* going to be famous." I laughed at him, but at least he was going to try. At the time, Creation were not popular in the slightest. This was six months before their success with the Jesus and Mary Chain.'

After a short instrumental album reissued as *The 17th Century*, he delivered a masterpiece in *Forever Breathes the Lonely Word*. Driven by Martin Duffy's whirling, optimistic Hammond organ, bright melodies brimming with smart pop artistry and a clear, unfussy production from John Rivers, this was the underground classic that gave Lawrence's poetic tendencies a chance to flourish.

He sang about the price of hanging onto your dreams in an unforgiving world on 'Rain of Crystal Spires', feeling eternally lost on 'Down But Not Yet Out', and finding comfort in the unthreatening legacies of the deceased on 'All the People I Like are Those That are Dead'. It had real crossover potential. The shimmering gossamer lightness of 'Gather Up Your Wings and Fly' was delightful, even when Lawrence offered cryptic Dylanesque put-downs like, 'It won't be long now while we're shaking your apple tree'. Everything was in place, even the cover photograph of one half of the young Martin Duffy's fresh, unsmiling face against a plain purple backdrop.

'It looked like we were going off with *Forever Breathes*,' remembered Lawrence. 'Alan said it was the best album he released on Creation. I was actually quite shocked everyone liked it so much because I assumed it would go the same way as everything else, but it seemed like the album really was going to be a hit.'

Even when it was all going right, it still went wrong. With *Forever Breathes the Lonely Word* so clearly being one of the great albums of the 1980s, the *NME* – that bible of all things credible – was set to give Felt the ultimate stamp of approval by sticking them on its cover for 8 November 1986. At the last minute, Felt were replaced, appositely enough, with a special report on youth suicide by the journalist Lucy O'Brien. Few could have known the profile in silhouette representing a dead body at the bottom of an otherwise black page was Lawrence's.

'They might as well have said we're not good enough to go on the cover,' said Lawrence of the *NME* debacle as we left the café to wander down Old Compton Street in search of both a toilet and the Saatchi Gallery, which, no matter how many times I told him was on the King's Road, Lawrence insisted was in Soho. 'Then we did *Poem of the River* in 1987 and it all went all wrong. Alan McGee wanted a Creation house producer and he got one in a guy called Mayo Thompson, who had been in a '60s art band called Red Krayola and it was a crazy idea, a disaster. We were his guinea pigs and it didn't work. People love *Poem* and I don't know why. It is a mess. They love it because it is tortured, I suppose.'

At least he had his fans, one of whom turned up at a Felt gig at the University of London Union and came back with the band to the Hammersmith house of its guitarist Phil King, thereby beginning her mission to become Lawrence's girlfriend through sheer persistence. Her name was Vikki.

'To me, she was a modern version of a girlfriend that hadn't yet been invented, and she fixated on me with stalker-like obsession,' said Lawrence. 'I would go, "You're not my girlfriend" and she ignored me until she was. By that point, I was sick of coming to London, sick of seeing who I would stay with that night, because then you have this awful moment of not being at home, you're scared to go to the toilet and their kitchen is messy. Maybe they leave butter on the knife, maybe there are toast crumbs in the butter dish – all the things that drive me mad and it is a nightmare. Vikki had her own place and it was very clean, so finally I had somewhere nice to stay. Vikki became a reality and the reality was good.'

Before returning to New Zealand and becoming a high-school teacher, Vikki, also known, by Lawrence at least, as Vikki Ball (Round), Vikki V-Sign, Spook, Mrs C.C. Felt and Cartoon Character Face, spent seven years in London, a few of them in an on-off relationship with Lawrence. She remembered it as 'dreadful, dreadful, dreadful. He's adorable – from a distance – but at the same time he certainly destroyed my confidence because he would say things like – I remember this one – he wanted to talk to my mother to find out why I was so annoying. He didn't want me to kiss him. He didn't want me to touch his hair. We had to sit in opposite corners of the room. He was very controlled, controlling, and extraordinarily aloof. I suppose that was the attraction, in the beginning at least. That and the fact that I thought he was so cool.'

Initially, Vikki was determined to get Lawrence's attention. She told him that she'd travelled all the way from New Zealand just to see Felt in concert; a complete lie, but one that was bound to appeal to his vanity. She took a bunch of fireworks to a gig with the intention of setting them off and causing a ruckus. She talked her way backstage and cornered him. She got a phone book and went through all the people with his non-existent surname in the Birmingham area until he answered. Having established there wasn't a Mrs Lawrence, she announced that she was calling because he had ordered a record from Harold Moores, the classical music shop she worked at in London, and she needed to make sure it went to the right address.

'He didn't know who I was, but he humoured me and, from then on, I was calling him all the time. Eventually I turned up at his amazing flat in Birmingham and insisted we watch a football game on the television. Then I went into the bathroom and changed into a Scotland football kit, because I was obsessed with the Scottish footballer Pat Nevin. That's where it all began.'

Vikki lived in a squat in north London alongside Douglas Hart from the Jesus and Mary Chain and a heroin addict from New Zealand, and once their sort-of relationship got going, she looked after Lawrence every time he came down from Birmingham. 'I would say to Vikki stuff like, "Now we're going to Stratford-upon-Avon, where Shakespeare came from." She would run me baths, cook me meals, and she had clean sheets, so although the rest of the squat was a heroin-infested hell-hole, I liked staying there.'

There were adventures along the way. On a road trip to Cornwall, they stopped at a hotel to stay the night, but not liking the look of the place and noticing there was nobody in reception, Lawrence dared Vikki to steal a convex gilt-edged mirror on the wall that was similar to one featured in Joseph Losey's *The Servant*. 'It was like Bonnie and Clyde,' remembered Vikki. 'I went in there and took the mirror off the wall, which wasn't very easy, and we ran back to the car and roared off. Lawrence loved that mirror. Do you know the Felt song, "Get Out of My Mirror"? It's that mirror he's telling me to get out of. Once I turned up at his flat in Birmingham uninvited and he wouldn't let me in, so I told him I was going to stand there and die on his doorstep. That became "Don't Die On My Doorstep".'

Lawrence got Vikki to do things for him. He got her to write to the food manufacturers Burtons as Mrs C.C. Felt of Rainham, Essex, and ask them to bring back onto the market Piglets, a crispy, crunchy bacon-flavour potato snack, because her son Lawrence couldn't face life without them. He got her to take records he had been sent by indie labels to record shops and pretend she had bought them from the shop so she could exchange them for ones he wanted.

'I would go into HMV in Birmingham or Virgin Records in London and do it because he was too embarrassed or scared to do it himself,' said Vikki. 'One time, though, he came with me and we got caught. I was captured on camera, peeling a price sticker off a record, and the two of us were taken to a back room and interrogated by the police. The end result was a lifetime ban from HMV Piccadilly. Taking records back to the shop was definitely one of my regular jobs.'

What Lawrence did for Vikki in return remains unclear. 'He had no interest in my body, and never tried to do anything to please me, while somehow making out that his lack of interest in sex was my fault. He certainly never touched my breasts. He told me he was saving himself for Natassja Kinski.'

Nonetheless, the relationship was, if not conventionally romantic, then at least providing Lawrence with the friend he had dreamed of for so long. 'Now I had the gang I always wanted, even though there were only two of us. I could be myself, which is hard with girlfriends – most of them didn't like my fastidiousness – and Vikki didn't want children, which was even better. I have to say, if I was a normal guy, she would have been the one.'

Needless to say, it couldn't last. Another problem was his terror of intimacy, which meant anything resembling a healthy conjugal relationship was out of the question. Then there was his diet.

'Occasionally he would allow me to get an Indian or Chinese takeaway, but Lawrence would decide they were disgusting and throw them away before I had a chance to even take a bite. He subsisted mainly on Uncle Ben's rice. I actually lost a lot of weight during the time I was with Lawrence.'

According to Lawrence, the real problem was Vikki's possessiveness. 'It got to the whole "You don't love me" point,' he sighed, as if reeling off a tragic inevitability. 'On top of that, she wouldn't accept my compliments, so when I told her she looked like a beautiful little pixie with a lovely round head, she didn't think I was serious. I even bought her a football once, in celebration of her head. I would say I couldn't love her because of the way I was, but I was happy for us to be friends, and then she would drive me mental by going on about it all the time. Then there was the jealousy. She thought I had girls hidden in cupboards. The truth is I did have something more important than her, which was the band.'

He also met, towards the end of Felt, a strange woman who had a profound effect on his life professionally, personally and psychologically. Rose McDowall left a violent childhood in Glasgow to form Strawberry Switchblade with her friend Jill Bryson, a vision of '60s gothic in polka-dot dresses, stacked black hair and wild overuse of mascara. She had an unerring if reluctant ability for fashioning perfect pop: Strawberry Switchblade's 1985 top-ten hit 'Since Yesterday' was filled with an innocent sense of loss, so joyful, sad and tuneful, you would never have guessed it was about nuclear war. Rose turned up at the Creation offices one day and, to Lawrence, this was a big deal: someone who had actually achieved a real hit record, entering the hit-free world he was a part of.

'I spent most of the time asking her what it was like to be in the charts and what actually happens when you go on *Top of the Pops*. She spent the rest of the time going, "Why do you want to know about that? It was rubbish." She didn't like it.'

Rose joined Felt on stage for a multi-artist Creation Records benefit concert called 'Doing it For the Kids' in August 1988, sang on the final Felt album (1989's *Me and a Monkey on the Moon*) and sprinkled some much-needed stardust onto Lawrence and his world. To his amazement, Rose hated rubbing shoulders with pop stars. She wanted to be in the Creation scene. She wanted to join Felt. It could have worked. A live photograph in *Melody Maker* from 'Doing it For the Kids' featured Rose and Martin Duffy under a spider light, evoking the kind of dark glamour Lawrence had been after for years.

'"Primitive Painters" is a classic defeatist anthem, a shamefaced confession of an inability to cope with life's most rudimentary demands (like eating vegetables),' wrote Simon Reynolds in a *Melody Maker* review of the gig, which elsewhere berated the entire Creation scene for its neurotic attempts to revive rock's past glories. 'Live, even without the stratospheric powerhouse of Liz Fraser's vocal, it's an irresistible, cascading surge, a contradiction of the vocal and its morose words. Lawrence's listless wisp must be the ultimate voice of deficiency and unrealised selfhood: a one-note range, and even then he doesn't sound in full command of that note.'

It amounted to high praise, and it seemed like Rose McDowall might be exactly what Felt needed. But there proved to be problems, not least when Lawrence first spent the night in a Muswell Hill flat that Strawberry Switchblade's record label had rented for them, with Rose downstairs and Jill Bryson, who hardly ever went out, in the room above. Rose and Lawrence went to a gig by some long-forgotten indie band in the back room of the Falcon, a pub in Camden which had become the fulcrum of the Creation scene. She gave him a tab of LSD and, after the concert, took him to some woods near her flat. The freaking-out began around midnight when Rose told Lawrence that sometimes, in the dead of night, she liked to come into the park, take all her clothes off, and clamber up a tree to perch on a branch.

'She wanted to be a fairy,' said Lawrence. 'She talked about becoming one of the fairies in the Arthur Rackham illustrations. She was thinking of getting her ears done to make them pointy, and would probably have got some wings too if she could find a doctor to do it. By this point I was thinking, *This girl is really weird.*'

Rose took Lawrence back to her flat, which was old and run-down; because she was Scottish, he assumed she was attempting to recreate the ambiance of the Gorbals, the famously deprived tenement blocks on the south side of Glasgow. 'She opened the door, we walked into the living room and this thing jumps from my toes all the way over my head and down the other side. I was on acid and a creature jumped on me. She hadn't told me she had a pet monkey.'

She hadn't told him she had two: marmosets who lived in a floor-to-ceiling cage in the corner of the living room, complete with tree limbs and foliage she'd lugged up from the local park. The fact that the flat smelt like a zoo alone was enough to twist Lawrence's psychedelically addled mind into terrifying contortions; that Rose shared her flat with two primates was too much to comprehend. 'She talked to them all the time, although I never found out their names. She liked those monkeys a lot more than she liked people.'

Lawrence resolved never to go in the living room again, apart from one time when watching a video compilation of all the times Rose had been on television proved too much of a temptation. But the monkeys were not the only creatures she shared the flat with. 'One time I woke up in the middle of the night and saw this big thing walking along the wall. I jumped out of bed and screamed, "There's a lizard up there!" Rose said, "It's in your imagination. Go back to sleep." But after the sight of that mini-dinosaur crawling along the wall, there was no way I was going to stay in the flat, so I got up to get dressed. Rose sat up in bed and went, "What are you doing?" I replied, "I can't stay here, I'm off to sleep in the car", and got out of that menagerie as quickly as possible. She was quite cross with me actually.'

With Rose in London and the rest of Felt in Birmingham, not to mention the complications wrought by her coterie of exotic pets, Lawrence knew it would never work to have her in the band. Besides, the ten-year plan was almost complete. Rose suggested they become boyfriend and girlfriend. 'I went "Nah". She liked boy-men and I suppose I fitted that description, but she wasn't interested in the films and books I was into. She was interested in magick.'

When she wasn't with the Creation crowd, Rose was hanging out with Thee Temple Ov Psychick Youth, a British association founded by Genesis P. Orridge, formerly of the art-noise wreckers of civilisation Throbbing Gristle, who explored mysticism, sex magic, ritual, the occultism of Aleister Crowley and other weird shit. 'She was into cuttings and pentagrams and so on. There was a girl on the fringes of the scene who Rose really hated and her big idea was, "Let's bring that girl round to the flat and sacrifice her". She didn't do it, of course. Rose was actually a very nice person and she was only saying it to get a reaction, but it freaked a lot of people out anyway. She also dressed like a witch for a while, with a pointy hat and a big black cape. She would put them on to go down the shops.'

Halfway down Old Compton Street, we bumped into an old friend of Lawrence's. Martin Kelly co-founded Heavenly Records and managed the pop trio Saint Etienne; his brother Paul made the *Lawrence of Belgravia* documentary. Martin had high hopes for Lawrence's long-overdue success with Mozart Estate.

'The Forum by the end of the year,' he predicted, naming the north London venue with a capacity of more than 2,000, the same place where Felt did the 'Doing it For the Kids' benefit back when it was known as the Town & Country Club.

'I don't know about that,' said Lawrence, staring at the ground and pushing a discarded nitrous oxide canister about with the tip of his brown suede shoe. 'We have a concert at the Lexington . . .'

'You've got to think bigger, Lawrence,' Martin commanded. 'It's building up, man. Best reviews ever, more and more people discovering Felt and Denim . . .'

'He's even got a Lawrence Thief,' I added.

'We're not ready for that kind of concert,' said Lawrence. 'We're not big enough, we've got to take it slowly.'

You had to wonder if Lawrence, for all his dreams of glory, really wanted to be famous. Douglas Hart said this was what made him fabulous: a total lack of compromise, even in the face of his own stated ambitions. As we leaned on a lamppost on the corner of Old Compton Street and Frith Street, and watched as a begging street junkie approached us before thinking better of it, Lawrence denied the suggestion entirely.

'Alan McGee used to say that all the time about me. He would go, "Lawrence doesn't really want to be famous and he would hate it if he was. He likes the way he is. He wants to be in the underground." It wasn't true. I certainly wanted to be famous, especially after people kept getting famous around me and we remained the band at the bottom of the heap. It happened for the Jesus and Mary Chain. It happened for Primal Scream. It never happened for Felt. Even John Peel wouldn't play us.'

Lawrence was very good at saying no, less good at grabbing opportunities when they came his way. McGee said that after a decade of dealing with truculent indie bands, he knew Oasis were going to be huge the moment they walked into the offices of Creation Records and announced they would do whatever he asked of them, whenever he wanted them to. An interview with some tiny fanzine nobody heard of? Tell us where to go. A slot on an unstylish mainstream television programme? Let's have it. With Felt, it was no all the way. We don't do this, we don't do that, no, no, no.

'When Oasis turned up, me and a few other people from Creation thought, *We've got it all wrong*,' accepted Lawrence as he shuffled towards the Tube and back to his council flat on Whitecross Street, about 60 miles from Noel Gallagher's mansion in Hampshire. 'We wanted to be big, but on our own terms. For example, we wouldn't do videos. How stupid. We could have been on MTV.'

The closest Felt got to a video was for 'Primitive Painters', which features a dimly lit Phil King, chosen for his lustrous locks of auburn hair, and Lawrence, standing on a staircase in Phil's flat, strumming guitars. 'Even "Primitive Painters" is not a real video. Creation and

Cherry Red were going to pay half each, but then Alan didn't want to and as a result we ended up with a half-finished bit of film that wasn't a video at all.'

As far as Lawrence saw it, not much had changed since then. Festivals didn't want Mozart Estate. Record shops didn't stock the album. At least Lawrence moved on when he said he would, sticking to his ten-year plan for Felt before calling it quits, but he thought he would have been at the height of his powers when Felt ended.

'I had dreams of the fans coming up to me in tears, going, "Please don't split Felt up, Lawrence. Now you are world-famous, won't you think again?" I would say: "It has to be this way. A plan is a plan."'

We joined the horde of commuters pouring down the steps of Leicester Square Underground like lumpy gravy. 'The one thing I will never do is reform Felt. Lou Reed reformed the Velvet Underground but I'm stronger than him.'

Lou Reed said he reformed the Velvet Underground to earn its guitarist Sterling Morrison some money.

'My answer to that is, "Give him some of your money then, Lou,"' said Lawrence, as a Tube worker kept a watchful eye to ensure we didn't barge through the barriers without paying. 'Of course, it wasn't true. I think Lou Reed wanted to reform the Velvet Underground to have his day in the sun and by doing so he dismantled the magic of the band. I would never dismantle the magic of Felt.'

And he never has.

CHAPTER FIVE

BACK IN DENIM

On the day the contract for the book came through, Lawrence and I were due to meet at our usual coffee shop rendezvous. It was one of those bright May mornings when a gossamer breeze passes through the toy-town sky and the scent of rose and lavender brings freshness to waking up and walking about.

'Are you meeting Lawrence?' asked the Italian girl with the long brown hair and oversized Chloé glasses, with a smile like the dawn of summer. I told her I was, ordered a cappuccino and a pastéis de nata, sank down deep into a cracked brown leather sofa and made a list of all the things we would talk about as Lawrence, after so many years of bad luck, hard times and missed opportunities, was opening up finally towards a new era of success. I waited in the brown leather sofa.

And waited.

As she cleared the cups and plates on the table, the Italian girl gave a sympathetic look, which for some reason isn't what you want when you've been stood up and everyone knows it.

I went through texts from Lawrence. The last one came the day before.

I've just seen dannie from towie walking down brentwood high st!!! I think she was with chloe brockett omg!!

Was it a coded message, a way of announcing the whole thing was off?

Further investigation suggested he was talking about Dani Imbert, mainstay of the fake reality show *The Only Way is Essex*, alongside a friend of hers who had also been on the series before continuing her television career with an appearance on, among others, *Celebs Go Dating*. Lawrence told me more than once he had a soft spot for bold young women aiming for fame at all costs, who he was familiar with because he was not only well read but also well televised. 'I like the *TOWIE* girls, the nail-bar girls, which you get in high streets up and down the country. They're yappy.'

Try as I might, I could find nothing in the message to suggest Lawrence had got the heebie-geebies because I pushed too hard on, say, Rose McDowall's mini-dinosaur. After forty minutes or so of sitting about in the coffee shop, I went round to ring on his doorbell. There was no answer. Eventually, after phone calls, doorbell abuses and increasingly exasperated texts, I gave up and went home.

The only person I knew with experience of this was Paul Kelly. Lawrence had no manager because he was unmanageable. He had no family to speak of, with both parents long dead, no children, wife or partner, and his having not spoken to siblings Sam or Beverly in years. But Paul had spent seven years making *Lawrence of Belgravia*. He was used to coping with Lawrence.

'First of all, he will now be feeling incredibly guilty about standing you up,' said Paul. 'The danger is that he'll be feeling so bad, he'll avoid you altogether because he can't face the thought of a confrontation. He used to do that with me all the time and it drove me mad. I would book a day, make sure I didn't have to deal with the kids, get the filming equipment together . . . For a while, I lived in a flat on a tower block near to Lawrence's. I used to see him on his balcony, smoking, while I was ringing him and he was refusing to answer the phone.'

Perhaps, instead of acting like an excited teenager at the sight of some women on a reality TV show, Lawrence could turn up, be professional. 'I think he's actually scared of success,' said Paul, mirroring Alan McGee's summation of Lawrence's forever nearly approach. 'If it happened, he would have to deal with it, and it is far easier to keep it as fantasy. Did you tell him about getting the contract for the book? It would be typical for Lawrence not to turn up if he heard about that because he would think, *Oh shit. Now it is actually happening.*'

I hadn't, but Paul wondered if it might also be the prospect of playing Glastonbury Festival that was freaking him out. After we bumped into him on Old Compton Street, Martin Kelly had got in touch with Nick Dewey, who was married to Emily Eavis, who was the daughter of Glastonbury's founder, Michael Eavis. The couple were now in charge of booking the acts for an event that had become cemented into the public consciousness as an inescapable and elevated aspect of British life. In 2023, Elton John, the Arctic Monkeys and Guns N' Roses had already filled the top slots, but Nick was amenable to the suggestion that Mozart Estate should be there too. Lawrence's band would not be playing on the world-famous Pyramid Stage, however, but a little canvas tent on a hilly peak called the Crow's Nest.

'He called me yesterday about it,' said Paul. 'Now that you've become associated with all the things he has to get on with, he might be avoiding you.'

The frustration was that, for the past two weeks, we had been hanging out, getting along and finding the right setting to talk about the transition Lawrence made around 1990, when he let go of the tasteful, ethereal dream realities of Felt and formed a band which took inspiration from both his '70s childhood in Birmingham and the novelty pop that formed its soundtrack: Denim.

We had returned to that era a week before our aborted coffee shop meeting, by taking a train to a place in south-east London Lawrence felt summed up the spirit of Denim. 'It is the land that time forgot,' he said of Welling, a once-wealthy suburb on the edges of London and Kent, where Kate Bush grew up in a large farmhouse and which had, by the '90s, become home to some of London's biggest immigrant communities – and to the headquarters of the British National Party. It was dominated by a long high street, there was a Russian tank from the Crimean War mounted on a stand at Welling Corner, and the misleadingly titled Cruisin' Records stood as the town's sole outpost of pop culture.

'You know that book I recommended you read, *People of the Abyss*?' asked Lawrence, citing a pioneering social history from 1903 in which the American adventure writer Jack London gave an account of his time among the 'bipeds' – the poor and desperate of London's East End – sleeping in workhouses and witnessing the cycle of poverty that saw men and women cast out like horses sent to the knacker's yard after heavy labour left them broken and nonproductive. It was the inspiration for George Orwell's *Down and Out in Paris and London*. 'Welling is the modern-day version while also being stuck in the 1970s. It is full of bipeds – hideous deformed human creatures living from day to day. You don't get beggars here. It would be a waste of their time.'

The moment we stepped out of the station, an old man sitting outside a red-bricked pub called the Plough and Harrow, pint in one hand and cigarette in the other, took one look at Lawrence and shouted with a toothless grin: "Ello, darlin'! Cam and sit on my knee.'

'This kind of thing happens a lot in Welling,' muttered Lawrence, ignoring further requests by the old man to engage in physical embrace as he sped down the road, past Chick Chicken and Best Kebabye, and towards the safety of the high street. 'Some men think I'm a woman. They whistle at me and shout, "Alright, luv?". Sometimes I'll go in a shop in the suburbs and they'll say, "Thank you, madam." I don't understand it. They think I'm an old crone.'

'But not in London?'

'Only in Whitechapel.'

If it weren't for the vape shops and the Polish supermarkets, the tanning salons and the nail bars, Welling was indeed stuck in the 1970s. In an electrical goods shop that specialised in intercoms, land lines with large buttons for the partially sighted and mobile disco lights – and where prices were displayed on yellowed, curling Post-it notes and the stock was piled so high in cardboard boxes that the dusty window display had not changed in a decade because there was no way of getting in there – I bought a Breville sandwich maker. I couldn't help but notice an uninviting carpet of newspaper on the doorway that appeared to have been turned into a feeding centre for the local pigeons.

'Animals come first,' said the owner, an elderly Indian man with oversized eyebrows called Terry, on the reason for his less-than-hygienic entrance. 'I feed the pigeons and my neighbours complain, but I don't care because animals are creatures of the God and somebody has to feed them. If everybody kicks them, it is not good. All the cats and foxes come to my house. I have two hairless cats.'

'If you saw a cat from outer space,' contributed Lawrence, 'it would be a hairless cat.'

'Look at these penguins,' said Terry, gesturing at two straw penguins occupying much of the shop counter. 'My customers, two elderly sisters, made them for me. I love penguins.'

'Some people like gorillas,' Lawrence observed.

'I don't think many people have them as pets,' I added.

'Maybe not.'

Terry could have formed the inspiration for a Denim song, while further attractions in Welling provided material for an entire Denim album. The Avenida Steakhouse, with its facade of white stucco oval windows and framed posters of forthcoming attractions ('Wine, Dine & Dance with Nicky Louise'), had a menu offering prawn cocktail, duck à l'orange and Black Forest gateau – delights rarely sampled since the '70s glory days of Fanny Cradock, the Galloping Gourmet and *Robin's Nest*. Further down the high street was a mustard-yellow shop sign for Wide Shoes: Specialists in Broad Footwear.

'Have a look here,' whispered Lawrence, gesturing in a furtive fashion at a window display of women's shoes. 'This is for those unfortunate ladies who have to live with the stigma of unusually wide feet.'

Wide Shoes faced the challenge head-on with an array of not unattractive footwear. There were peep-toe leather pumps, wedge-heeled sandals and pastel-blue Mary Janes, with reasonable prices, from £29.99 to £99.99, that catered to Welling's broad-footed community on all scales of the economic ladder. Next door was Dream

Curtain Designs, whose speciality was the kind of net curtains busily being ripped from the homes of anyone under the age of eighty. Further along was Hair of Dreams – there was a lot of dreaming going on in Welling – and the Bellegrove Social Club, which was festooned with Union Jacks and appeared to be the drinking establishment of the area's more patriotically minded residents.

A smirking boy, with tracksuit trousers slung so low his boxer shorts-bedecked bum was hanging out, and two girls, with big pink nails and tight, unforgiving ponytails, made sniggering noises as we passed the bus stop.

'Weirds!' shouted the boy, inspiring cackles of laughter to ring out from under the bus shelter.

'The schoolkids around here always give me a hard time,' muttered Lawrence as we carried on up the high street. 'Did you see that lot, giving me attitude? I don't know why that boy thought he was so superior. One touch of his trousers and they would have gone down to his ankles. It is the reverse of the reality. These tracksuit kids think I'm something to laugh at when really they should be laughing at themselves. They should stop, take a good, long look in the mirror, and ask: "Why am I so boring?"'

Lawrence took a mini towel out of his bag, wiped the sweat from his brow, and sniffed with bleak truculence.

'That's what they should do.'

Observing this kind of thing, pulling his head out of the clouds and sticking it back onto the street gave Lawrence the impetus to reinvent himself with Denim. Not long before Felt came to its necessary end, he decided he had to get out of Birmingham. He had started work on a Felt album that was going to have horror film music on one side and pornographic movie music on the other.

'We had titles like 'The Sound of Death Above a Garage', 'She Cried Until Her Eyes Came Out' and 'Kitty Likes It'. I was up for the challenge of making an album for use in horror and porno films, but out of kindness I thought, *Let the others do an album instead. Let them have their own Felt album.*'

That became *Train Above the City*, an eight-track, twenty-six-minute anomaly in the Felt universe: a slow, plaintive collection of instrumental jazz and super-soft rock featuring Duffy on piano. The only clue to Lawrence's involvement came in the song titles. 'Seahorses on Broadway' and 'Press Softly on the Brakes Holly' could only have come from one person's mind.

'It is a shame the horror porno album didn't come out,' Lawrence reflected as a one-legged pigeon pecked at a chicken carcass in the gutter. 'But then it might have cast a shadow on my otherwise unblemished character. Independent music fans can be very prudish.'

During the making of the final Felt album, *Me and a Monkey on the Moon*, in 1988, Lawrence relocated to Brighton. His intended plan of moving in with Vikki went wrong when her squat was boarded up by the council, metal sheets hammered to the walls and doors to ensure no further entry, and he told Alan McGee he didn't know what to do. McGee suggested he come down with him and Primal Scream to Brighton, where Lawrence was given the job of cleaning McGee's two-bedroom flat and writing down any messages that came in for him while the Creation Records founder was busy building his empire and discovering rave culture in Manchester. It would have been the ideal arrangement, but for one terrible mistake.

'I didn't know you weren't meant to keep the central heating on twenty-four hours a day. We never had central heating in our house when I grew up, so I didn't know about that kind of thing and when Alan got back, he went mad. We had a big to-do about the enormous gas bill and I ended up having to pay it.'

Culturally, it wasn't a great time for Lawrence because McGee, Jeff Barrett and the rest of the Creation gang had discovered acid house to such an extent that they couldn't pour a cup of tea without making shapes in the air as if in the throes of ecstasy. 'The attitude seemed to be: you're either on the buzz or off the buzz. You weren't part of the gang if you weren't into it, which didn't work for me because it didn't resonate. I didn't want to go on the mystery tour. And by the time I got to Brighton, it seemed like the independent world were finally waking up to something that had been happening in the clubs for two years. Everyone was going around, saying, "Are you into it yet? Are you into it yet?" And I wasn't. I'm not a disco person anyway. I'd been to clubs in the past where Bobby Gillespie and the rest of Primal Scream would get up and dance the moment "Street Fighting Man" by the Rolling Stones came on and I would go, *Wow. They're all jumping about.*'

In his book *Creation Stories,* McGee claimed Lawrence's legendary fastidiousness was all an act because when he was meant to be looking after the flat, the kitchen was a total mess. 'That's because the only place I wouldn't touch was the kitchen,' protested Lawrence, who was inspired to walk extra-fast down Welling High Street the moment his commitment to cleanliness was called into question. 'Alan would eat Heinz Macaroni Cheese in a tin and I couldn't go near it because as far as I was concerned, the tin was infected. The kitchen was not my domain and there was no way I was going to touch Alan McGee's used cutlery.'

In August 1988, a property boom meant the value of Lawrence's two-bedroom flat in a modernist block in Edgbaston – which he got a mortgage on two years previously for £21,500 after landing a £5,000 publishing deal, and which was similar to the home of Roger Moore's suave spy in the TV series *The Saint* – doubled overnight. As a result, he had money to put into a place of his own in Brighton. 'I thought, *This is good, this property thing*. I was advised against it because people kept saying there was going to be a crash, but the only crashes I knew about were car crashes, so I ignored them and bought a tiny basement flat in Brunswick Square, right in the heart of Brighton. It didn't actually have a bedroom. I slept under the stairs.'

As it turned out, there *was* a massive property crash at the end of the 1980s and, in 1990, Lawrence's flat ended up being repossessed by the building society. Saddled with a £22,000 debt, he came to an arrangement to pay it off at a rate of £1 a week for the next 424 years, before it was written off. Before that happened, he put the flat in the hands of a solicitor and started a new life: he was going to New York.

* * *

Something I had to learn, the more time I spent with Lawrence, was that nothing was ever his fault. 'You have to call me the night before we're meeting!' he squeaked, when I yelled at him for failing to turn up at the café or answer his door. 'I can't be expected to remember everything. I must have been asleep. I did have a good long sleep that day, come to think of it.'

When I suggested he might invest in a diary, he pointed out that he did document forthcoming arrangements on those Post-it notes on a wall. I guessed the one about meeting me had fallen off. He said he wasn't spooked by the book happening, or the looming prospect of Glastonbury, or the pressure of long-awaited fame coming his way. Instead, he turned up at the café the following Friday and announced we were to go to Plaistow and Canning Town in the East End. This was the destination of the first of his suburban walks, back in 2016, when he made a pilgrimage to Terence Stamp's grandmother's house. It was also the place the *EastEnders'* actor Danny Dyer called his spiritual if not his actual home, and Lawrence wanted to visit Queen's Market in Upton Park because it was, he claimed, the worst market in Britain. As with Welling, going there would illustrate his journey towards Denim.

After coming out of the station, and after relieving ourselves on a barren scrub of land lined with industrial units on one side and neat rows of council houses on the other, we saw a man in a long blue coat, clutching ten bars of Dairy Milk, being chased by a security guard from the local Sainsbury's. Blue Coat dropped the Dairy Milks in the road and peeled off down an alleyway.

'He's got good taste, that robber,' said Lawrence, inspecting one of the discarded bars as the puffing security guard wheezed down to pick them up and carry them back to their rightful place. 'He went for the best.'

Canning Town connected to the realism, nostalgic but rooted in the everyday, of Denim. Lawrence went to New York because a photographer he knew called Donna had a place on 13th Street in the East Village, so he wrote a letter to her to announce he was coming to New York forever and wanted to stay with her. She suggested he had a holiday first, check it out, see what he made of it, given he had never left Europe before. He said no, this was it: all or nothing.

'I wrote to Donna to ask "When we get there, can we take photos of me on the street with Allen Ginsberg, William Burroughs and Jim Carroll?"' said Lawrence, as we went down the alleyway in the hope of catching Blue Coat Robber and asking why he had chosen to lift so many bars of Dairy Milk. 'I had this idea she would know them all. As ever, the reality was totally different.'

The first thing Lawrence saw, as he waited to pick up his one-pound laundry bag from the carousel at JFK airport, was a group of giant African men, laughing at him.

'These guys were pointing at me, doubled over in hysterics. I went to New York to change my life with a one-pound laundry bag and to these people it was the funniest thing they had ever seen. Then I got a taxi downtown and it was like I was in an episode of *Kojak*, with sirens going everywhere. Suddenly I was thinking about Bob Dylan in the Village, and Television and Richard Hell in burned-out buildings in the Lower East Side, all soaking into those first few seconds I got out of the cab. It was like being in a movie. It went downhill rapidly from there.'

After a few days on Donna's sofa, it became clear the new life wasn't all it was cracked up to be. 'Donna was going, "You're not like you were in London." I said, "What did you expect? I've only been here five days." She said it wasn't working. She was chucking me out! Luckily, she found me a great big room I could look after while the person who owned it was away. All I had to do was paint the walls white.'

Lawrence's new apartment was on Sullivan Street in Lower Manhattan, where Martin Scorsese grew up: Mafia territory, which meant all the bins were collected on time. It started out as Lawrence's ideal home, a vast empty space with white walls, wooden floors and nothing in it whatsoever except for a wooden construction in the middle of the room with stairs walking up to a bed.

'The first day I was there, I thought *What do I do now?* There was no television and no radio, and all I had was a cassette player and a mixtape a girl I had been seeing in Brighton made me with a few songs from Duran Duran's first album and some ELO on there. That's when I decided to buy a guitar because I was missing it, really. I found an acoustic in a pawn shop, sat on the bed, and wrote the first Denim album.'

Boredom set in. Lawrence knew nobody. He went to a deli on the corner that sold, alongside packets of Arm & Hammer detergent and enormous cans of beer, hot soup: a new phenomenon. 'In England at the time, you could only get soup in a can, but at this deli they had a big cauldron of minestrone soup, which I would have every day. It was beautiful.'

Apart from that enriching culinary experience, New York proved a terrible disappointment. It was the era of the Club Kids, druggy narcissists who lived from party to party and look to look, which would have suited Lawrence right down to his black leather brogues, but he wasn't hip to them. 'Donna didn't know anything about the Club Kids and instead she took me to see terrible bands like Ultra Vivid Scene playing in front of ten people, the very thing I had come to New York to get away from.'

The nadir was a solo show by Ian McCulloch of Lawrence's post-punk heroes Echo & the Bunnymen. 'It was so depressing. When he walked off stage I said, "Great gig, Ian", in a way that I thought was obviously sarcastic, but he said, "Yeah, I know. Got any chewing gum?" What a conceited guy! Meanwhile, Donna had a regular Thursday night with her girlfriends where they would watch Johnny Depp in *21 Jump Street*. This wasn't the New York I hoped for at all.'

A single man with his soup, Lawrence would visit the launderette on the corner, go for long walks through the city, attend a Marlon Brando season at a repertory cinema, and wonder if he had made a massive mistake in coming to New York in the first place, not least after the girl who made that mixtape started sending poetic, moving letters declaring her love for him. Her name was Michaela.

'I didn't even think she liked me,' said Lawrence as we passed a group of Muslim men smoking cigarettes outside a café. 'She was one of the girls who used to hang around Primal Scream and we had a bit of a fling in Brighton, nothing much. Then, the moment I got to New York, she was sending me all these amazing letters going on about how much she missed me. There's a Denim song called "Don't Bite Too Much Out of the Apple". It is about Michaela.'

That's from 1996's *Denim on Ice* and it is an appealingly synthetic, sentimental MOR ballad. 'It's about how, when I was young, I couldn't find the girl I liked. Now I've gone to New York and maybe there is somebody back home, who writes letters to me, as sweet as can be, and they say, "Don't bite too much out of the apple and forget about me". I came up with that superb line myself, of course, but nonetheless these letters were making me think: Michaela.'

He also received a telegram from Vikki, who had heard about Michaela and was spiralling into jealousy. It consisted of three words: Leave me alone.

'He wrote back with a letter in which he said he would gladly leave me alone and called me a pathetic little baby,' said Vikki. 'The strange thing was that he went on to say how excited he had been to receive a telegram. I thought, *Well, that's the last I'll hear from him.*

110

Actually, he kept sending letters, probably because he needed a place to stay if he came back to London.'

The deciding factor on leaving New York was not Michaela, but cockroaches. Lawrence did not want to live with them and realised that, in Manhattan, it was not an option. 'It was actually during one of those Marlon Brando films. I was in the cinema watching *The Nightcomers* when the biggest cockroach you ever saw crawled over my foot. I ran to the back of the cinema and sat down again, where there were balls of rolled-up newspaper on the floor. I heard this terrible scratching, and out crawled a rat. I thought, *Now I can't even go to the pictures.*'

The only thing left to look forward to was picking up the latest edition of the *NME* from a specialist magazine shop each Friday, and it seemed like the Stone Roses were on the cover every week. Against all expectations of acid house wiping them out of existence, guitar bands, of the sort Lawrence had been plying his trade in for the past ten years, were exploding. The alternative music scene Felt helped inaugurate was spilling over into the mainstream.

'I thought, *Oh God, if ever there was a wrong time to be in New York, it is now,*' Lawrence moaned, shortly before spotting a sports casual-wear shop called Club JJ, which he had been wanting to go into for ages but had been too scared to enter by himself. 'Alan McGee turned up in New York one day and said Bobby was going to be on *Top of the Pops* with Primal Scream. "Loaded" was a hit record! I sat on that bed in the middle of the flat and thought, *I've got to get out of here.*'

After apologising to a woman in a headscarf for bumping into her, explaining that he liked to be over-nice on the street (and over-horrible in the studio), we went into Club JJ. 'I want to find out what the smart boys in Canning Town are wearing,' he proclaimed. 'The amount of times I've stood next to the window of this place, trying to find the confidence to go in.'

We tried on pairs of sliders, inspected a velour tracksuit from Ellesse, and, following the dictates of the man who ran the place, appreciated the superior quality of a three-button top in West Ham colours. 'We do well with all of the major brands,' proclaimed the man, having announced that his father opened the shop in 1978 and it had been in the family ever since. 'You won't find better prices for tip-top sportswear in Britain.' He was beginning to sound like Lawrence.

'Have a look around, then think about buying that Ellesse velour top,' commanded Lawrence, after picking up a Lyle & Scott jumper and running a papery hand along its downy contours. 'Do some groundwork before making your purchase.'

I didn't want to, and instead found myself dragging Lawrence out of the shop before something bad happened. Actually, the owner didn't actually seem to mind us hanging about the shop – perhaps in places like West Ham they're less freaked out by someone of Lawrence's appearance – because his parting shot was to tell us to go to his sister shop over the road and consider buying an Ellesse ladies top for our wives or daughters. Instead, we carried on up the high street.

Lawrence came back from New York with his one-pound laundry bag, his guitar and a stack of '60s *Playboy* magazines he found on the street. With Vikki's flat being unavailable, he went to Windsor, where an old friend called Johnny Male, a few years away from forming the briefly massively successful Britpop band Republica, had a house.

'Johnny Male lived with his mom, although I never saw her, and I wondered if it might be like *Psycho* with the skeleton of the mother in the basement. He was one of those people who left butter on the knife and a big mess everywhere, so I asked, "Aren't you going to clear that up? I'll help you." He told me not to worry about it. Then I came down in the morning and it was all done. The secret mother crept out in the dead of night, tidied everything, and scurried back to her lair.'

It was time to turn Denim into a chart-busting major label act, so the first thing Lawrence did was find a lawyer. 'I read somewhere that all the big bands get a lawyer first, and guess what? I found one of the most corrupt lawyers in London.'

The corruption worked in Lawrence's favour. He ran up around £10,000 in legal fees, but didn't have to pay any of it because his lawyer got struck off around the time a deal was landed with Boy's Own, a subsidiary of the major label London Records. Then, wandering around Sloane Street one day in the hope of working out where Terence Stamp once lived, Lawrence saw a board advertising a studio flat for rent. With a bit of jiggery pokery that meant he got the whole, then-extortionate £125 a week paid for by housing benefit, and Lawrence achieved what he had long dreamed of: a central London pad with an impressive postcode.

'Bobby Gillespie said the flat was completely horrible and I only got it so I could tell everyone I lived in Sloane Street,' said Lawrence, after making us stop to admire some chickens rotating slowly on a spit, hot grease splashing onto the pavement. 'Of course I did! Why the hell else would I live there? A flash address was part of the plan.'

In the pages of *Melody Maker*, Lawrence saw a new bands page consisting of a very large photo with a very small article attached, so he contacted Bob Stanley, the music journalist and one-third of

Saint Etienne, who wrote the piece. 'Bob said you had to play live to get onto that page, which meant I had to play a gig, which had not been part of the plan at all. We wanted to launch Denim in this page in *Melody Maker*, and to do that we needed photographic evidence of a live scenario.'

We took the bus up to Queen's Market, sitting on the lower deck as Lawrence told me how Denim duly landed a support slot with Johnny Male's pre-Republica outfit Soul Family Sensation, in a band concocted hastily of himself and Siobhan Brooks, Male's girl-friend at the time. 'I asked her to be in the band because she had hair like Nico. That got us onto the page in *Melody Maker* and then everyone – Elektra Records, London, the lot – rang me. It took off.'

Lawrence pointed to an unremarkable terraced home on Barking Road. 'That's Terence Stamp's grandma's house.'

Boy's Own were an acid house crew who had been given their own label and wanted to put out a rock band. Denim fitted the bill and, as soon as Lawrence mentioned he was friends with Felt's old producer John Leckie, now the man of the hour due to his success with the Stone Roses, London Records were happy to get behind it all. Besides, Lawrence had two songs everyone thought sounded like hits. 'Middle of the Road' was a statement of intent, rejecting the cannon of cool music, from the Rolling Stones to Otis Redding, for the much-mocked '70s singalong sensations of the title. 'The Osmonds' went deeper. It begins as a harmless, I-remember-Spangles-style, eight-minute journey through a groovy, primary-coloured past, listing left-over hippies, skinheads, Oxford bags, Chopper bikes and kung-fu fights. Samples of Herbie Flowers' ultra-slow bass thump for 'Rock On' by David Essex and Lee 'Scratch' Perry's dub reggae oddity 'Kojak' add to the flavour, while Lawrence sings in the affectingly melancholic chorus about a time when there were lots of little Osmonds everywhere. Then it all changes.

'In the '70s, there were lots of bombs,' states Lawrence in his understated way. 'They blew my hometown up and lots of people were killed.' He was returning to the evening of 21 November 1974 when bombs attributed to the Provisional Irish Republican Army went off in two pubs in Birmingham city centre – the Mulberry Bush and the Tavern in the Town – killing twenty-one people and injuring 181. Lawrence remembered the evening as a warm one; 'a no-jacket affair', as he put it. He was twelve, on his bike in Castle Bromwich, one village over from Water Orton, when the news came through. As he sang in 'The Osmonds', 'everyone knew someone who'd died.'

We got off the bus and, after almost being run over by two speeding mobility scooter drivers with cans of Tennents Super rattling about in their cup holders, came to Queens Square, which is next to Green Street, famous for being the former home of West Ham FC, a legendary epicentre of football hooliganism. 'Isn't it amazing? This building means everything to me,' said Lawrence, gazing up at the residential monolith overlooking the square, with its balcony-free blocks of flats with green window sills and concrete awnings at the edges. To the right was a pub called the Queen's Function Room, which someone had recently painted white, but in such a slapdash way that splodges of paint were splashed all over the pavement.

Lawrence gazed up in wonder. 'Doesn't it knock your socks off? The fact that it is home to the most horrible market in all of humanity really adds to it all.'

We entered an urban bazaar, a concrete casbah, selling everything from sari fabrics to dried sheep's intestines to white T-shirts for

£2.99. It was here that in 2012 a market stallholder called Muhammad Nazir came up with a novelty tune called 'One Pound Fish' as a way to attract customers. It came to the attention of Warner Brothers and ended up being a top-thirty hit, but unfortunately the song's success also alerted the UK border agency to the fact that Nazir was living in Britain on an expired visa. He had to go back to Pakistan when 'One Pound Fish' was still riding high in the charts, never to return. Proof, if it was needed, that a smash hit can have unexpected consequences.

'You'll get the most hideous fishes, highly synthetic West Ham tops, and enormous knickers for big fat women,' listed my emaciated guide. Lawrence had worked on markets himself, helping his dad sell 'chemists' goods' from his stall in Birmingham's Corporation Square, before hitting puberty and becoming too embarrassed at girls from his school seeing him there on a Saturday morning to continue. 'I love this market. I hate it too. Don't bother saying hello to anyone, they'll look at you like you're going to mug them. Why don't you get some nice fruit for your family? It's much cheaper than Waitrose.'

With Denim, this kind of thing became inspirational material. 'Suddenly my eyes were opened,' said Lawrence as we passed a stall selling knock-off Rolexes. 'I was looking for a London that wasn't there any more, Terence Stamp's London in particular, alongside bands like Middle of the Road, the Glitter Band – but not Gary Glitter – and *Opportunity Knocks*. TV in general was important, and we were an ITV house so I would watch *Magpie* rather than *Blue Peter*. On top of this, I liked short songs, fifteen minutes on each side of the album. Put it all together and you end up with Denim.'

With its mix of nostalgia, realism and '70s glam/MOR pastiche, 1992's *Back in Denim* was a blueprint for Britpop, three years ahead of its time. And making the record was never going to be easy; Lawrence saw Denim as his big chance and it had to be right. During early sessions with the producer Brian O'Shaughnessy at Bark Studios in Walthamstow, he passed a pub called the Royal Standard and saw that the Glitter Band were doing a concert there. He made all his compatriots come along to see them, and was so impressed with the Glitter Band's guitarist Gerry Shepherd and drummer Pete Phipps that he got them into the band. As recording continued at Mickie Most's RAK Studios, then at Abbey Road, the costs mounted. After an engineer at RAK wiped nine seconds of an intro to a song, Lawrence went crazy and demanded the engineer be sacked immediately. But RAK's owner, Mickie Most, not known as the most lenient of men, told Lawrence that the man had been there since the studio opened and in no way was he going to be booted out for a mistake that was actually Lawrence's fault. He had failed to replace the 'leader', the empty section opening a master tape, meaning recording started the second the tape ran.

John Leckie, now on board, re-recorded the entire nine seconds note for note, an incredible feat, but working with Lawrence proved too much of a challenge even for this legendarily magnanimous producer. Leckie was attempting to deliver to London Records a finished product that didn't go over budget, but he hadn't counted on the wilfulness of the man he was making the album with.

'I made him cry,' Lawrence confessed. I couldn't help but sense a hint of pride in his subdued tone. 'Here is a guy who worked with John Lennon, Phil Spector, Pink Floyd, Mark E. Smith, and I was the one who drove him over the edge. The problem is that John was trying to make an early '90s record and I couldn't allow that to happen. For some reason, he liked to submerge things in a wedge of sound – listen to the Stone Roses' first album for proof – and I wanted every single riff, every single bass note to ring out.

'What's more, he was rushing it. I brought musicians in who hadn't got the parts yet and he was going, "Yes, yes, very good." My attitude was the exact opposite. It didn't matter how long it took. We had to get it right. Every last detail was a matter of life and death. Eventually, John Leckie went: "Okay, let's stop and go to the café round the corner." That's when he broke down and said he couldn't take it any more.'

Lawrence returned to Bark Studios to finish the album with Brian O'Shaughnessy, and by the time it was completed, *Back in Denim* cost so much to make that it actually succeeded in bankrupting Boy's Own. Creatively, however, it was a triumph.

'I'm back!' Lawrence shouted, opening the album in declamatory fashion with the title track, 'Back in Denim', seemingly unaware that hardly anyone noticed he went away in the first place. Inspiration came from 'Thunderstruck' by AC/DC, from the Australian heavy rock primitives' 1990 album *The Razor's Edge*, on which the producer Mutt Lange came up with biggest guitar sound Lawrence ever heard. He knew *Back in Denim* had to start with a similarly massive rock moment to show he meant business, so he hummed the riff to the guitarist until he got it, told Leckie to emulate AC/DC's monolithic perfection, and then, having never managed to get past track three, chucked *The Razor's Edge* in the bin.

Lawrence even found the time to be a Svengali along the way, dreaming up a band called Shampoo that would consist of two stroppy teenage girls before finding the ideal candidates in sixteen-year-old Jacqui Blake and Carrie Askew, best friends from Plumstead in south-east London who had been annoying everyone at their comprehensive by obsessing over the Manic Street Preachers and acting like pop stars before they had done so much as a turn at the end-of-year concert. He wrote a song for them called 'Blisters and Bruises', which was put out on Bob Stanley's Icerink Records in 1993. Shampoo hit the big time on EMI two years later with the naughty kids' anthem 'Trouble'.

'What impressed me about Shampoo is that they lifted lyrics from Tin Machine,' said Lawrence, citing David Bowie's much-unloved early '90s rock band. 'They were hip enough to realise that Tin Machine were so bad, they were good.'

At Upton Park, we got the Tube back into town, where Lawrence reflected on how Denim could never really benefit from paving the way for Britpop. There was a famous *Select* magazine cover from April 1993 featuring Pulp, Suede, the Auteurs, Saint Etienne, Denim and the headline 'Yanks Go Home', but soon afterwards, Britpop morphed into the ironic and/or straight-up laddish abandon of Blur and Oasis, with *Loaded* magazine appealing to a newly hedonistic mood, accompanied by middle-class people talking loudly about football in pubs and boasting about how much ecstasy they had taken on the weekend. The only place that really shared Lawrence's Denim aesthetic, with its playlist of easy listening, show tunes, glam rock and film soundtracks, and camp reworking of 1970s light entertainment culture, was a nightclub in central London called Smashing.

Set up by a flamboyant Jesus figure called Matthew Glamorre, a sharply dressed mod-skinhead-beatnik DJ called Martin Green, a shiny-pated, voluble DJ called Michael Murphy (who went on first and had tantrums when nobody danced to 'Beat the Clock' by Sparks) and a drunken man on the door called Adrian Webb, who ended up managing Britpop flash-in-the-pans Menswear a few years later, Smashing occupied a series of down-on-their luck venues in early '90s Britain. The best was a gentleman's club in St James, complete with plush velvet banquettes, fringed table lights and etched mirrors with naked female silhouettes, called the Gaslight.

Martin Green would play 'Jesus Christ Superstar' and everyone pretended to have a moment of spiritual epiphany before attempting the dance routine to 'The Rhythm of Life' from *Sweet Charity*. A variety of cabaret turns did short sets at midnight, the worse the better. I met my wife on the dancefloor at Smashing, jumping along to 'Vicious' by Lou Reed, and Lawrence's girlfriend Michaela, a rock chick with cropped black hair and leather trousers, tough but sexy, was there most weeks too. Lawrence made the odd appearance, motionless and uncertain in his satin bomber jacket and Levi's, watching the whole thing from the sidelines, forever one step removed from abandoning himself to the ritual.

Martin Green remembered Lawrence turning up to Smashing at the Gaslight some time around 1993. 'Michaela brought him down and, for some reason, we started talking about Serge Gainsbourg, because he had all the Serge Gainsbourg albums from the late '60s to the early '70s and you just didn't meet people who owned them in those days. I had a copy of *Histoire de Melody Nelson*, which I picked up in Paris, so I was interested in him immediately and made him a list of records to seek out. *Female Animal* by the Clay Pitts Orchestra, a soundtrack to an American soft porn exploitation movie, was on there.'

Lawrence got back together with Michaela on returning to London, but unfortunately the yearning she felt when he was in New York dissipated rapidly into irritation. This meant she usually wanted him to stay at home while she went to Smashing on her own so she could tell him all about it at the end of the night without having him cramp her style by actually being there. Lawrence dealt with the unsatisfying arrangement by writing about it. 'Put a plus one on the door,' he begs on 'Fish and Chips', a song from *Back in Denim* that he initially titled 'Smashing' before thinking better of it. She rarely did.

'Michaela moved to London and found that club straight away,' said Lawrence as the Tube arrived at Mile End. A baby cried a few feet away from us and rows of slack-jawed people stared at phones, inert to the world around them. 'Later on, Smashing was full of pop stars, but in the early days there were these unusual characters who knew about Denim and were happy to welcome me in. When I met Martin Green, I was amazed that there was a guy who was into middle-of-the-road music just like I was, because back then nobody liked it, nobody talked about it. It was considered a not particularly funny joke. And Smashing seemed like something Michaela and I could do together because, apart from that, we didn't socialise. We just went round to each other's flats and slept with each other.'

'Actually,' claimed Michaela, 'he only went once. After that first time he was so horrendous, so nasty about everyone, that I refused to take him again.'

On this, Lawrence demanded a right of reply: 'It's simply not true. I went loads of times.'

Elsewhere, *Back in Denim* held revelations not only on Lawrence's mindset but also his ambitions. 'Here is My Song for Europe' was a blatant if ultimately unsuccessful attempt to provide the UK with a potential winning entry for the Eurovision Song Contest. 'American Rock', its muscular chord sequence recalling the street swagger of 'Spanish Stroll' by Mink DeVille, was designed with US audiences in mind, a boy-meets-girl tale with shades of both '70s New York and *West Side Story*.

'I realised many of the songs were unique to the UK and thought, *I'll be big worldwide so I'd better have a song for the Americans too*,' he reasoned of 'American Rock'. 'I was catering to all parties, in preparation for fronting one of the biggest bands the world had ever known.'

'I'm Against the Eighties' was Lawrence's rejection of the indie scene he had been a part of, 'partly because it hadn't happened for me, partly because a terrible band called the June Brides were on the cover of the *NME* in 1985, and suddenly independent music became indie, which was weak music for weak people. Just my luck to be in the worst decade of all time for guitar music.'

Then there was the big love song of the album. 'I Saw the Glitter on Your Face' recalls, with its gentle twanging guitars and shimming synthesisers, the soft-rock smoothness of the American band Bread. It was an ode to a fictitious glitter girl, but there was a lot of Michaela in there too, with Lawrence announcing in his typically non-committal way that they're through, he doesn't love her any more, she'll get over him, they always do. But the melody tells another story, its melancholic cadences suggesting he's only saying this because the glitter girl has already lost interest in him and he's trying to protect his emotions. According to Lawrence, the relationship was fraught from the start, the first major challenge being Michaela's choice of underwear.

'Her getting caught up in the ladette culture of the '90s went all the way to wearing boys' pants,' Lawrence remembered. 'I made her realise, in a nice way, that there's nothing wrong with being feminine. I said she's a good-looking girl and there's no shame in that.'

Whatever happened to Michaela? She wasn't in Paul Kelly's film. I hadn't seen her in two decades, and I wanted to speak to her because Lawrence's attitude to girlfriends took some getting used to. He didn't want to admit that they were actually his girlfriends. Perhaps he was happier on his own. Perhaps he was a hopeless romantic, always let down when reality shattered the dream of love, because his back catalogue was littered with songs about chaste unavailability. Felt's 'I Can't Make Love to You Anymore', a pedal steel-enlivened country rock lament from *Me and a Monkey on the Moon*, pretty much captured his general outlook vis-à-vis relationships of a sexual nature.

Soon after I said goodbye to Lawrence, a message came through.

'If you want the truth, Lawrence is not the sweet and gentle person he puts himself over to be. There is lots to talk about and I'm not sure Lawrence will be happy about what I have to say. There were some good times but, ultimately, he was an absolute nightmare. I'm very happy to set the record straight.'

It was Michaela.

CHAPTER SIX

HORRIBLE PLASTIC WINDOWS

A few minutes after we walked out of Beckenham station, Lawrence was struck dumb by a semi-detached, four-bedroom house in the Victorian mock-Tudor style, complete with original latticed lead windows, a sunny conservatory, and a sloping front garden bright with hollyhocks, roses, lavender and foxgloves. A knobbly wooden bench sat unused in the middle of a bright green, weed-free lawn and an enormous shining Range Rover stood in the gravel drive, like a proud, haughty stallion ready to roar into action whenever its master or mistress demanded.

'Flesh and bones don't do it for me any more,' said Lawrence, after declaring that he had lost his heart to a house that estate agents would have described as 'imposing'. 'Now I'm in love with bricks and mortar. When I find a house that really does it for me, I scream at it, "I love you!"'

Once a year, Lawrence's family would drive slowly through Solihull, the richest part of Birmingham, to gawp at the houses of the wealthy. Just as various girlfriends hurt Lawrence's feelings by failing to live up to his impossible standards, however, so too did houses.

'Look at these horrible plastic windows,' he said, recoiling at a series of white UPVC frames on the front of a steep-roofed, half-timbered house painted in a fetching shade of cream and topped off with a little round turret. 'This house takes my breath away. It could be straight out of *Hansel and Gretel*. Then they went and ruined it by putting plastic windows in and my love is tainted forever.'

We passed a lone bungalow amid this sea of suburban opulence, its overgrown lawn and rotting, wood-framed windows suggesting ownership by someone, an older person perhaps, who did not share the wealth and status consciousness of their neighbours. 'You see, I like this one just as much, if not more, than the rich people's mansions,' said Lawrence, as we stood outside the bungalow to admire its modest charms. 'The tragedy is that a rich person will buy this plot of land and knock the bungalow down to build a horrible affair with five plastic windows in a row. We need to start a campaign: No Death To Bungalows. I will always stand up for the bungalow. For one thing, if a mad axeman comes in and you're upstairs, you are far more likely to get your head chopped off. With the humble bungalow, that isn't an option. I've always been paranoid about being murdered. It is why I wouldn't live in the countryside. Or the suburbs for that matter.'

Beckenham was the place where David Bowie launched his assault on the world at the end of the '60s and the early '70s, living in a section of a vast, long-gone mansion called Haddon Hall with his wife Angie and their baby son Zowie. He put on a festival in a nearby park, ran a folk night called the Beckenham Arts Lab in a room above the Three Tuns pub – now a branch of the pretend Italian restaurant chain Zizzi's – and fascinated the locals with whatever flamboyant creation he would wear for the purpose of pushing little Zowie in his pram down the high street. Lawrence suggested we came to Beckenham to try to understand Bowie – and perhaps understand himself a little better in the process.

'Bowie was never a central London person,' he said as we walked up a wide, quiet, gravelly road lined with modernist mansions and geometrically satisfying blocks of flats. 'He immersed himself in suburban dullness and drove into the centre every day to see his manager. Apparently, he was a very poor driver. That's what his song "Always Crashing in the Same Car" is about.'

Lawrence also wanted to get to grips with why the locals were nice to Bowie but horrible to Lawrence. He had complained to me in the past about going into a sweet shop on the high street for his beloved Drop Fruit Duo liquorice sweets, only to be given the cold shoulder by the man inside, or walking past the kids at the bus stop to a chorus of jeers. Perhaps the blandness of suburbia forced Bowie into flamboyance and the people of Beckenham loved him for it. Lawrence, on the other hand, with his bloodless skin and vampiric frame, was a reminder of the sickness of the city they had escaped from.

'I think that line from "Kooks" – "I'm not much cop at punching other people's dads" – was Bowie through and through,' said Lawrence as we carried on up the quiet street. 'The people of Beckenham recognised it and I get the impression that he was admired for it. It was a case of, "Look at the strange, kooky guy", not "Let's get the freak". But Bowie didn't have to do the things I have to do. He didn't have to go into supermarkets.'

We stopped at the top of the gravelly road to reflect on Bowie's early reality.

'Angie would do the supermarket shop for him.'

Would Michaela go into supermarkets for Lawrence? I had to wonder what was in it for both of them during their on/off, four-and-a-half-year relationship. Towards the end of it, Lawrence achieved his dream of having a girlfriend who lived near him but not with him, after both he and Michaela managed to find flats on Butler's Wharf, in a residential block in the shadow of Tower Bridge. Not that it helped matters.

Michaela had announced, after some caution at raking the coals over what was clearly a difficult time for her, that she was happy to talk. She was also busy. She was a set painter and designer for film, adverts and videos, and did long hours on shoots before returning to her house in Eastbourne, where she typically spent weekends sewing fabrics together for the following week's commissions.

'I've still got all those letters Lawrence sent me when he was in New York, bundled up somewhere,' she said, down the phone from the house, while working on a drape she was putting together for a hotel lobby. 'By the time I split up with him for good, it was a massive relief. There was a point, though, when I really was in love with him.'

Michaela met Lawrence shortly before leaving home for university, heading out from her mother's house in Worthing most evenings to hang out in indie clubs in Brighton, about 12 miles along the south coast. 'Initially, Lawrence was extremely attractive to me, not only because of Felt's music – I remember thinking how beautiful "Crystal Ball" was – but also because he seemed so gentle and unthreatening. I was looking for someone who was the complete opposite of my dad, who I felt had rejected me. When Lawrence was off in New York, I probably built up an idealised vision of him, which is why I was writing letters every day. Then he came back.'

The first sign that this was not going to be the greatest love affair since Cleopatra and Mark Antony came in the summer of 1991 when, down from Nottingham University, Michaela asked if she could move into Lawrence's flat in Sloane Street for a week while she tried to find somewhere of her own. Naturally he refused and they split up after a massive row so, after staying with friends for a few weeks, Michaela found a studio flat in Holland Park in west London, where post for a Mr J. Kerr and a Miss P. Kensit started coming through the letterbox. Jim Kerr, of Simple Minds, and Patsy Kensit, former child actress and the burgeoning face of Swinging London's '90s renaissance, were living upstairs.

'I made the mistake of telling Lawrence about this and because he loves anybody famous, he wheedled his way into us seeing each other again,' said Michaela. 'Worse than that, he lost the place in Sloane Street and was living in the spare room of some woman in Putney with a load of cats who were driving him mad, so he wanted to move in. This was after he wouldn't let me move in for *one week*. Of course, he guilt-tripped me into letting him, saying I was his only friend and so on. Oh God, it was a nightmare. All he did was sit in the room and smoke pot while I was off working.'

Michaela had a job as a cleaner for various homes in Holland Park and Notting Hill, and among her clients was Riggs O'Hara, an Irish actor who had been something of a friend and mentor to Marc Bolan in the late '60s. Bolan's early single, 'The Wizard', had been inspired by O'Hara, whom the glam-superstar-in-waiting had imbued with all manner of magical powers. 'So, of course, Lawrence wanted to meet him. I had to explain that I was only his cleaning lady and couldn't exactly start bringing my friends round.'

There were good times. An incident in Worthing involving a cheese omelette made Michaela feel great affection for Lawrence, if only for a while. She credited him with inspiring her to set a goal and achieve it: he said they would live in central London and then he found a way to make it happen. There were long walks through the city, conversations on everything from architecture to books to music, and visits to the cinema, which added to Michaela's conviction that the Lawrence of then would be a perfectly nice companion to a middle-aged woman, but not a twenty-one-year-old girl out for good times. And Michaela felt that one of the biggest problems was Lawrence's tendency to overreact massively to the slightest problem.

'When Lawrence gets frustrated, he throws his toys out of the pram, and he couldn't control me and it did his head in. The day before my birthday, he had made me shampoo his carpet. The following morning, we were in a café near Harrods when he blurted out: "I haven't got you anything! It's pointless, it's useless, I can't do this!" Apparently it was my fault he hadn't bought me anything because I'm so hard to buy presents for, so he finished with me on my birthday morning. After I shampooed his carpet. After we had sex the night before.'

There was also Lawrence's ideal of femininity to contend with. 'He would say things like, "You're actually really nice and quiet, not the laddy girl you pretend to be." He would go, "You're going to get married and have children," which I never did. He was always telling me who I was and predicting what I would become. He would say, "I don't believe in love," and when we would meet someone, he went, "This is my friend Michaela," never "This is my girlfriend". I ended up feeling very inadequate because of

Lawrence, and thought, *Well, you're offering me nothing and apparently I'm not your girlfriend, so I may as well go out on a date with this guy I've met.'*

Michaela wasn't overly enamoured of Lawrence's talent in the first place. 'It is more that I was never so impressed with who he was. Early on in our relationship, he took me to the offices of Creation Records, to show off really, and handed me a stack of Felt albums. I did listen to them, and thought the lyrics were fantastic, but he couldn't sing to save his life. He couldn't hit the note. He couldn't even talk the note.'

Nor did Michaela think she was going out with a pop star-in-waiting, despite the breaks coming Denim's way. 'I never, ever thought he had a chance of mainstream success. He was too weird, too selfish. There was no bend, no give, wouldn't play live, wouldn't do this, wouldn't do that, so self-limiting that the only person who stopped him was himself. He wanted something so much that he destroyed his life over it, while at the same time ensuring he could never actually get what he thought he wanted. I used to look at him and go, *Do you know what? You're a real idiot. If you stopped wanting to be the star that you also don't want to be, Denim could be huge.'*

Lawrence and I came to a council estate next to Beckenham Park where a large common, overgrown enough to be classified as a meadow, backed onto a row of beech trees. Perhaps the trees would be pulled down soon, to be replaced by a cul-de-sac named after them. 'I identify with boring places,' Lawrence announced, as we stood in the shadow of the trees and admired the scene. 'Sometimes I think I'm on a mission to find an exact replica of the boring suburb I grew up in.'

He compared his childhood situation with the lives depicted in *The Only Way is Essex*, in which former working-class families from the East End of London played out an altered version of reality amid the new wealth of their Essex environment. 'You watch *TOWIE* and realise they were doing the same thing as my mom: moving out of the council estates and into the pretend countryside. It makes me think, after all these years, perhaps I shouldn't be so angry with her after all.'

Although Michaela never got to meet Lawrence's mum and dad, she once spent an evening with his sister Beverly and her boyfriend at their home on the outskirts of Birmingham. 'My eyes were really opened by that night. Lawrence was acting completely normal: no phobias, no "I can't eat this", just laughing with his sister, taking the piss out of each other, both being really funny in that Brum way. I thought, *Wow, the mask is off. Who is the real Lawrence?* I saw beyond the facade, the person he was before he effectively allowed mental illness to take over. It was the moment I realised that this man was not a complete moron. He was not someone who couldn't do things for himself. This was someone who once had a job and a mortgage and a normal life, but who sacrificed everything for his own vanity. Needless to say, we had a massive argument and he finished with me the next day.'

Back in the '90s, Lawrence did everything he could to escape suburban normality. After *Back in Denim* came out in 1992 – to the excitement of music journalists and fashionable nightclub types but not to the public at large – Lawrence set about building the next stage of his urban would-be pop-star existence. He found a flat in Covent Garden, even deeper into the molten core of the metropolis. He bought an album called *The Best of Cliff Volume 2*, mainly because he liked its photograph of a lustrous-haired Cliff Richard trying to look cool in a brown leather jacket and oversized cross medallion, which led to him taking Cliff Richard seriously and wanting to pay tribute to this much-mocked figure on record. The plan was to record an EP of Cliff Richard songs that would feature a cover image of Cliff's head, carved out of rock. He would call it *Cliff Rock*. The EP was recorded, but then London Records dropped Boy's Own entirely and *Cliff Rock* never came out.

'Boy's Own became Junior Boy's Own and had massive success with the Chemical Brothers and Underworld,' said Lawrence. 'Once again, there was no room for me.'

We walked on in the heavy afternoon light and heat, Lawrence speeding his little body up the grassy hill towards Beckenham Place, a vast Georgian mansion at the centre of the park. Not only did he never appear to eat anything, he rarely drank water either. His only sustenance appeared to come from the milky tea he liked to buy from Costa Coffee towards the end of our long walks. I, on the other hand, was a mere human, in need of water at the very least. I said to Lawrence that we had to stop at the café at the park so I could get something to drink.

'Don't panic,' he commanded, marching onward. 'You're not going to die of exhaustion. If we were walking up Snowdonia, maybe, but not in Beckenham Park.'

Lawrence was still marching towards fame after *Back in Denim*, undeterred by the collapse of his Cliff Richard tribute record, his label and possibly his career. Instead, he started working with a young engineer called Gerard Johnson, whose production company was touting Freaky Realistic, a happening funky dance-pop band with shades of Denim's '70s nostalgia, as the next big thing. Led by a pale young man from Peckham called Justin Anderson, Freaky Realistic landed a slot on the post-pub youth culture show

The Word for their debut single 'Koochie Rider' and shot a video for a tune called 'Leonard Nimoy' at Smashing, which featured some of the more interesting regulars as extras. As Freaky Realistic were on Polydor, Lawrence saw a connection with them as his route back into the game.

'That didn't work out either,' said Lawrence as he sat down at a picnic table, having relented and allowed me to pop into the café for a can of Sanpellegrino. 'Freaky Realistic split up, but I started doing demos with Gerard Johnson and that's where *Denim on Ice* began.'

Denim's second album had a very different tone from the first: more embittered and cynical, with drum machines and synthesisers bringing in a cold, metallic quality and Lawrence pushing the permissive sensibilities of his listeners to the limit. The self-explanatory 'Glue and Smack' was a reaction to the fact that there had been so many songs about marijuana and LSD, so he wrote one about the nastiest drugs imaginable.

'The idea with *Denim on Ice* was to write songs that made people talk,' said Lawrence. 'But it backfired because nobody noticed and nobody cared. Not one reviewer said it was close to the bone or in bad taste. We were desperate for attention. Desperate!'

Lawrence was trying to get attention, not just from the music press and the public at large, but from people he knew. 'Mrs Mills' is a jolly '70s-style novelty pop tune in which he mentions various women, some of them girlfriends, some of them not, in the hope that they might be flattered or at least annoyed. The line 'Miki's looking pretty in the city' referred to Miki Berenyi, the flame-haired singer and guitarist of the indie band Lush, who Lawrence had known for years.

'I wanted to see if anyone was taking note. I wanted Miki to say, "Why did you put me in that stupid song?" She didn't, of course, and neither did anyone else. Donna from New York is in there and so is Michaela. Not that she cared. She didn't say anything at all. I'm not sure she ever bothered to listen to it.'

Denim on Ice was a product of Lawrence's years in London in the early to mid-'90s. He spent his days walking around the West End, looking in estate agents' windows, going to a newsstand on Tottenham Court Road every Tuesday afternoon to pick up early editions of the *NME* and *Melody Maker*, and surviving on very little indeed. After buying the music papers, he would go to the café of the National Portrait Gallery in Leicester Square and spend the rest of the afternoon reading them. Here, an old man with wild staring eyes and a shock of frizzy white hair gawped at him and shouted, 'My God, young man! You look like an understudy from Dante's *Inferno*!'

'I didn't even look that bad in those days,' said Lawrence. 'I got all my clothes dry-cleaned, I looked smart, I wasn't trampy or weird in the slightest. So there has to be something about my face that makes certain people react in a violent fashion. The guy who worked in the tea room of the National Portrait Gallery used to give me abuse too. He stared and he stared.'

What was happening to Lawrence's great hope for the future of music between *Back in Denim* coming out in 1992 and *Denim on Ice* finally making it into the world in 1996? Not a great deal, because his revelation was that gigs were over, DJs were the thing, nobody was interested in bands any more. This was shortly before the 1995 Oasis vs Blur race to number one made the *BBC News* and put bands into the heart of the biggest story in music for the past thirty years.

'It was my big mistake,' accepted Lawrence. 'Instead of getting a four-piece together and going for it, my big epiphany was that it was all about DJs now. I couldn't have been more wrong.'

Lawrence was signing on the dole – a rousing pub singalong on *Denim on Ice* called 'Job Centre' celebrated the hinterland between work and unemployment – and after he and Michaela moved to separate flats in Butler's Wharf, he found himself so broke that when word came that a new label called Echo, a subsidiary of Chrysalis, were interested in Denim, he had to convince a friend to meet him at Tower Hill Underground to give him the fare to get to Echo's offices in Latimer Road. It was worth it. Echo offered Lawrence a deal for *Denim on Ice*.

There was a reason for the album's caustic tone. Lawrence had come to London to pursue his dream and he was bored. Bored of an unchanging routine, bored of going to see bands at the back room of the Falcon in Camden, bored of ordering minestrone soup in the Stockpot, a low-budget restaurant offering a facsimile of home cooking with branches in Soho and Chelsea. A young hanger-on, desperate to find a role in the indie scene, became his personal joint-roller for a while, with Lawrence offering the guy £50 a week to pop into the toilets of the Falcon and knock him up a joint whenever he needed one. Michaela was around, and she and Lawrence were 'going out but not' as he put it; sleeping with each other, hanging out at each other's flats, occasionally arriving together at Smashing or a short-lived Saturday-night club at the Café de Paris in Piccadilly. The main problem, as he saw it, was that they looked like such an unlikely pair, Michaela with her black hair and leather trousers, and Lawrence with his shades and brightly coloured leisurewear.

'You would never think we were a couple,' said Lawrence. 'It was never going to work with me and Michaela. Imagine Terence Stamp and Jean Shrimpton, or David Bailey and Penelope Tree . . . That's what I wanted, to be one half of a great-looking couple who looked like they were meant to be together.'

'Not wishing to cause offence,' I said to Lawrence, as we sat down at a picnic bench next to a muscular man doing one-armed press-ups on the grass, 'but do you mind if I make a comment?'

'Please, go ahead.'

'Weren't you a bit superficial in your search for love?'

'That was just with Michaela, and the tragedy of the fact that we could never really be boyfriend and girlfriend because we looked so silly walking down the road. She started laughing every time she saw me coming. When it was just the two of us, we had a great rapport, but then she would go on about other men all the time, as if she was trying to make me jealous. "Oh, I walked across Tower Bridge and saw this group of boys with bikes . . ." "This man came up to me in the café and he was so good-looking . . ." She was man- and boy-mad. I think she wanted to be a boy.'

When she headed out to Smashing, Michaela certainly didn't find Lawrence to be the ideal companion. 'I was sociable,' she said. 'I liked dancing. Lawrence was totally inhibited, he didn't drink, and he set himself up to spoil the whole night, particularly as afterwards he would be horrible about everyone. Nobody was cool enough for him . . . nobody apart from Primal Scream and rich people. He loved rich people. They didn't even have to do anything for him to love them.'

At Smashing one night, Michaela met a good-looking Liverpudlian called Andrew Meeson after going up to him with a cigarette in her mouth and asking, 'Will you light my fire?' Two weeks later, she moved in with him.

'I went from someone who refused to live with me to someone who was six foot three, in a rock 'n' roll band, played guitar amazingly. You could take him anywhere, everybody loved him, he was great. I had been unhappy with Lawrence for a long time so finally I ended it, and that's when he tried to make me feel guilty. "I haven't got anyone but you . . ." – all that. I was still living in Butler's Wharf at the time and his big one was "Can you come over and bring your Hoover?" "Get your own!" One day, I was with my friend Petra outside the flat, drawing, when Lawrence shuffled up with his carrier bags, all red and flustered, and went, "Why won't you lend me your Hoover?"

'The final time I saw him was on a traffic island in Holborn. He said, "But I love you!" By then I had met this hunk of a guy, and I looked at Lawrence and thought, *What was I ever hanging around you for?*'

Lawrence remembered it differently. He remembered seeing Michaela with an enormous biker who may or may not have been Andrew Meeson at a festival. 'She looked at me and said, "God, you're thin." That's the last time we saw each other.'

However much Lawrence liked to say how little he cared about Michaela, how ill-suited they were, how he would never get jealous in the slightest when she went off with other men, he didn't half talk about her a lot. And an awful lot of songs from *Back in Denim* and *Denim on Ice* are about her. Not only 'Fish and Chips' and 'Don't Bite Too Much Out of the Apple', not only a sorrowful mention of his nickname for her in 'Mrs Mills' – 'Eddie's flown the nest, she's found another / With her Liverpool lover, I guess I drew the short straw' – but also 'Romeo Jones is in Love Again', on which he begs a woman, Michaela as it turns out, to keep him company. He wrote 'Best Song in the World' one afternoon when he was annoyed with her about one thing or another, so he included a line about how she looked not only like her mother, who was a glamorous lady, but also her father, who was not.

'I'm not sure she even knew,' said Lawrence, when I asked what Michaela thought of all these songs about her. 'She certainly didn't care. She didn't care at all about anything I was doing. I got some-one else pregnant for God's sake.'

The someone else was Vikki. 'I didn't want a baby, so no worries there,' said Vikki of the incident, 'although Lawrence used to tell me I would go back to New Zealand one day and have a load of babies, which I never did. Actually, it is a miracle I got pregnant in the first place because we hardly ever had penetrative sex. He certainly had very little interest in my body.'

It is recounted in 'Brumburger', one of the angriest songs Lawrence has ever written. Alongside verses on getting mugged by his girlfriend's family, going on a date with a girl who looks like she has just walked out of the '70s cartoon about hippie bears *The Hair Bear Bunch*, and stealing a cat who falls out of the window and gets run over by an old man's lawnmower, he complains about how Michaela is out every night without him, looking for attention and not getting any. And, in a clear case of protesting too much, he sings about how he couldn't care less and he never thinks about her at all anyway. Halfway through his declaration of ambivalence he announces: 'I once killed a baby before it was born, babe / I don't think it's murder / It's up to us, isn't it?'

Vikki had the abortion. 'I was really angry about it,' said Lawrence, a statement that doesn't get close to matching the complexity of emotions battling it out in 'Brumburger'. 'In real life, so many girls have abortions and yet it is looked down upon. You never see it in soap operas. But, in a sense, that song was about the fact that every affair, every relationship I ever had, always went wrong. It didn't matter if I was nice to them, horrible to them, no matter what I did, it just didn't work. When the French girl I really liked walked out on me at the end of the '90s, I couldn't take it any longer. I've been asexual ever since.'

There is a song by Lawrence's great hero John Lydon, from the Sex Pistols' one and only album proper *Never Mind the Bollocks*, which goes even deeper in its confusion and rage over the same moral torture as 'Brumburger'. 'She was a girl from Birmingham / She just had an abortion,' snarls Lydon in 'Bodies'. 'She was a case of insanity / Her name was Pauline / She lived in a tree.'

Her name was indeed Pauline, but she didn't live in a tree. She lived in the village Lawrence grew up in. She was the Water Orton carnival queen for 1968, a role that Lawrence's own sister Beverly was elevated to seven years later. Like so many villages in Britain in the 1970s, Water Orton had one hippie family and Pauline was a part of it.

'The whole family was weird,' Lawrence remembered. 'They had the only overgrown garden in the village, windows that were always black, and loads of kids, with Pauline I think being the eldest. Her brother was known for his Mick Jagger impersonations. When the pubs closed at 10.30, the big boys would turn up for the last half hour of the youth club disco in the church and everyone would stand back and clap as Pauline's brother did his routine to "Jumpin' Jack Flash".'

Lawrence went out with Pauline's younger sister Jane when they were both fourteen, but he had to break it off because Jane took to wearing three-and-a-half-inch platform shoes. 'I got too embar-rassed about walking down the street next to a giant the whole time. It was actually at the youth club disco that I ended it. I looked up and delivered the news, and she was crying as she towered over me. The tears were raining down and splashing onto my face.'

Pauline had by then achieved a degree of local fame and notori-ety after a man in an open-top Jeep turned up one day to take her out on a date. It was John Peel. 'He was in the park, the high street, everyone saw him as they drove off together. That was a really cool day in the history of Water Orton.'

Not long afterwards, Pauline had an extremely bad LSD episode and ended up being sent to a psychiatric institute. 'She went crazy. She would come out of the mental home, go back in again, and we saw her wandering about the village looking haggard and not engaging with anyone, a beautiful girl who had gone too far with acid and was now troubled and tramp-like. It was really sad.'

The punk rock scene spoke to Pauline's sense of alienation, although Lawrence remembered her still dressing like a hippie girl with long brown hair and tasselled skirts even when she was hanging out at Barbarella's or travelling down to London to be with the Clash. 'She turned up at Johnny Rotten's house and tried to hang around with him, but he wouldn't stand for it. He wrote "Bodies" instead.'

Denim on Ice was intended to deliver Lawrence his much longed-for hit, with even the name of the album suggesting greatness achieved. Inspiration came from a famously disastrous 1975 con-cert at Wembley's Empire Pool by the progressive keyboard wizard Rick Wakeman called 'The Myths and Legends of the Knights of the Round Table on Ice'. An inebriated horn player attempted to chase after Guinevere as she glided past, a pitched battle between two knights proved impossible when one failed to show up, overuse of dry ice meant various mythical figures on skates crashed into each other, and Wakeman was so distraught by his grand folly that he had a heart attack at twenty-five.

Denim, however, would be such a massive band by the time of the album's release that staging an ice spectacular was the only way to go. In preparation for this, Echo Records told Lawrence that Denim had to do some live dates, so he relented and asked Jarvis Cocker if they could support Pulp, so massive after the success of 'Common People' that by February 1996 they were filling arenas. Cocker was not familiar with Felt, chiefly because John Peel didn't play them, but he was moved deeply by Denim's 'The Osmonds' as an emotional ballad about the conflicted realities of childhood, so much so that it gave him goosebumps. By the Britpop days, he was making a beeline for Lawrence at parties, intrigued by his typically unusual take on any given subject.

'There would be all these drunken people doing my head in, and then Lawrence would come along and talk in great detail about, say, his visit to the factory where John Smedley made their jumpers,' said Cocker, who at the time was renting a flat in Maida Vale formerly owned by Gilbert O'Sullivan that still had its original '70s furniture and wallpaper. 'For the most part, he kept himself to himself, sitting in the corner but with a smirk on his face, as if he was thinking about something quite interesting. I was intrigued about what that might be.'

So intrigued, in fact, that when Lawrence asked if Denim could support Pulp, Cocker jumped at the chance, not least because he felt this was a band more people should know about. There was some similarity between the frontmen, although Cocker was a more natural star, extremely good at playing to the crowd and knowing how to take minor details of British life and use them as material for songs that reached out to a lot of people. Lawrence's eccentricities made him a harder sell, but perhaps he was being protected from the thing he thought he wanted. After Cocker enacted a stage invasion during Michael Jackson's messianic performance at the 1996 BRIT Awards, sticking his bum out, hopping about and generally mocking the quasi-religious pomposity of it all, he went from indie star to tabloid sensation, finding the experience so terrifying that he retreated from view entirely. He even dealt with having to be at a festival in 1997 by walking around in a gorilla suit.

'Not that I'm the Queen, but 1996 was my *annus miserabilis*,' said Cocker, explaining his lack of recollection of the Pulp arena tour and Denim's part in it. 'The Michael Jackson thing changed my circumstances and there was nothing I could do. I wanted to be famous – I don't know where that came from – and you think fame will fill some hole in you. Then you achieve fame only for that hole to still be there, and it is really disappointing. As a result, I became so wrapped up in myself that I wasn't taking much notice of anything else going on and I never saw Denim because I was not in a great state at the time. I never left the dressing room until I went on stage.'

It was strange to hear Cocker talk about the realities of the one thing Lawrence professed to want so much. I thought about the way Lawrence was so controlling about what he ate, where he went, how he managed his life on a day-to-day basis, right down to not allowing me to stop for a drink in Beckenham Park if it didn't fit in with his plans, because the one thing guaranteed to accompany fame is a loss of control.

'You think you will be in control when you're famous, because you'll be like a king or something,' said Cocker. 'What actually happens is that a lot of people start seeing you as a big bag of money, and all of a sudden you have to hang around with the kind of people you would never normally hang around with. So, yes, you do lose control of your life, and I'm not sure how much Lawrence was willing to talk to industry types to further his career. Ultimately he is committed to the music he loves and he is uncompromising as a result.'

In 2011, Lawrence came onto a BBC Radio 6 Music radio show Jarvis Cocker was presenting called *Sunday Service*, turning up with his records out of their sleeves because he didn't want to get them damaged. 'There were a load of amazing things I had never heard before and that's a whole other side of him,' said Cocker, 'someone who has this deep and specific knowledge of popular music and is not operating from a "success = quality" mindset. He is listening very specifically to what the music is saying, and he finds elements within that music that he likes and make sense to him. I'm not saying he would consciously decide to not be popular, but it is not something that actually matters when he is following his own creativity.'

As we left the shadow of the tree to walk through the park and into the town, I told Lawrence about the reason Jarvis Cocker never saw him on that Pulp tour. 'That's good because I didn't know what was wrong with Jarvis back then,' he said, once he got over a panic about which direction to go for the high street, having refused to countenance my suggestion that I get out my phone and have a look, instead mapping the route by working out which bushes he went for a wee against on his last trip. 'I thought, because Pulp were so big, he didn't have time to come out and say hello and that's what happens when you get really famous. To be honest, that tour was ridiculous. We were playing as people were filtering into the arenas with their jumbo Cokes, and we had the worst sound because we were at the bottom of the bill. Nobody was bothering with us. The idea was that it would be something good to look back on in the official Denim biography. People would say, "Did you hear about that tour Denim did with Pulp back in the '90s? Can you believe it, that they were actually supporting *them*?"'

There must have been some pride for Lawrence in the arena tour, however, because he told his sister Beverly about the support slot and she came along to witness it, the first time she had shown any interest in his musical career. 'I told her that I was using the Glitter Band, because she fancied Pete Phipps back in the day and we both liked Gerry Shepherd. She had heard of Pulp because they were big, so she did come along to the NEC and that was the extent of it. I never sent the family records or anything.'

We made a pilgrimage to the place where Haddon Hall once stood and found a secret passageway that Bowie would use to get away from the fans and into his limo without anyone seeing. We visited the rusty Edwardian bandstand in Croydon Road Recreation Ground where a twenty-four-year-old Bowie sat down one day and wrote the tale of a girl with mousy hair who escapes the constrictions of suburbia by going to the cinema, watching sailors fighting in the dancehall and lawmen beating up the wrong guy. '"Life On Mars" was so easy,' said Bowie years later. 'A really beautiful day in the park, sitting on the steps of the bandstand . . . "Sailors bap-bap-bap-bap-baaa-bap" . . . Middle-class ecstasy. I started working it out on the piano and had the whole lyric and melody finished by late afternoon.'

Our own middle-class ecstasy culminated in a visit to Mr Sims' Olde Sweete shop on the high street. The man appeared to have thawed in his attitude to Lawrence, not least after he bought the entire stock of Drop Fruit Duo liquorice to the tune of £28.50.

'Oh, he's my friend now,' Lawrence concurred afterwards. 'He was non-verbal for so long, but that has changed. I think he respects my dedication to liquorice, because I truly believe I've got to be one of the world's leading liquorice experts. It could be my job. I would like to work for Red Band Liquorice. It's the brand that makes the Drop Fruit Duos.'

He didn't have such luck in Holland & Barrett, where we popped in to get some RJ's Choco Logs Liquorice. The man at the shop, after coming out from the counter to hover behind us, declared they were out of stock. 'I reckon all the RJ's liquorice is stuck some-where on a boat from China,' Lawrence posited. 'They're stuck in the Malacan Straits. The pirates have got them, and they're feast-ing on Choco Logs because they're so good. Good luck to 'em.'

That got Lawrence thinking – as we went from Holland & Barrett to a branch of Costa Coffee, where he bought a millionaire shortbread and instructed the Costa girl to pour out a third of the hot water in his disposable cup of tea and fill it with milk – about the kind of jobs he might be able to do should he move away from the whole pop star thing once and for all. At the top of the list was working in a supermarket as a basket supervisor.

'I would like to hand out the basket to the old ladies as they come in,' he said, poking at the tea bag with a little wooden stirrer. 'I would stand at the door all day, going, "Basket, madam? Lovely day, isn't it? Yes, it is a bit windy I know. I SAID, IT IS A BIT WINDY, I KNOW."'

'Would you also . . .' I began.

'"You again?"' he interrupted in loud, clear, slow tones, inhabiting his imagined role as the supermarket's senior citizen liaison officer. '"You've been in three times already today!" That kind of thing.'

He pointed into the nothingness.

'"Yes, Mrs Humphries. The cat food is still located in aisle ten."'

'I want to wear a tie and one of them brown overalls, old-fashioned, with pens in the pocket. I would stand there, giving out the baskets. I'm sure that used to be a job. You don't see it any more. I suppose because of cutbacks.'

One famous fictional character did have a similar job, and that was Ken Barlow of *Coronation Street*. His dream of being a novelist crumbling to dust (the discovery of a decades-old manuscript in the attic intact prompting Blanche, his *bête noire* of a mother-in-law, to snip that even the moths rejected it), Barlow took up a position as trolley attendant at the local supermarket. When I told Lawrence about this, he looked at me as if I suggested he get a job cleaning dog turds off the pavement with a toothbrush.

'Have you gone mad? Ken had to collect all the trolleys in the car park, where there was a young kid giving him stick the whole time. I'm not rescuing trolleys from the bushes or any of that shit. I'm at the front door, giving out the baskets.'

He approached another imaginary senior citizen.

'"Madam! Would you like a basket?"'

He took a sip of tea and stared into the distance.

'I've got a respectable job.'

We passed a group of kids at the bus stop. Maybe these particular children of Beckenham were too polite to say anything because there was not a snigger among them. 'That's my ultimate goal: to not be laughed at by schoolkids,' said Lawrence with a jaunty skip, as if he had just achieved something remarkable. 'Schoolkids are horrible people. They'll laugh at me, or nudge their friends, and I don't like it. I want them to think *That old guy is cool. As old men go, he doesn't look too bad. Maybe he was in a band once. Maybe his photograph is on the back of one of those things our parents had . . . What are they called again? Oh, yes, records.*

'Still, that was a good result just now. Not a single comment. Maybe I can start hanging out here on a regular basis, or at least until five in the evening. I have to get out by five because otherwise bad things happen.'

We made our way to the Three Tuns pub, or rather the local branch of Zizzi's, where a Bowie-esque lightning bolt was painted on the pavement outside and a mural of Bowie in his curly haired phase from 1970 adorned a wall. We sat on a bench, where a big unshaven man in a shiny black tracksuit with a rip in the crotch patched together with silver duct tape, came up and asked for a cigarette. After Lawrence gave him one, the man got out of his bag a tub of Palmers cocoa butter moisturising cream – he had a few in there – and offered it to his new friend.

'Nah, it's cool,' said Lawrence, raising a narrow palm.

'I want you to have this,' said the man, intensifying his gaze. Lawrence accepted the moisturising cream and put it in his multi-use vintage WH Smith bag.

'You having a good day?'

'Not bad,' said Lawrence with a shrug.

There was a moment of silence. It felt awkward and complicit at the same time.

'Alright, geezer,' said the man with a sigh, getting up. 'Good luck.'

It was only after he left that we realised: that the man thought Lawrence was a fellow shoplifter. He was asking how that day's lifting had been going.

'People think these bags are for nabbing things,' said Lawrence. 'In fact, I carry them around for more innocent purposes.'

He took from one of them an unused tea bag.

'Observe my foresight,' he announced, holding up the tea bag. 'You can't trust these Costa girls, because if you're not vigilant they might throw anything in the cup in that split second of preparation. They can put too much milk in the tea, so it ends up being the wrong shade. For this reason, I always carry around a spare tea bag in order to bring it back to its perfect hue. In the event, my tea is fine. But I bring this in case of emergencies.'

In the event, back in 1996, the unpleasant subjects addressed on *Denim on Ice* proved too much even for the irony-loving Britpop generation. '*Denim on Ice* bombed big time. I wanted to write songs about horrible people doing horrible things in a way that would turn them into hits. It didn't happen, but I wasn't about to give up.'

To Lawrence, it was inconceivable that his songs didn't take over the world and Denim's third album, the appropriately titled *Novelty Rock*, was intended to do just that. Even when he was emulating the inappropriate joyfulness of TV commercials for female sanitary products on 'Tampax Advert' ('Being on is no hassle, girls love it, yeah, it's really great'), even when he came up with a bouncy tune called 'The New Potatoes' in which a squeaky voiced spud details its journey from the earth to the plate ('I lived in a field and now I live in a tin'), he fully assumed he was making not only masterpieces, but smash hits.

'I've always thought that every single thing I've ever done is the best, probably because I'm very good with tunes,' he crowed. 'I'm a melody man. Inspired by Barry Manilow's "I Write the Songs", which he didn't write, I once came up with a song called "I'm the Melody Man". It could have been a massive hit. Unfortunately, I forgot how the melody went.'

Lawrence realised that if he really wanted to become the greatest pop star the world had ever known, he had to give up on songs about horrible people and horrible things and apply his melodic gifts to more uplifting subjects. Now Denim would leave behind lyrics that might turn off listeners of a sensitive disposition. Now it was time for his songwriting to utilise more acceptable words and, like David Bowie before him, become the star that destiny intended him to be. It was time to write the song set to become the number-one hit of 1997: 'Summer Smash'.

CHAPTER SEVEN

SUMMER SMASH

Summer was here and that meant something I never thought would happen: Lawrence playing Glastonbury.

In fact, it had happened before. In 1987, Felt played a Sunday-night slot at what was then known as Stage Two, one down from that day's headliners, the psychedelic jokers Doctor & the Medics. Lawrence's Creation stablemates the Weather Prophets were there as well, living out their rock 'n' roll fantasies by watching the Rolling Stones documentary *Gimme Shelter* in their van before taking to the stage in leather trousers. There were no such fun times for Felt. In *The Creation Records Story*, the late David Cavanagh reported that Lawrence arrived at the site to gaze out in dismay at the fields of mud, the tents crammed up against each other, the notorious drop toilets with their clanking metal cubicles raised above an odorous pit of effluent, and asked: 'Where are the cottages? Where are the cottages, for the stars?'

When told by a fellow Felt member that he would have to sleep in a tent like everyone else, he revealed the reason for his fear of a night under canvas.

'What if a lizard runs over my face?'

Now came the chance to do Glastonbury all over again, thirty-six years after Felt were busy reaching their peak in popularity. A Glastonbury performance could make or break a career, not least because so much of the festival was televised and broadcast all over the world. Alongside the Saturday-night slot at the Crow's Nest, Mozart Estate landed a gig at a place called the Bimble Inn. And when I asked Lawrence if he would interview me for my own event at the Crow's Nest, a midday talk on a book I had written on the history of '70s singalong pop, to my amazement he said yes. Both venues – or, rather, canvas tents – were in an area at the top of Glastonbury called The Park, which looked over the rest of the site in a way that made you appreciate the yawning scale of the place and the beauty of the Somerset hills beyond.

'I've discovered, to my shock, that Glastonbury don't provide the artists with accommodation,' he said in a shaky voice, seemingly having forgotten about his prior experience. He called one evening, just as I was making pasta with tomato sauce for the children and trying to ensure the pasta wasn't too hard or over-cooked, the tomato sauce was thickened to the right amount and the Parmesan was grated and ready to be sprinkled on top. I tried not to think about the fact that Lawrence once told me how Parmesan reminded him of vomit. 'Can you believe it? I think it's unfair. It's not like they're paying us or anything. The least they could do would be to give the band a cottage within walking distance – and a car service to and from the site would be a bonus. You're going to have to find somewhere for us. I don't mind sleeping in a chair – I do it all the time – but the band will need beds.'

Before they put up a million-pound fence to keep the crusties out, even more years before the EE phone-charging lounge became the festival's most popular attraction, Glastonbury was a haven of mystical, magickal weirdness. In 1971, the Pyramid Stage was built following the festival's co-founder John Michell's calculations on where two ley lines met, and from there it developed into a mecca of druidic worship, Pagan ceremony and rock 'n' roll abandon. It had been growing ever since, and one of my jobs involved writing regular reviews from across the site throughout the weekend. It meant I had enough on my plate without sorting out Lawrence's accommodation arrangements. Nonetheless, he was blessed with an amazing ability to make his problem your problem.

My first suggestion that he book a bed & breakfast in Glastonbury town fell on deaf ears. He said he didn't have the money for that kind of thing. I explained there weren't really that many cottages sitting empty, waiting to be filled with influential but obscure novelty bands on a budget of zero, but I could ask around and see what might be available.

A couple of weeks passed.

'How are you coming along with the Mozart Estate house?' Lawrence asked on the Tuesday before the festival. That was the day I had to find a campervan to hire, sort out the insurance, deal with a few hundred emails, write a newspaper feature on a different subject entirely and prepare for the next five days of life in a field.

'I've tried but I don't have one for you,' I said, and it was true.

'Oh, well,' he replied, in an unusually reasonable fashion. 'I'm sure we'll work something out.'

'Lawrence is a grown man,' said NJ, who I had been married to even longer than I had known Lawrence, over supper that night after I told her about the Glastonbury problem. 'It isn't your job to find him somewhere to stay. He could have dealt with this months ago.'

'But we're not dealing with a normal person,' I pointed out. 'There are many aspects of existence that provide serious challenges for him.'

'You always do this. You adopt these difficult people, and then you get yourself all stressed out trying to deal with them. You've got enough to cope with at Glastonbury. Concentrate on the work you're there to do.'

What about the work I wasn't there to do? The Mozart Estate set at the Bimble Inn was on Friday afternoon, my talk at the Crow's Nest was at midday Saturday, and there was the second Mozart Estate gig at the Crow's Nest on Saturday evening. They couldn't just not happen, could they?

NJ and I got there on Wednesday, having found a place for the campervan up a rocky track surrounded by trees, fifty feet or so from the towering metal fence at the top of the site. On Friday morning came a call from Lawrence. Following some garbled complaints about having to walk a long way from the car park and nobody telling him where to go, he announced he was here.

'Come and get me.'

'Where are you?'

'In a field.'

After half an hour or so, I spotted a lone figure in a Wrangler denim jacket, denim jeans and blue-and-white baseball cap, clutching his vintage WH Smith multi-use carrier bag on a sloping patch of grass near a crowded bar, jumping to one side as a large woman with fairy wings careered towards him. 'I'm dying for a pee,' he cried. Unsurprisingly, he wasn't going to go near the drop toilets or the compostable ones backstage, but he wasn't averse to finding a quiet tree to relieve himself against. I took him up to the spot where the campervan was parked. And, from there, a miracle happened. After wandering back down the rocky path, we bumped into my brother Tom, who announced that some friends of his, a couple called Andrew and Henrietta, lived in a stone cottage with their various children about twenty minutes away. They offered to put Lawrence up for the night.

'They're really lovely people, but the house is very messy,' Tom warned Lawrence.

'I'll clean it up for them,' he offered, miming a sweeping movement.

'You might have to sleep downstairs in the living room. Kids are running around upstairs.'

'I'll sleep in a chair. I'm good at that. People tell me their grand-dads sleep in chairs, so it must be something that happens in old age. This is a bit of good news for once. When I told everyone that there would be empty cottages near Glastonbury to provide me with a temporary home, they laughed.'

He drank a Coca-Cola and stood alone before the carnivalesque throng.

'Who's laughing now?'

While Lawrence went off somewhere, Tom introduced me to Andrew and Henrietta. They showed me photographs of a country cottage with roses and hydrangeas poking over a dry-stone wall, rich in downy moss. There were tiny pink flowers growing out of the cracks, a greening wooden garden gate freed from its hinges leaning against the wall, and an ancient slate roof that looked like it could do with a bit of upkeep but would do the essential job, perhaps aided by a few buckets in the attic when there was a really heavy downpour. I never got to see the inside of the house for reasons that will become apparent, but an hour or so in their company gave an idea of the kind of people Andrew and Henrietta were: generous, unfussy, intrigued rather than dismayed at the thought of having a would-be superstar in their midst. I imagined their car to be an old green Volvo, never washed, with an interior thick with lurcher hairs and a disintegrating rug that turned out to be an 18th-century family heirloom covering cracked leather upholstery on the back seat. They were good-looking too, with the kind of aquiline, fine-boned, make-up-free faces so redolent of English upper-middle-class bohemianism. That was bound to appeal to Lawrence's deep-rooted deference and love of beauty.

Henrietta gave me details to pass on to Lawrence, although since his phone was not capable of satellite navigation, I would have to get him to write it all down on one of the pieces of cardboard he scrawled important things on and lugged about with him in his WH Smith bag. The Old Rectory, as the rambling pile was known, was a short walk away from a gate at the top of the festival site that led to the local village. Henrietta would leave a key in a flowerpot by the door, and she gave exact instructions on how to get to the house and what to say to the stewards on the gate in order to get in and out of the festival.

What could possibly go wrong?

An hour or so before Mozart Estate's set at the Bimble Inn, Lawrence appeared outside the campervan. 'I can't remember any of the words!' he fretted as he got NJ to tie to his boyish, or maybe girlish, wrist an oversized white paper luggage tag containing many of the words he couldn't remember. As we opened up the hatchback and pulled out various things for lunch, from salads to yoghurts to little balls of mozzarella packed together with olives and sun-dried tomatoes, we tried to get Lawrence to eat something, but he wouldn't. Eventually he relented and accepted the offer of a caramel wafer. He inserted it into a clear plastic sandwich bag and sealed the top, to be consumed at some point in the future.

'When I was ten,' said Lawrence, standing up and leaning on the campervan as NJ and I sat on the grass and dug into our picnic, 'my sister pinned me down on the living room floor and forced me to eat cheese.'

Surely, I said, if Beverly was doing that, his horror of cheese was well under way.

'My reasoning is this,' he declaimed. 'We know that in nature if something smells, it is dangerous to eat. Cheese is extremely smelly. For that reason, we are not meant to eat it. Actually, the way I was treated as a child was unfair because everyone made out that I was being unreasonably fussy when in fact I belonged to a cult of religious people, who refuse to eat dairy products for ethical reasons, without knowing it. There weren't many of them back in the early '70s, but there were some, pioneers of this way of thinking, and it turns out I was one of them. Now they are common and highly respected. You get a lot of young people joining this sect.'

'What are they called?' NJ asked.

Lawrence looked up at the bright blue sky.

'Vegans.'

While I pondered on this, Lawrence tried to remember some of the lines other artists had spoken that he wanted to use in his own performance. 'There was a great one Freddie Mercury used. It went, '"We are Queen. What do you think of that?" I'm thinking of coming on and saying, "We're Mozart Estate. What do you think of that?" Freddie Mercury said it in Buenos Aires in front of half a million people. I have noticed, though, that when you say it at the Trades Club in Yorkshire, it has a very different effect.'

He had another one he wanted to try out, by a figure who was rather less popular among Glastonbury's right-thinking regulars. 'I'm going to come on and say, "Nobody said it was going to be easy." You're guaranteed to get a massive cheer when you say something like that, aren't you? Then I'll tell them, "Donald Trump said that." They won't know what to do.'

Mozart Estate did their Friday afternoon slot at the Bimble Inn. It was a sweet spot: a brown canvas tent festooned with Moroccan lamps, parachute drapes and frayed rugs on which children with scabby knees and straw in their hair lay about. The backstage area was occupied by dreadlocked, tattooed men and women alongside an ancient lorry, a dressing room/tent with an old brown sofa, a collapsing caravan and an enormous cast-iron fuel burner. The audience wasn't exactly huge on the hot and sunny afternoon, comprising mostly of the straw-haired children who hadn't managed to get out in time and about thirty fans who danced and punched the air, but nonetheless the set was a perfect amalgam of punk energy, singalong charm and brutal commentary.

'It's like a dream, it's like a four-leaf clover,' shouted Xav and Charlie, poking the sky with index fingers to the beat. 'He's gonna rock ya and then he'll take over.' Deputising on bass guitar – Rusty Stone had a wedding to do – was a cheerful mod called Andy Lewis, whose regular gig involved playing in Paul Weller's band. Tom Pitts, wearing oversized shades he picked up at a Spanish petrol station for five Euros, bashed the cymbal-free drum kit with a ferocity that belied his placid demeanour. Lawrence would clearly have liked to have run on stage after emerging from the wings to the deafening roar of 20,000 hysterical fans, but unfortunately the stage of the Bimble Inn was accessed by three steps that went straight into the crowd so he had to make do with hovering about the drum kit and keeping his back to the audience before spinning around. Still, it was an entrance of sorts.

I couldn't believe how good Mozart Estate were. You could hear every bass note, every keyboard motif, every word of Lawrence's funny, poignant, redolent lyrics. 'You live in fear that friends will call,' he bemoaned on 'When You're Depressed', surely the world's most uplifting song about living in abject misery. It was also one of the least sentimental: when you're depressed, you're depressed. There is no point in feeling sorry for yourself.

'I want to share your wonderful applause with the guys in the band,' Lawrence announced, borrowing a line Shirley Bassey once used during a concert at Carnegie Hall in New York. 'You know that washing machine?' he asked during Go-Kart Mozart's 'West Brom Blues', a portrait of broken hearts and domestic mundanity in his native Midlands. 'It don't half get things clean.' And who else at Glastonbury had a raucous should-be hit like 'Relative Poverty', which featured the statement, 'I'm living on a tenner a day / Goodness gracious a tenner a day'? Certainly not Elton John.

There was a visual appeal to the set too. Lawrence was a slight, cadaverous figure in his bright red Mozart Estate T-shirt tucked into the dampened Wrangler blue jeans he had never washed once since buying them two years previously, his blue-and-white baseball cap and large-scale, metal-framed shades topping off the ensemble. The profile set him well against the other band members: Xav in a white shirt festooned with bright red strawberries, the muscular Charlie in a sleeveless paisley vest, Andy in a red T-shirt and denim flares over monkey boots, and Tom in white shorts and T-shirt featuring the tormented visage of an alcoholic singer from Manchester called Jim E. Brown. They looked, in fact, like a group of civic-minded youths who had been tasked with helping a man on a Care In The Community scheme realise his dream of becoming a pop star, which, in a way, they were.

'Good evening,' said Lawrence, doing his best to ignore the blinding rays of sunlight pouring onto the stage. 'Hey, welcome to our music. I'm glad the songs mean as much to you as they mean to me.' That turned out to be a bit of between-song banter cribbed from David Bowie and it served as introduction to 'Donna and the Dopefiends', a cheerful tune about trying to cop heroin on the New York streets from a junkie dealer and her terrifying girl gang. Lawrence named it after Donna, his friend in New York who was definitely not a dope fiend, after being annoyed with her about something or another.

'Syringe street kids are fixing by the Hudson River,' sang Lawrence as Xav and Charlie supplied the vigorous backing vocals. 'There's an old guy with no shoes / It's like I'm looking in a mirror.' Why was nobody noticing the literary richness, the imagistic power, the capacious evocation? Perhaps Lou Reed would have appreciated them, having gone down a similar path in his time. But that was no good to us, because he was dead. Then Lawrence sang the words that pretty much summed up his last thirty years of life here on the planet:

You know I still want to be a star
But I just sold my guitar
And you know the way things are

Why was Nick Cave allowed to sing about dabbling with the darkest drug of all and proclaimed a genius? Why was Elliott Smith's 'Needle in the Hay' celebrated as a powerful metaphor on the downward spiral of addiction and 'Donna and the Dopefiends' not? Maybe Lawrence needed a manager. Maybe the novelty aspect of his music, the similarities it shared with unsung geniuses like Chicory Tip and Lieutenant Pigeon, proved a problem for modern audiences.

But there was always novelty pop of a kind and, in the last decade or so, they tended to be global rather than national: the Korean smash 'Gangnam Style' came to mind. Perhaps Lawrence's lyrics about murder, crime, cash, homelessness, poverty, despair and horrible people in general were too much for sensitive audiences. But that's what the great rappers concerned themselves with, wasn't it?

What did it take?

After the set, Lawrence announced he was going to spend the next hour following the strict instructions given to me by Henrietta and find the house so he didn't have to worry about looking for it in the dark later on. I told him he needed to head to somewhere called Kingshill Gate, at the very top of the site, and he would find it by going through Strummerville, a wooded area with a twenty-four-hour campfire surrounded by logs that was set up by the late Joe Strummer of the Clash and retained his spirit of communality and gentle anarchy. 'You see that field?' I said, pointing to a hilly area 100 metres or so from where we were standing. 'Go up there, turn right, you're in Strummerville. You can't miss it.'

'Up there, turn right, you're in Strummerville,' Lawrence repeated, nodding. He picked up his WH Smith bag. 'Got it.' Then he shuffled off in the opposite direction.

That night, having spent hours bashing out reviews on various acts throughout the vast space of the festival, I ended up at the Crow's Nest somewhere around 1 a.m. NJ, Tom and I were sitting at a rickety wooden table, drinking beer after a long day, when the phone went. It was Martin Kelly. He was, against all the laws of what should have happened by then, with Lawrence.

Lawrence never found the house that afternoon. He did find Strummerville and the Kingshill Gate, but a teenager in a high-vis jacket told him he wasn't allowed to go through it. When Lawrence explained that he had instructions to head that way, the teenager said, 'What do you want to go up there for? There's nothing apart from a load of brambles.' Lawrence pointed out that his house was past the gate, but he appeared to have lost the strength to argue the point because then he headed back into the festival. At some point later, I wasn't sure when or how, he found Martin Kelly. Somehow Martin found himself agreeing to walk all the way to where his car was parked, at the opposite end of the site, about an hour away, and drive him to the house. But they couldn't find it.

'That postcode you gave Lawrence took us to a tree,' Martin complained. 'I can't see the house anywhere and we've been driving around for the past hour.'

Many of the smaller roads surrounding the festival were cut off by metal barriers and security guards, so it was likely Martin and Lawrence had been sent off in the wrong direction, unable to argue their way to the right place. I sent Martin a photograph of the house in the hope that someone might recognise it. He called back to say one of the security guards claimed it was a photograph of Worthy Farm, home of Glastonbury's founder Michael Eavis.

'Yes, I know, Lawrence,' I heard Martin snap, against the background burble of a Midlands mumble. 'Let me try and talk to Will.'

I explained that I had given them the right postcode, that the photograph was not of Worthy Farm, that they had better keep looking. But if they couldn't even locate the house, what were the chances of finding the key? They would have to bash on the door and terrify a few children in the dead of night. Martin said he would call back.

He never called. Eventually, we turned in and I assumed Lawrence was in there by now, perhaps doing a bit of late-night Hoovering before sitting upright in a chair in the living room with a cup of tea prepared to his usual specifications. The important thing was that he made it to the talk at the Crow's Nest at midday, not least because I had been going around telling everyone about it.

The Crow's Nest was a scout hut-like tent at the very top of the site. Could Lawrence even get up that hill? I had noticed on our regular walks through the suburbs that upward gradients could prove a challenge, so it was definitely a concern, but not one I had time to think about the following morning as I skimmed through the book and tried to remember some choice stories to roll out and get the laughs. It was a good spot: the Crow's Nest was a hang-out for people not far outside of Lawrence's universe, people who were interested in original ways of thinking, like the guys who ran Heavenly Records, or fellow survivors of the '90s indie scene like Miki Berenyi of Lush and Jarvis Cocker of Pulp. Lawrence, I imagined, would do a very good job as the Michael Parkinson of Glastonbury.

He knew '70s singalong pop inside out, he had bothered to read the entire book, and you never knew which way he was going to approach a subject. It kept things fresh.

He just had to get there.

'Will,' said the slight Birmingham voice down the other end of the phone, half an hour before we were due on stage. The voice had that tinge of hesitancy, mixed with panic, which always made me nervous. 'We don't know where we are. We don't know how to get to where we've got to be. And we don't know where we're going. Where are we, Martin?'

Martin said they were in the car park. It took an hour to get from the car park to the Crow's Nest.

I gave rudimentary directions and told them to run.

The phone went again.

'Where is the Magpie's Nest?' Lawrence asked. 'None of these people on the gate know where it is. They've never heard of it so you've obviously got the name wrong. Are you sure it's not called the Pyramid Stage?'

There was not much to do except take a deep breath and collapse onto the ground in despair. I told Lawrence there were thousands of stewards at Glastonbury, most did the job in exchange for a ticket, and they couldn't be expected to know every corner of the vast site.

'You'll have to send a car,' he commanded. 'Or a golf buggy at the very least. Send one immediately and we might be able to make it on time.'

'But where are you?'

There was a long silence from the other end of the line.

'We're in a crowd of people.'

Incredibly, in one of those miraculous events that only seem to happen to Lawrence and ensure that, for every twenty times he is cursed, there is one when he is supernaturally blessed, someone took him down a secret route, away from the public, which got to the production office of The Park in ten minutes. 'Stay there!' I screeched. 'Do not move! We're coming down to pick you up right now!'

'Let's go,' said a harried but remarkably capable man who ran the place called Tony Crean, jumping into the driver's seat of a golf buggy. The metal chain-link fence in the backstage area of the Crow's Nest opened up and we bounced down the hill, through another secret spot, before stopping at the production office. Lawrence and Martin were nowhere to be seen.

The phone went. It was Hannah, one of the people from the Crow's Nest.

'Lawrence is here.'

We made it to the stage just in time, coming on to 'I'd Like to Teach the World to Sing' by the New Seekers and talking for the next hour before – well, maybe not the biggest crowd in the world, but among them was Miki Berenyi, who said afterwards that seeing Lawrence at Glastonbury was something she had long assumed to be completely impossible. And Lawrence was a superb interviewer. He wanted to know about the young female stars of the '70s singalong scene like Linda Lewis, Tina Charles and Ayshea Brough, he talked about the influence '70s pop had on Denim, and the impact the Birmingham bombings had on everyone he knew. He wanted to know how social and political forces in Britain shaped the music of the decade. You couldn't have asked for a more erudite host.

When it was over, we passed a row of empty wooden benches to sit on some foldaway metal chairs under a handwritten sign on a sheet of A4, Sellotaped to a plastic awning, which read: ARTIST'S AREA. I cracked a beer and he lit a cigarette.

'Thanks, Lawrence,' I said. 'I can't believe you got there in time.'

'Don't know what you were worried about,' he said lightly, leaning back and puffing a plume of smoke into the sky. 'Really, you need to calm down because you'll get a heart attack the way you're going. It happened to Rick Wakeman, you know.'

He looked down at his jeans. Faint traces of steam were rising.

'I think I might smell of damp,' he observed. 'I like hot weather, but this is a bit of a problem. I've never washed these jeans, ever, and now the humidity is turning me into the human equivalent of a musty basement.'

Inspired by reports of Hells Angels who never washed their denims no matter what grime, sweat, oil and blood got caked into them over the years, Lawrence resolved to do the same. 'I'm scared of denim. Scared of washing it and losing the colour. I intend to keep wearing these jeans until they collapse entirely and I have to throw them away, but I'm not sure if it is a clothing policy that works particularly well at Glastonbury.'

The evening performance by Mozart Estate at the Crow's Nest shone so much brighter than any number of sets by so-called stars over the weekend. Once again, there were fewer fans than I hoped or expected, but I couldn't help but feel like one of those forty or so people at Manchester's Lesser Free Trade Hall when the Sex Pistols played there in 1976: witness to a historic moment. A man who was dancing wildly at the front of the stage got thrown out when he lit up a joint.

'Don't go,' said Lawrence to the man. 'You're our only fan.' But he wasn't. As the small, enlivened crowd shouted along to

'When You're Depressed' and sang the chorus to 'Relative Poverty', I thought, *There's something happening here. What it is ain't exactly clear. But it was happening.*

I asked Lawrence about his feelings on the whole affair.

'Glastonbury is a highlight of the year for sure,' he reflected, as Xav and the boys collected up the leads and put the guitars and keyboard back in the cases. 'Knowing what happens in my life, I naturally assumed it was going to rain, but with such unexpectedly beautiful weather, the whole adventure has been very good for band morale. Most importantly, when I told people I was going to find a cottage to stay in, they mocked me. But we *did* find a cottage. There *are* cottages for the stars.'

'I forgot to ask about that,' I said. 'How was it? Did you meet the kids? What is the inside of Andrew and Henrietta's house like? Were you a good guest or an awful one? Did they make a cup of tea according to your requirements?'

'Oh no, we couldn't actually locate the house,' he announced airily. 'After an hour or so of driving around, we gave up and went to a Premier Inn. But the point is that it turns out I was right all along. There was going to be a sofa bed made up for me in the living room, while the woman and her children would be asleep upstairs. They were incredibly trusting, which just goes to show it is a good thing I'm not a mad axe murderer because it would have been the perfect opportunity for a crazed killer to do his worst. A detached house in the countryside, an invitation to a complete stranger to come and stay the night . . . You're asking for trouble, aren't you?'

As for Glastonbury itself, it reminded Lawrence of *The Hobbit*. 'Mr Blank read us *The Hobbit* in English class and afterwards you went into the woodlands to look for hobbit holes or wherever they lived. That's what the countryside here reminded me of, and Glastonbury is where the hobbits let it all hang out for their annual festival.'

Less attractive were the food stalls everywhere. 'The food looked disgusting,' said Lawrence, and it didn't occur to me at the time that he was speaking in the past tense, even though it was only Saturday. 'The smells were coagulating in the air, creating a big fug of awful aroma, with hordes of people gorging on whatever they could find. Luckily, I found a stall selling sweets and bought some Candy Kittens. That is a minor detail in what has turned out to be a remarkable event. Yes, I feel like Glastonbury will be a turning point in my life.'

There was a turning point in the career of Denim back in 1997 and it was called 'Summer Smash'. Around the time that the deal with Chrysalis was ending, Bob Stanley, the man who gave Denim their first break with that new bands feature, was putting together his own label called EMIDISC as an offshoot of EMI and he was keen to sign Denim. Bob spoke to a producer/A&R/product manager at EMI who was overseeing the project called Tris Penna, and he agreed to promote Denim on one condition: that they deliver a hit. So Lawrence went off to work on a song with Terry Miles, cousin of Martin Duffy and an all-round wizard on the synthesiser. A week later, he had 'Summer Smash'.

'EMI was in Hammersmith at the time, and walking through the revolving door of the offices felt like this could be it: my life-long ambitions realised. I was confident "Summer Smash" was a hit, maybe the biggest of all time. But would EMI think so? They hadn't seen the potential in "Tampax Advert", not even in "The New Potatoes". I walked in there and said, "Here's your hit single."

I put it on and, at the end of it, Tris said, "That's a hit." I said, "I know." From there, it was all systems go.'

Justin Anderson of Freaky Realistic contributed to an electro-pop B-side about going on holiday to Paignton and catching a show by the British comedians Little & Large called 'Sun's Out', and there was an instrumental version of Terry Dactyl and the Dinosaurs' '70s singalong hit 'Seaside Shuffle' included too. The Radio 1 DJs Mark and Lard made 'Summer Smash' their single of the week and played it every day. It was guaranteed to go top thirty and had a pretty good chance of going all the way to the top. 'Summer Smash' was smashing its way through the summer of '97.

On the Sunday before the week the song was due to be released, news came of Princess Diana being involved in a car crash with her boyfriend Dodi Fayed in the Pont de l'Alma tunnel in Paris. We all remember what we were doing that day. I was in bed with NJ, in our flat in King's Cross, when she said, 'Di and Dodi are dead.'

'I was up all night, watching television, when the news broke,' said Lawrence. 'At first, I thought, *Wow, that's unusual. I wonder if she's actually dead?* Shame about Diana, but didn't think much of it. Next morning, however, came the news that "Summer Smash" was cancelled. They melted down all the copies in the warehouse. There were boxes of records in the EMI offices that they threw in a skip and I got there just in time to grab some 7 inches, cassettes and CDs. Apart from that, nothing got out. We had been speeding along, everything was going well, and then EMI's foot came off the Denim pedal. When they cancelled "Summer Smash", alongside "Impossible Princess" by Kylie Minogue, my attitude was "This is bad but it is not the end of the world. We'll do another one." But they lost interest entirely.'

Lawrence did manage to get *Novelty Rock* out on EMI, but the dream was fading fast. Tris Penna moved on to work for Andrew Lloyd Webber, EMIDISC was dropped, and only the punky indie band Kenickie made it from Bob Stanley's label onto EMI proper. Lawrence asked if he could come too and was told he couldn't. He asked Tris Penna if he might be an exciting new signing to Andrew Lloyd Webber's label and that wasn't happening either.

'It was over,' said Lawrence.

What happened next?

'I had a mental collapse.'

CHAPTER EIGHT

WEREN'T YOU IN A BAND?

It was a glorious day in the city, one of those sunlit afternoons when being alive seems like a great idea. A perfect day, then, to go clothes shopping with Lawrence.

'I've discovered the greatest men's clothing shop in the history of humanity,' he announced. 'It is so fantastic. The last time I went there, I couldn't afford any of the clothes. I had to plump for a magazine consisting entirely of photographs of vintage sweatshirts. It cost £70.'

The shop was on Great Portland Street in Fitzrovia and it was called Clutch Café. It specialised in Amekaji – replications of American workwear from between the 1940s and the 1970s by small-scale Japanese brands. The clothes were extremely well made, obsessively authentic and staggeringly expensive. There were 1950s-style lambswool cardigans on sale for £500, work boots going for £699, and satin souvenir jackets with ornate dragon embroideries for a face-melting £1,335.

It was an appealing-looking place too; a world of exposed brick walls, weathered oak cabinets and seersucker overalls folded neatly on ancient tea chests, presided over by serene men in well-cut denim shirts and off-white Japanese sneakers with rubber soles. Unlike our experiences in Benetton, the men here not only seemed undisturbed by Lawrence, they actually welcomed him as a valued customer.

'We've got the Sturdy black leather car coat back in,' said a slender fellow with glasses, loose white trousers and a cheerful bright blue Hawaiian shirt. 'It's downstairs. My colleague will point it out to you.'

Sturdy turned out to be a Japanese leather brand and the item in question was an extremely heavy, blanket-lined coat of washed cow hide leather with brass buttons and scalloped pockets: a snip at £2,000. 'Appreciate the superior quality,' commanded Lawrence, running his narrow fingers along the thick leather. 'It's beautiful.'

With the help of a slight Japanese man with shoulder-length hair, he tried it on. You could imagine Marlon Brando swaggering about in the jacket in *On the Waterfront*. On Lawrence, the coat looked like it might eat him.

'I like it,' he said, striking a series of poses in the mirror as the Japanese man made adjustments.

'It's far too big for you,' I pointed out.

'You like clothes that are too tight. I wear them loose,' he corrected. 'Clothes look good on me when they're big. They make me look a bit trampy.'

'At this rate, you're going to be the most expensively dressed tramp in Britain.'

I had visions of Lawrence wandering up and down a Tube train in his Sturdy coat, beginning the familiar refrain of 'Sorry to bother you, ladies and gentlemen', only to be called out by some

Amekaji freak who couldn't help but notice the craftsmanship under the layer of dirt encrusting Lawrence's leather outerwear. I directed him towards some leather gloves.

'They are nice,' he mused, handling the soft material. 'There's something quite sinister about them, like Dirk Bogarde in *The Night Porter* . . . Yes, I like them. And they're only . . .' He turned them over to find the price. '£300.'

His eyebrows went up in shock.

'What a bargain!'

His attention was drawn towards deep indigo jeans by a Japanese brand called Anatomica, a relative steal at £270. 'I've got a serious problem with denim,' he told the Japanese man as he studied the 1960s American Navy work pants-style jeans. 'I can't wash it.'

'I never wash my jeans either,' said the clean-looking assistant. 'Instead, I use this.'

He produced a spray can of Japanese denim conditioner.

'It kills 99 per cent of bacteria dead,' the man announced, brandishing the £25 can. 'It works as a deodorant and a sanitiser. Hang up your jeans and give them a couple of sprays. Full Count Denim Conditioner will get rid of that damp and musty jeans smell immediately.'

This place was Lawrence's spiritual home.

'Take a look around, inspect the stock, before making a purchase of your own,' Lawrence commanded. 'You may be interested in the Henley shirts they have upstairs. Go and have a look.'

For some reason, I did what he told me, throwing away a crazy £110 on a three-button oatmeal Henley shirt with tubular cuff ribs. It was only when we left, with Lawrence not having bought anything at all, that I realised: he was having a vicarious consumer experience. He was making me buy things, rather than spending money he didn't have himself. He did the same thing in Terry's electrical shop in Welling, when I ended up buying a Breville sandwich maker under his supervision. And he almost did it in Club JJ in Canning Town. It was quite impressive, really.

We walked to Regent's Park and sat on a bench in the shade as exchange students laid checked picnic blankets onto the grass, vigorous men and women leapt at a Frisbee, young mothers pushed prams along the gravel path, and kids walked home from school in their grey-and-blue uniforms, their merry chit-chat catching in the breeze. Lawrence stared ahead into some kind of void, somewhere beyond everything.

When I first met Lawrence in 2005, he was in the little flat in Belgravia. There was a dirty-looking mattress on the floor of the living room, a television on the floor next to a video machine with a few tapes by its side, and bare walls painted in a durable shade of cream, peppered with angry brown stains of indeterminate origin. The only sign of domestic pride was in the corridor, where Lawrence's French pop, underground middle-of-the-road, punk, glam and Bob Dylan records were arranged on shelves behind a clear polythene sheet next to his books. They included a set of the *Skinhead* novels by Richard Allen and a few cult classics like *Hunger* by Knut Hamsen, *On the Road* by Jack Kerouac and *Ask the Dust* by John Fante. It looked like the lair of a man who had all but given up on his own life, but not the lives of others articulated and captured down the decades.

'After it all went wrong with "Summer Smash", I moved into the flat in Belgravia and went, *What the hell will I do now?*' said Lawrence, popping a Drop Fruit Duo into his small round 'O' of a mouth.

'The mental collapse started in 1998 and it continued, going down and down and down, for the next four years.'

Aware he was facing a serious catastrophe, and accepting his major-label dream and the chart fame that went with it was over, Lawrence's first intention was to get back on the horse and keep going with a smaller project. He would do his own label, West Midlands Records, where he would release records by friends while also having a home back at Cherry Red for his new band Go-Kart Mozart, the world's first B-sides pop sensation, into which Lawrence would throw any obscure or novelty idea without worrying about whether it was commercial or not. It is how 'Drinkin' Um Bongo', a song named after a popular children's soft drink but about one of the worst genocides in African history ('Plenty of anger in Rwanda'), from Go-Kart Mozart's 1999 debut *Instant Wigwam and Igloo Mixture*, came to be.

'After *Wigwam* was released, I thought, *How did I actually do that?* Because, by then, I was so far down in the tunnel I couldn't do anything any more. I was finished. It was the new decade and, for the first time ever, I thought, *What am I going to do?*'

What he did was become a heroin addict.

'I'm not sure I want to talk about it.'

It was understandable, I said, as we sat side by side on the bench and watched the people go by on a sunny afternoon in the park. It must have been an incredibly painful period. Maybe there was guilt involved, of talent wasted, of the endless struggle of trying to write brilliant songs and facing the agony of putting them out into the world only for the world to react with indifference, exchanged for the icy comforts of annihilation.

'It's not that,' said Lawrence. 'It's such a cliché, isn't it? I can't stand all those "my drug hell" stories by pop stars.'

Michaela thought Lawrence wanted to become a junkie. 'I knew how obsessed he was with the whole Richard Hell/Lou Reed/New York punk scene and he wanted to emulate it in the most obvious way imaginable. There was loads of cocaine floating about in the '90s, and heroin was the next step. I remember catching him at it for the first time. I turned up at his flat to find Lawrence and the guy he used to pay to roll joints for him doing heroin, which of course he denied, but it was pretty obvious to me what was going on. That guy is a drugs counsellor now.'

I wasn't so sure. Real addiction – as opposed to the druggy transgressions countless band members indulge in before straightening out and either becoming rich and famous or entering into civilian life – is so frequently a symptom of severe trauma. Lawrence was blocking out the pain with self-medication, blanketing the broken dreams by turning to the one thing guaranteed to make all your problems go away – for a few hours at least, before introducing a new set of problems the likes of which you never got close to before.

In the early 2000s, Lawrence ended up in a psychiatric institute on Vincent Square in Victoria after missing a couple of visits to his local doctor. 'The doctor thought, *This guy is mad*, so he sent a mental health team round to the flat. They knocked on the door and said, "We've been sent by your doctor. We think you might need some help. We have a facility around the corner if you'd like to come along." At first, I went, "Yeah, doesn't seem like such a bad idea." They took me there and it was straight out of *One Flew Over the Cuckoo's Nest*: people with massive bunches of keys, going through doors and doors and doors, and this strange, silent atmosphere interspersed with the odd scream in the distance. They showed me a room I could stay in. I was on various medications from the doctor and they let me be an out-patient in the end, so it was okay . . . for a while.'

One afternoon, Lawrence's care worker had arrived in the foyer to say a smiley hello when there was shouting from down the corridor. Suddenly, a man burst into the foyer and punched her in the face so hard that he knocked her out. 'She went down, the man was jumped on by orderlies, the police came and told me to go home, and by the time I came back, the care worker had left for good. She decided there and then that she didn't want to work in the profession any more.'

The worst times were yet to come. Lawrence's biggest fear was realised when a psychiatrist he was in a consultation with looked at him with squinted eyes and asked: 'Weren't you in a band?' The psychiatrist had been to a Felt concert and bought a couple of their records during his university years. 'Then he said: "We're snowed under and there's nothing we can do for you right now." He thought I was there under false pretences, because as far as he was concerned, I was a successful figure. The one guy who knew who I was had to be my psychiatrist.'

Lawrence skulked out of the psychiatric institute feeling like a fraud. Not a fraud pop star, but a fraud mental patient. On two separate occasions afterwards, police broke his door down because the doctors assumed he had committed suicide after they hadn't heard from him. Nobody wanted a suicide on their watch.

'These burly policemen burst in and shouted, "Are you okay?". I said, "Yeah, why?" I was sitting on the floor, watching the telly. *The O.C.,* I think it was. But however bad things got, I never thought about killing myself. That would be an admission of failure.'

The ambition was still there, the drive to stardom ongoing, even it if had taken a detour down a needle-strewn alleyway. But something had to change because Lawrence reached a state of total junkie stasis. When there was a notification that the building was infested with mice, he told the building manager that there certainly weren't mice in *his* flat. As his friend Pete Astor commented, they were probably dancing around his toes, and he didn't even notice.

Lawrence was busy losing himself to *La Maman et la Putain*, or *The Mother and the Whore*. Jean Eustache's black-and-white film from 1973, one of two full-length features the director made before killing himself in 1981, consists of little more than three and a half hours of French people talking, but it serves as a summation of both the French New Wave and hippie-era bohemianism, which found itself unmoored after the great heroic revolution of the Paris '68 riots. It concerns Jean-Pierre Léaud's Alexandre, a self-absorbed would-be intellectual in a white shirt and long scarf who spends his days hanging out at Les Deux Magots, drinking J&B whisky, chatting up women, smoking cigarettes and jumping between Marie, the fiery mother of the scene who supports him by running a boutique, and Veronika, a promiscuous nurse facing a serious case of existential despair. There are endless scenes of the three sitting on the big mattress or the bare floorboards of Marie's apartment, drinking wine and eating *lapin à la moutard* cooked by Marie, who is struggling to reconcile the free love, unbound from emotion, which they're meant to be embracing, with the values of the bourgeoisie from which she came.

The Mother and the Whore captured a time when everything was meant to change in France, when young men like Alexandre were going to be elevated to a deeper understanding, a deeper experience, way beyond the material concerns and unquestioning conventions of the Occupation-scarred generation that came before. In fact, they turned out to be just people, subject to the same jealousies, immaturities and insecurities as everyone else. Alexandre is a revolutionary who doesn't do anything revolutionary. All he does is talk and sit around in a bare apartment. If he wants money, he has to sponge off his girlfriend. He philosophises, he looks cool, he is good-looking, he sleeps with beautiful women. He realises, only at the end, that it isn't enough. The women realise it earlier on. The selfishness Alexandre mistakes for enlightenment has left him with nothing. Alexandre was the great hope, the great hero, the genius, but it is all a fantasy.

'There was a video shop at the back of a newsagent's in Pimlico,' said Lawrence. 'At the time, I couldn't do much more than stay in my room, but each day I did manage to visit that newsagent's and have a look at the videos. I went through whatever could be good in that shop, like anything with Julia Roberts's less successful brother Eric in it, an amazing actor specialising in terrible action films. In among the selection, for some strange reason, was *The Mother and the Whore*, which I used to rent so often, I ended up buying the copy off the guy. This came at a time when things were getting worse, everything slipping away, year by year, until there was nothing left. When I look back in it now, I imagine someone saying, "Why the hell didn't you get yourself together? Why didn't you sort yourself out? Why didn't you get a job like normal people?"'

The answer lay in *Hunger* by Knut Hamsen. The Norwegian writer, who won the Nobel Prize in Literature in 1920 and ended up being charged with treason for supporting the Nazis' planned invasion of Norway, poured his conflicting feelings of self-hatred and superiority into a fantastical vision of the *übermensch*. *Hunger* is the tale of a starving writer attempting to hold onto respectability as he wanders around the city of Kristiania, and whose concept of intellectual and artistic purity means he would rather eat his own finger as he goes mad with hunger than get a job. Hamsun's unnamed protagonist gets to the point of not even writing anything. It is the idea of his commitment to the life of the writer that counts.

We had been on the bench for over an hour and now it was early evening, which meant that men and women in smart functional clothes were crunching along the path, the signs of tension accompanying them: a crumpled back of a suit here, an uneven hem of a skirt there. Unlike the kids coming back from school, unlike the foreign students and their Frisbees, they were rushing past, heads down, eager to reduce the intersection from work to home as much as possible.

'Of course, I could have changed my life,' said Lawrence as the people went by. 'Lots of my friends were getting jobs around the time. Pete Astor got a job. Douglas Hart started making films. But if you want to know what was going on in my life, read *Hunger*. Knut Hamsun could have had a full belly. He ate paper at one point, he was so desperate. But he's an artist. He'd rather starve to death than do something as banal as get a job. If someone saw him, say, washing dishes, his credibility would have been dashed and that was me entirely. No matter what happens, I am a songwriter and a musician, and it is what I must do. However long I have to sit in this room with no money whatsoever, no matter how many times the police break down my door to check I'm still alive, I cannot admit I'm not an artist.'

Or as Paul Kelly saw it, Lawrence gave up everything for his own singular cause. 'He has a deep knowledge of film, music and literature, partly because he has more time to indulge it than most of us, and he turned his life into an art form. He sacrificed his wellbeing, any kind of real security, for his art. He makes a lot of other people work for it, but the dedication is something to be celebrated.'

Lawrence was living on unemployment benefit, which didn't go very far, and by now had cut himself off from pretty much everyone he knew. He hadn't seen his family for years. If an old friend – Pete Astor, say – turned up at the flats and rang the bell, he went to pieces. The big fear was that they could somehow get in and knock on his door and he would have no choice but to open it, at which point they would see the mess he was in, the mess he was living in.

There was an improvement of a sort around 2003 when Lawrence started attending regular appointments at the Drug Dependency Unit. He even wrote a song about it, 'At the DDU'. It's quite catchy. He got off heroin and onto methadone, and after a while he could collect his own script from the chemist rather than have to go to the Unit. In 2004, he started attending Narcotics Anonymous meetings in the basement of a church in Notting Hill, an area he chose because he had a much better chance of meeting a supermodel or a rock star who partied too hard than the standard run-of-the-mill junkie (in the event, he met all three). And Lawrence even had his own *La Maman et la Putain* romance in the years of isolation. In 2000, stuck in his room, he received a letter from a French woman. She was the singer in an indie-pop band called Spring, she was the girlfriend of the editor of a French magazine he had done interviews for called *Magic*, and she was a chic beauty with the air of a Nouvelle Vague screen icon.

'There was a time in Paris when it was me, Bob Stanley and Pete Wiggs from Saint Etienne, the guy from Magic, and his girlfriend,' Lawrence recalled. 'I was looking at the girlfriend and thinking, *It's a pity she's so tight with him because I'm actually in love with her.* Then a letter came. It said, "I'm coming to London. I can't stand Paris any more. Can I come and see you?"'

The French Girl arrived to announce she had split up with the editor of *Magic* and was building a new life. At the time Lawrence was back in touch with Alan McGee, now not only clean of drugs but also a multi-millionaire after Creation's generational success with Oasis, so they went around to see McGee at his enormous house in St John's Wood. He told them he had started a nightclub on Oxford Street and he would put The French Girl and Lawrence's names on the door. He told them to get there by ten.

'We started getting ready at seven, but somehow we didn't leave the flat until three in the morning. Eventually we got a taxi, and when we finally got there, Alan was furious. He said, "Where the fuck have you been?" – that was the end of me and Alan for a few years – and then The French Girl says she's going to the toilet. After a while, a guy comes up to me and asks if she is my girlfriend. When I say yes, he goes, "She's out cold with blood coming out of her head." She had fainted, or gone mad and smashed her head on the sink – yes, we had been taking drugs – and that's when Alan said something like "I can't do this any more" and left. I tried to take The French Girl to hospital, but she refused. The following day, she screamed: "Why didn't you take me to hospital? Were you going to leave me to die?"

'That was the beginning of our crazy relationship.'

Nonetheless, some semblance of normality, of productivity, was coming back. Not least because Lawrence was planning to put out on his West Midlands record label an album by Milla Jovovich, the Ukrainian-born model soon to launch her career as a massively successful star of futuristic box-office blockbusters like *Resident Evil* and *Ultraviolet*.

'We were going to call the album *Diamonds in a Jewel Case*, with a beautiful picture of her taken by a top photographer,' said Lawrence of a collection of folky lo-fi recordings Jovovich made over a few nights in a Los Angeles apartment in 1997. 'It was all good. Then The French Girl was looking at it and suddenly, out of nowhere, she went, "You just want to sleep with her!" What was I meant to say to that? It was the first of our massive arguments in which she made my life hell. I put the project – the whole label, in fact – on hold.'

The relationship was strained further by the fact that neither The French Girl nor Lawrence had any money, and on top of that, he was increasingly retreating from view. They should have been doing the things Lawrence had always dreamed of doing with a girlfriend, like going to galleries, discussing cult novels, wandering about the city looking moody and mysterious. Instead, Lawrence shut down. They might leave the flat to look at some magazines in Victoria station, but he could manage only a few minutes before having to head back home.

'I could cry thinking about it. It's so sad, what I put her through,' said Lawrence in a weak voice, a pale, spectral figure on a park bench, sitting there, unmoored from the speed at which the world turns. 'I would tell her she had come at a really bad time. I couldn't go out. This period I was in wasn't going to last forever, so she would go off for a walk down the King's Road while I stayed inside.

And the physical side of the relationship stopped pretty soon. She would say, "We're like brother and sister, aren't we?" Sometimes we were happy, sometimes we were sad, and she was there with me but not there.

'I felt sorry for her because I had absolutely nothing to offer and yet, like most of the girlfriends I had, she was jealous: jealous of the musical world, jealous of my dedication to the songwriting life. Michaela was different – she couldn't care less – but with the other girlfriends, you would think they would want me to succeed. Not at all; quite the opposite, in fact. She would throw my lyrics back at me as if they were a personal affront. She would say, "I want songs about fields and flowers and trees and nice things and you write about death and horrible people." Then you wonder: why did you want to be with me? I've never written about nice subjects, so why would I start now?'

The French Girl wanted to pour her problems into creativity in the way Lawrence did, but couldn't seem to do it. Whatever happened in his life, even in his least productive, most stymied years, Lawrence could write a song. Even in the thick of addiction, mental illness and agoraphobia, he made an (unreleased) album for Alan McGee. There were Go-Kart Mozart albums on either side of the darkest times: *Instant Wigwam* in 2000, *Tearing up the Album Chart* in 2005. While Lawrence worked away with his guitar in the tiny flat, The French Girl got books out from the library in the hope that they would inspire her. But the songs never came.

'I would say, "I'll do some chords, you use your lyrics, let's see what happens." Then she wouldn't want to use the lines she had written, so I would come up with something and it would be, "It's not fair! You can do it straight away!" The whole thing collapsed.'

Could it have worked out? Probably not. Whether it was drugs, depression, jealousy or a mixture of all three, Lawrence no longer found himself attracted to The French Girl, or any woman for that matter. It doesn't sound like she was particularly attracted to him either.

'At the end of 2003, she left for good. I'll take the blame, because it must have been hell for her to wait for someone to come back into the world.'

Lawrence endeavoured to give up on relationships entirely. It was the same old story: an initial attraction, a gradual disappointment, a rage at the very thing that attracted his girlfriends to Lawrence in the first place, which was a dedication to his own singular cause. Felt's 'Get Out of My Mirror' might have been about the mirror he got Vikki to steal from a hotel because it reminded him of one in *The Servant*, but it also said a lot about his approach to life.

'That was the way it went with me and girlfriends, and I don't even think about it any more. I know the way I am. I'm not a catch. I'm not fun to be around. I'm easy going for sure, but what have I got to offer? These days, I never meet anyone who even likes me and I'm fine with that. I can't even imagine doing it now and I'm relieved, knowing that I no longer have to look at girls that you're never going to get anyway.'

He stared at a smiling couple blessed with lustrous auburn hair and excellent dental arrangements, passing arm-in-arm before us.

'All I've got to offer girlfriends is a load of rules. "You can't put that in my fridge" – not that I've got a fridge, but if I did – or, "Why don't we sleep in separate rooms?" Things like that. I got it all wrong with girlfriends anyway because I was looking for someone who was just like me, and that's a silly approach to take. And there's something even worse about me as far as girlfriends are concerned. I have an inability to enjoy myself. It was really exacerbated on the rare occasions I went to a rave, when everyone would be having a great time and I would be thinking, *How come I can't have at least one decent conversation?* What happened to me in the early 2000s was a product of what happened to me throughout the '90s, particularly during the time I was with Michaela and we were meant to be going out to nightclubs together and having a great time. I was on a major label, I had a great band, everything was going well. But even then I couldn't enjoy myself. It was only when The French Girl walked out and never came back that I realised.'

He popped a Drop Fruit Duo into his yawning void.

'I was better off alone.'

A squirrel appeared, twitching its way towards Lawrence and his bag of sweets. He gave the squirrel a piece of chocolate, which it jammed in its mouth before scarpering off with a distinct lack of gratitude that, I couldn't help but suspect, Lawrence admired. A magpie arrived to get in on the action.

'Do you want one too, Mr Magpie?' he asked, but the chocolate proved too much for the magpie's beak and it poked at it a few times before hopping off elsewhere. 'Oh, he doesn't like it.'

The sound of children laughing mingled with the rustle of the branches, and the birds singing in the trees.

'I'm just a Glum Brum.'

CHAPTER NINE

WON'T YOU MARRY ME, BILL?

The phone went.

It was Lawrence.

'I've got some great ideas for the book.'

Oh no.

He had been out for lunch with Bobby Gillespie at a fancy Japanese restaurant. By that, I mean Bobby Gillespie had lunch while Lawrence sat there and tried not to look at all the food everywhere. A couple of years previously, Gillespie had a hit with *Tenement Kid*, a memoir of growing up in working-class Glasgow before discovering rock 'n' roll and all that went with it. Gillespie told Lawrence that writing a book was a great endeavour and it did wonders for your confidence. All this proved encouraging for Lawrence. Too bloody encouraging, as it turned out.

'I now see that my writing my book will be very good for me.'

'But Lawrence, you're not writing this book. I am. You haven't actually written a word of it. You are the subject, I'm the writer.'

After a tense, steely pause, he continued. 'But I'll be making so many notes and changes that I *will* be writing it, which reminds me.

It's a good idea if you send it to me chapter by chapter. You don't want to send the finished version, only for me to have to rewrite the entire thing. It will be a terrible waste of your time.'

There was little point in telling him I had already got to chapter eight. I simply pointed out that if he was going to take that approach, then he had better be prepared to fight some battles, because I wasn't going to be the literary equivalent of his £50-a-week joint roller.

'I won't be allowing that anecdote with Michaela and the cheese omelette,' he continued. 'For a start, it isn't true. Secondly, it isn't the kind of thing the fans want to read.'

'What fans?'

'The fans,' he proclaimed, adding, a little less boldly, 'the fans around the world.'

'The cheese omelette is going in.'

'No omelette is going in *my* book.'

Why shouldn't I include the omelette story? It concerned something Michaela had told me, something that happened early on in their relationship. Besides, it had the ring of truth, which meant I found myself believing Michaela, not Lawrence.

'When I think about the omelette incident,' said Michaela, 'I'm reminded of how much Lawrence used to make me laugh. At the same time, it also makes me think I must have been mad. How are you meant to be romantically involved with someone who has that reaction to an omelette?'

Paul Kelly had faced all kinds of challenges in completing *Lawrence of Belgravia* because of the whims of his leading man. The first taste of what to expect came when Kelly shot Lawrence for *Finisterre*, his 2003 homage to London and the various creative people who had made it their home. 'He didn't want his interview to be filmed. Then I mentioned how in Julien Temple's film on the Sex Pistols, *The Filth and the Fury*, John Lydon is interviewed in silhouette. He said, "If John Lydon's done it, then it is fine." If you reference one of his heroes, he can usually be persuaded.'

Kelly made it clear at the beginning of shooting *Lawrence of Belgravia* that it was only going to work if Lawrence let him get on with it. 'Initially, he was fine with that, but then I received a letter containing a list of rules on what I could and couldn't do. I couldn't film him without his hat on. All the interviews had to feature people looking directly into the camera, like on the news. No comedy – that was a good one. Apart from the rule about the hat, I ignored the lot.'

I don't know why Lawrence was fussing about the book anyway. He had more pressing things to worry about, like the fact that we were more than halfway through the year and his great masterpiece, his three-minute pop classic that would deliver the ultimate hit after four decades of trying, was nowhere to be seen. I was yet to hear a note. On top of that, we had not found a home for his giant head. The little man from The Gallery of Everything turned us down. There had been talk of an exhibition at a gallery in Whitechapel, but that went quiet too.

'Why don't you ask Corin?' I suggested. 'He's a sculptor. He must have some ideas.'

'I can't ask Corin!' he yelled in outrage. 'He'll do it in the depths of Camberwell! He'll do it in a garden shed! The only refreshment will be tea brewed in a cement mixer and served in paint pots! What if Kate Moss turns up and Corin ends up clubbing her over the head?'

I had to wonder about the impression Lawrence had of this highly sophisticated and successful sculptor. He seemed to picture

Corin as some kind of south-east London caveman, emerging with his faithful hound Charlie every now and then to hunt for meat, perhaps barging into one of the chicken shops littering the high street and gnawing on a fried chicken leg before yelling 'Yabba-dabba-doo' and dragging some poor unsuspecting art student back to his lair. From what I could tell of Corin, who had no shortage of admirers only too willing to become his she-woman, it wasn't a particularly accurate impression.

'We've got to have it in a smart West End venue. We need to impress Corin with how important this is. It must be in a top gallery, where the fans can troop in and pay their respects. Martin Green said he had one lined up, but now he's not answering my calls. Oh, why does this always happen to me?'

Lawrence's fellow easy-listening enthusiast Martin Green had been putting on all kinds of exhibitions over the past decade, pulling out of obscurity under-represented pop art-style painters like Duggie Fields and Luciana Martinez. He was ideally placed to curate a Lawrence exhibition and he might have even found the place for it: a little gallery on Soho Square, with one room to be occupied solely by Lawrence's head and another for associated things to sell. But the woman who ran the place had gone on some kind of endless holiday. Further in-roads into the art world had to be made.

As it happened, one of Lawrence's biggest champions was having an exhibition of her own. Daphne Guinness was a singer, fashion figure, designer and aristocratic scion of the Guinness clan who, in ways that were perhaps not obvious, formed a female upper-class mirror image to Lawrence. Both were polite, if possessed by some kind of immovable inner force. Both were slight figures with complicated attitudes to food: Lawrence had his abiding fear of cheese,

Daphne had to wait until around five in the evening to have her first meal of the day, which typically consisted of comforting nursery food like fish fingers and mashed potatoes. Both suffered early trauma: he was recovering from leaving inner-city Birmingham for the provincial wastelands of Water Orton only to witness his sister almost being killed; she was dealing with the aftershock of being kidnapped at the age of five by a schizophrenic man who dragged her through the family house in Kensington with a knife to her neck before releasing her and killing his mother instead. Both presented fantastical versions of themselves to the world. Perhaps Daphne might have an idea on where the head could end up.

'They have a clear idea of what's acceptable,' said Malcolm Doherty, an old musician friend of Lawrence's and a sometime member of Go-Kart Mozart. Having met in a Bowie tribute band with the old Spiders From Mars drummer Woody Woodmansey and Bowie's regular producer Tony Visconti, Malcolm had become Daphne's producer, manager and musical director. 'They have their favourite bag, for example. Okay, Daphne's will be a Birkin bag and Lawrence's will be a WH Smith's carrier bag, but it amounts to the same thing. They operate in their own worlds.'

Now we would witness those worlds colliding. An exhibition called 'Drawing Daphne' was being held at a studio on Ebury Street in Belgravia, around the corner from the tiny flat Lawrence had been in with The French Girl twenty years previously. Daphne had one of the best couture collections in the world and the exhibition was to feature not only a series of paintings and drawings of her by various artists, but also the premiere of a video for a disco-tinged song called 'Hip Neck Spine', in which the photographer Nick Knight filmed her wearing as many of her outfits as possible.

She was an early supporter of Alexander McQueen, worked as an advisor to Karl Lagerfeld, and had in her archive one-off pieces by everyone from Chanel to Jean Paul Gaultier. She wore enormous hoof-like shoes by a Japanese designer called Noritaka Tatehana, which, coupled with a towering black-and-white hairstyle, transformed her height, just as Lawrence's blue-and-white baseball cap transformed whatever was going on at the top of his head. Now all Lawrence had to do was make it to the exhibition launch, and we might be one step closer to finding a home for his enormous marble bust.

Even that simple task, though, could prove a problem, because it didn't matter how many times I told Lawrence where Daphne's launch was – not that he should have needed me to tell him, considering he was invited of his own accord – he still had to call several times for the address, the time to arrive, what to expect, who would be there, what would happen. Then the texts came:

Lawrence: What tube is nearest?

Why was he asking? He knew the launch was a street away from the flat he lived in for five years.

Will: Victoria

Lawrence: ?Where r u?

Will: Round the corner. Hang on a min

Lawrence: Nobody here wots going on

Lawrence: I dont like this

Lawrence: Oh god this isn't good!

The problem, it transpired, was that there were shiny-haired women with clipboards on the door and Lawrence got spooked at facing them on his own. So we went in together and there was champagne for me, elderflower juice for him, and enough gothy fashion students, arty types and collar-up toffs to make him feel he was somewhere important, not least after Daphne made a bee-line for him, leaning on a metal post so as not to topple over on her foot-high heels as she chatted away about microphone brands and recording techniques. One will-o'-the-wisp of a woman was particularly arresting. Slight, with alabaster skin, not much in the way of eyebrows and a stack of streaked blonde hair over a face of sophisticated innocence, she was one of those early twentysome-things with a beauty that is not entirely human. Lawrence gave Malcolm a prod.

'Who's she?'

'I don't know her name,' Malcolm replied. 'I think she's a famous model.'

'Can you introduce me?'

'Here we go.'

'I'm just interested!'

'There's a big fat ugly guy over there,' I said to Lawrence. 'Would you like me to introduce you to him instead?'

'I'm not interested.'

I was tempted to ask Daphne and Nick Knight if we could hire the space, ideally for no money whatsoever, for the unveiling of Lawrence's massive head, but they did appear to be rather busy and, besides, perhaps it was a bit unrealistic. Instead, we wandered off into the streets of Victoria, past the block of flats that had been witness to Lawrence's years of seclusion. 'There is a certain stage in a pop star's life when you have to go to jail, or live on a desert island, basically disappear for a few years and do something which isn't music,' he reasoned. 'You've got to get away from it all. Then you come back when the fans are ready.'

Some time around 2007, Lawrence found himself on the streets. Arguably he achieved the goal of the true artist in the tradition of Knut Hamsun's *Hunger*, rejecting complacency so totally that he ended up in the ultimate nightmare of the bourgeoisie: homelessness.

'It all began when some guy in the block reported me,' said Lawrence as we headed towards the Tube. 'They said a big, menacing-looking man is coming round to the flat all the time and they were worried. I came back one afternoon and someone had been in the flat. God, that's bad. It was the only day – ever! – that I hadn't cleaned up and there was paraphernalia all on the floor, sitting there, waiting for someone to find it. And they found it. A letter announced that my lease was being terminated, even though the rent was paid for. They wouldn't give me a reason. But I knew the reason: the superintendent had come in with the landlord and they didn't like what they found.'

Didn't like it?

'Not one bit.'

Prior to the incident, Lawrence had not caused the building and its residents any trouble. He never played loud music. Apart from regular visits by mental health professionals and a daily visit from the big, menacing-looking drug dealer, he didn't have house guests and never held parties. He paid his rent in full, thanks to it arriving at the £125-a-week threshold of housing benefit he was entitled to receive back then. 'I was a little dormouse, never saw the other residents. I was at the end of the corridor in one room, on my own, and everything was cool. Then the day came and I really had to leave.'

Lawrence was evicted. His perfectly ordered records, clothes and books were taken by the DHSS and put into storage. 'It's a really good service actually,' he pointed out, with surprising perkiness. 'At least, it would have been if one of the guys hadn't dropped a box of records down the stairs and another one hadn't broken the neck of my guitar. As I watched my records tumbling down the stairs, pristine editions of rare albums by Jane Birkin and Michel Polnareff, I wasn't even sure if I cared any more. That was the point I gave up entirely.'

A year before he got chucked out, I made that visit to the Belgravia flat to meet Lawrence for the first time. I was about to take a record from the collection when he raised a wagging index finger, said, 'Hold on', and took from a drawer a pair of surgical gloves. He insisted I put them on so as not to run the risk of leaving fingerprints on the record sleeves. When I asked which records he would grab if the flat were on fire, he said he would rather burn with them. For him, to no longer care as a big lug sent his most beloved possessions hurtling down the stairs suggested Lawrence had by then reached a state several notches below total despair.

When a tenant has been made homeless, the DHSS have a policy of paying the cost of six months' storage for the person's possessions, after which they are thrown out into a skip on the street. 'You go to this place on the edge of London, a great big storage unit in Romford, and there are incredible things, brand-new sofas and so on, sticking out of the skips. We got there just in time to save the record collection I had been building up over my entire life.'

For one night – 'armed with a bag they give you to be homeless with' – Lawrence stayed at Paul Kelly and his partner Debsey's two-bedroom flat in a tower block in Clerkenwell. But with two young children, one of them living on a bunk bed in the corridor, there was no space for Lawrence on any kind of long-term basis and he had to go elsewhere. So he stayed on the street by Victoria station, sitting on an orange bench outside Sainsbury's until dawn, watching the homeless community gathered around Westminster Cathedral, night after night, bonding themselves into an alternative society parallel to, and yet a world apart from, the ever-shifting morass of life in the city centre.

'I almost merged into it all, but I found out that you have to spend a week or two on the streets to be registered and once you have been spotted three times by the homeless agents, they start doing something about it,' said Lawrence, referring to CHAIN, the Combined Homelessness And Information Network, a database recording people sleeping rough and the wider street population – those in a 'street lifestyle' of begging and street drinking – of London. 'You get registered and, once a place comes up, they offer it to you. A lot of people don't take one though.'

Why not?

'They like it on the street. They like the freedom. Had I stayed, eventually I would have made that fateful journey and mingled with the people around the cathedral . . . or they would have come to me, for sure.'

I was reminded of a book Lawrence recommended some years back. *Stuart: A Life Backwards* is an account by Alexander Masters, a recent graduate working in the early 2000s in a homeless hostel in Cambridge, of his friendship with Stuart Shorter, a once happy-go-lucky boy who ended up, by Masters' description, as an 'ex-homeless, ex-junkie psychopath'. After dismissing the original manuscripts as 'bollocks boring', Shorter suggested Masters start the book in the present and work back to the beginning of his life. That way the reader would get a sense of how the people they see crouched outside a Tesco Metro, watching the world from the bottom up, or working their way down a train carriage with tales of woe, got to be in their situation. Stuart belonged to the chaotic homeless, a community for whom the stability of a home, even when offered, is an impossible bind. These were the people Lawrence was talking about.

'Beyond their own governance, let alone within the grasp of ours, they are constantly on the brink of raring up or breaking down,' writes Masters of the chaotic homeless. Alcohol and heroin is usually involved, although addiction may come before or after arriving on the street. Rough sleepers have a life expectancy of forty-two years, they're thirty-five times more likely to commit suicide, men on the streets outnumber women ten to one, and trauma – in Stuart's case, being sexually abused by his brother – has generally brought the chaotic homeless to the conclusion that a life on the streets is better than one within society. As Masters puts it, 'many of Stuart's friends would rather die than take a shower or pay debts, and quite a few do'.

Lawrence did not like it on the street. He did not belong to the chaotic homeless. Nor did he belong to those groups whose circumstances had pushed them into the urban wilds: teenagers who fell out with parents or carers, ex-soldiers and ex-convicts dealing with the loss of rigid structures, schizophrenics and manic depressives living inside fogs of psychic torment. He had more in common with people who became homeless after suffering a crisis: the loss of a child, the collapse of a business, Princess Diana dying days before your breakthrough single is meant to come out. 'Self-confidence is their main problem,' reasoned Alexander Masters of this group. 'If the professionals can get hold of them within the first few months, they'll be back at work or at least in settled, long-term accommodation within a year or two.'

'After discovering that I have to spend at least eight to ten nights on the street to get into the system, I simply couldn't do it,' said Lawrence. 'I can do a lot of things, but not that. On the second night outside Victoria, sitting there with my bag, Pete Astor's wife Eve turned up in her car and found me. She leaned out of her window, staring at me.'

Eve and Pete lived in a big house in Muswell Hill and, at the top of it, was a separate flat converted from a loft, which the couple were preparing to rent out. It meant Pete Astor of the Loft had Lawrence of Felt living in his loft.

'It was the strangest thing. They had put in a bathroom, a bedroom, a sink and a cooker into this tiny space, and they were just about to rent it out when I turned up. Eve's thing was: what are we going to do? Throw him onto the street or let him stay there? They let me stay there.'

Lawrence was still an out-patient at the mental health unit on Vincent Square and he was told by one of his care workers that he had a good chance of being moved into residential housing on the square within a month or two, so he told Eve and Pete he wouldn't have to stay long. Then, on one of his regular visits to the unit, he was told by the same psychiatrist who recognised Lawrence from his days as an alternative music-loving student that the hospital accommodation was completely overstretched and there was not much wrong with him anyway, so they couldn't help him.

'It took me another month to build up the nerve to tell Eve and Pete. I ended up living with them for a year.'

In his more fanciful moments, Lawrence imagined himself to be like James Fox's gangster Chas in the 1970 cult movie *Performance*, hiding out from the world after killing a gang member by renting a room in a tumbledown house in Notting Hill Gate alongside Mick Jagger's reclusive rock star Turner, who is living in the basement with two beautiful women.

'Chas becomes a part of the world of the house and that's what it was like for me. I went out each Wednesday afternoon for my appointment with a doctor at the hospital in Victoria, and apart from that, I hardly went anywhere for the next eight months to a year. My life shut down. Something was wrong, big time. I was in a state of inertia.'

He stared into the middle distance of the Tube carriage. A line of people sitting opposite stared deeper into their phones.

'It was my period of seclusion.'

On the first night, Eve and Pete welcomed Lawrence in by inviting him to have a meal with the family, unaware of – or, at least, momentarily forgetting about – his relationship with food. Eve's fifteen-year-old son Wes was there, alongside Nancy, three, Otto, four, and an Affenpinscher called Bill. 'They cooked me a meal, which I wasn't going to eat, of course, but they weren't to know that. This little dog was appearing at my leg and I thought, *He will like me if I give him food and, on top of that, I don't want to eat it myself, so I'll slip it to him when they're not looking*. That sealed it: Bill fell in love with me.'

So began what proved to be the purest love affair of Lawrence's life. Bill was a small dog with a big attitude, a foot-high ball of fur with a stubborn, independent character and a clear idea of what he wanted, whether the people who helped him in his day-to-day life without asking for anything in return liked it or not. Prior to being adopted by Eve and Pete, Bill had been in a bad way. He had, it is sad to say, been practically reduced to begging, wandering the streets as a stray before the kindly couple took him in and provided him with every comfort he could possibly wish for. Not that he showered them with gratitude for it.

'Bill was human in every way apart from one small detail: he was a dog,' said Lawrence. 'He was an emotional character: highly sensitive, prone to sulking if he didn't get the attention he felt he was due. In the morning, I would walk him to the local wood, which was generally as far as I went outside of the house, and after a while the kids were going, "Bill loves Lawrence". But, of course, they didn't know what had happened between me and Bill during the welcoming meal. On the second or third night, he followed me up the stairs and that was it: he never left. Eve was going, "Get down here, Bill!", but he wouldn't listen. Bill was one of those characters who, once his mind is made up, there's no going back. Before I arrived, he had slept in the marital bed, which Eve liked, so she was furious about this new arrangement. She said to me, "First you took my room and then you took my dog."'

Bill scampered up the stairs the moment Lawrence showed signs of ascending to his quarters, paving the way in preparation for quality time with his buddy. Lawrence was going through one of his intermittent periods of not sleeping at night, merely dozing off every now and then on the cushions on the floor as the television flashed dispatches from the world of news and entertainment until the morning. So it made sense that Bill should take the bed. 'I was on the floor and he was in the bed, which meant he was top dog in our relationship. Nonetheless, he showed me the real love which I had been dreaming of having with humans all my life but never found. I would have married Bill. If only he'd asked.'

Unfortunately, Bill never found the words to pop the question. 'Yes, it was a language problem,' sighed Lawrence. 'It is a shame, really, because beyond that, we understood each other perfectly. If I was watching telly at night and got up to get a cup of tea, he followed me. If I went downstairs, he came down with me. Everywhere I went, he was there, looking up with love and devotion. I only had to move and he would wake up, any time of day or night. I had never known dedication like it. I certainly didn't get it from the other members of Felt.'

There was a routine to the day. Pete would go to work as a lecturer at Goldsmiths College, Eve took the kids to school, came back to do some exercises and get a few jobs done around the house, and Lawrence and Bill watched daytime television. *Cash in the Attic* was a mutual favourite. Once the kids returned from school, the inseparable duo came downstairs and everyone would hang around in the kitchen until Pete came back, at which point they might go with Bill for a walk in the woods. Lawrence integrated himself into family life, doing his best to chat with the kids, to remember to ask everyone how their day went. As long as he didn't have to eat with them, the relationship worked out very well. For the most part, he lived on potato cakes, which he stuck in the toaster and embellished with a dab of butter.

The Underground chugged along the District Line. People came and went.

'I did nothing. Didn't write a song, didn't write a note of music. Chas in *Performance* is doing all his stuff in the criminal world before he stops and hides away and it was the same with me. Muswell Hill was far enough away from the centre to hide away from it all and the only real thing I did the entire time was drive Wes around. He left school at sixteen and formed a band called Let's Wrestle, who started getting gigs. He was talking about it one evening when I said, "I'll drive you around." Everyone was very surprised about that.'

So began Lawrence's short-lived career as a driver. 'Not just for Let's Wrestle, but for Eve as well. Eve didn't particularly like driving, so I would take her to pick the kids up from school or do the supermarket shop. Then I would take Wes and his bandmates to whatever gigs they might have. I was the family driver. And each time I returned home, Bill's little head was staring out of the living room window, waiting for me.'

The Buddhists say suffering is a product of desire. If that is the case, a total collapse of hopes and dreams could well lead to contentment. Sometimes the kids would come up to Lawrence's room, sometimes he cleaned the house, sometimes he sat in his attic cell and did nothing at all. After being told by Westminster Council that he was a low priority for rehousing, he was assigned a charity lawyer who agreed to take his case to the High Court. Her argument was that he was homeless and the council had a duty of care, but the judge overruled it and Lawrence was back to square one.

'Then, one day, the charity lawyer said to me: "I've just seen you on YouTube. What the hell is going on?" She had seen footage of Go-Kart Mozart at a concert in Holland, just before I was made homeless. She said if I was capable of being in a group and going on tour, she couldn't help me.'

Once again, homelessness and stardom proved a terrible combination. 'I promised her it was a one-off, in the past, that I wasn't doing music any more and I couldn't look after myself. But it was no good.' Even pointing out that he didn't learn to tie his own shoelaces until he was twelve failed to melt the lawyer's heart. 'This is how it is. For the system to work, you can't get better.'

In other words, Lawrence had to give up on being a functioning human being, let alone the leader of a cult band, in order to be granted the most basic right of all: a home of one's own. And while this was going on, Eve told Lawrence the family had to let out the flat and he was moved into the living room.

'Sad for me,' he lamented as we got out of the Underground and made our way up to street level. 'I felt in the way. I was down there in the living room, even though nobody moved in upstairs, with the family running in and out the whole time. It was obvious from then on that I couldn't stay there for much longer.'

Eve knew a woman who worked at a hostel in Highbury & Islington in north London and a solution found itself. 'It wasn't easy, though. I had to get three Islington residents to write letters to say they had seen me outside Angel Underground station, and I was homeless.' Eventually he was given a place at the Highbury hostel, and then in another one on Holloway Road, in small, featureless rooms with sturdy MDF fittings and fortified glass on the windows for the next one and a half years.

'On the first night in the Highbury hostel, I was eating a biscuit, sitting on the floor as usual, when a mouse jumped over my shoe. I ran back to Eve's. "I can't stay there! They've got mice!" But I had to get used to it because now there really was no choice and there was nowhere else to go. There was a kid in the room next door and I told him about the mouse one morning when the two of us were smoking downstairs. He took a drag of his cigarette and went, "Yeah, I know. Woke up this morning and there was ten of them, having a party." The two of us went to a hardware store to buy spray foam, which you use to plug up any holes in the wall, and without asking permission from the hostel, I took all of the furniture out of the room, stacked it on the landing, and filled every single crack and crevice with this stuff. They didn't care because the building was condemned anyway and we were moving up to the new hostel on the Holloway Road in a couple of weeks.'

This was Lawrence's life: subject to circumstances dictated by institutions he had no control over. Initially, the kid next door, he of the visions of the dancing mice, seemed to be Lawrence's friend, but Lawrence soon discovered the first law of institutions: if you do a favour for someone, they will ask you for another favour, and another, and another until you are entirely in their power. 'It was awful, like going back to school. I thought we were going to have a fight at one point, like you do in the playground when you have no choice but to get into a scrape so the other kids respect you. The moment I got to the hostel, the staff said: "Whatever you do, don't give anyone a cigarette." So what do I do the moment this kid asks for a cigarette? I give him one. Then it was: "Can you lend me a fiver?" It carried on until eventually he said, "It's my sister's birthday, I need thirty quid." That was the final straw as far as I was concerned. We had a big to-do and I went, "What do you think I have? I'm in the same position as you. I'm living in a hostel. I've got nothing!" Incredibly, it worked and he didn't bother me again.'

It was a good thing he didn't, because the teenage boy had a history of violence, which is why he was there in the first place. He kicked and punched his bedroom door in the hostel so many times, the door frame collapsed. His family only lived around the corner, but they couldn't handle him so they asked the council to house him instead.

'That was hostel life, with people coming and going for all kinds of reasons,' said Lawrence. 'There was a guy who thought he was Richard Branson. You had to pretend he was a multi-millionaire, otherwise he got really upset. We had a paedophile for a bit, which I didn't know about until afterwards. He came up to me one day and said, "I've got some girls coming at five o'clock. Would you mind signing them in for me?" "Yeah, of course." By the evening, he was back in jail. Turns out he had been accosting girls in the park. And he asked me to sign them into his room!'

For a man of such psychotic fastidiousness as Lawrence, hostel life brought its challenges. When he saw a turd in the washing machine one morning, he resolved never to use it again. He took one look at the kitchen and decided it was best if he never enter it. At least Paul Kelly was making the film, which began shooting around the time Lawrence was getting thrown out of the flat in Belgravia and wrapped as he was being ensconced into the new one in Clerkenwell.

'Among the bad things happening, the catalogue of errors, the ever-worsening series of indignities, I did have the film to hang onto. So I could put up with all these terrible events because I knew it would look good in the film.'

Paul Kelly remembered visiting Lawrence at the hostel on Holloway Road and witnessing him pretend not to be in his room as someone – the boy with the dancing mice, most likely – hammered on the door, demanding money and cigarettes. 'It was hard for Lawrence not to be spotted as a soft touch for all these junkies. He would go walking in town for hours, just to keep away from them.'

Lawrence disappeared for weeks on end during the times when Paul was trying to get on with filming, particularly around Christmas. 'It was always a concern because I assumed he had died. Usually someone had seen him, but one year I really started worrying because people were calling, asking if I had heard from him. It turned out he had curled up in a ball and not engaged with the world.'

Finally, the chance to bid for a flat in the borough of Islington came through. When Lawrence was packing up his boxes, getting ready to leave the hostel for good, his teenage tormentor came up, gave him a fist bump, and told him to look after himself.

'I liked him, actually,' said Lawrence of the boy, as he headed off to his flat with its records in perfect order, the wooden cupboards without handles, his collection of designer clothes and ultra-cheap supermarket-branded apparel behind wooden cupboards with glass doors. 'There was no pretence. He never said, "Give me your number" or "Come and see me when you're in the area." We knew it was over. His final words were "Have a good one". Fist bump and that was it.'

CHAPTER TEN

ON THE HOT DOG STREETS

Deciding on the one abiding Lawrence masterpiece is not easy. The Felt albums, *Ignite the Seven Cannons* in particular, are the easiest to appreciate in terms of tasteful shimmering brilliance and transporting atmosphere. The three by Denim contained some of Lawrence's most musically sophisticated and lyrically sharp moments. 'The Osmonds' is a moving song about the comfort and weight of childhood memory, while 'I Saw the Glitter on Your Face' captures jealousy, heartbreak and the glamour of the everyday with soft-rock subtlety. Besides, the emotion at the heart of it was real, chiefly because it concerned Michaela, who probably suspected her relationship with Lawrence was doomed the moment she suffered through that early encounter in Worthing involving her, him and the cheese omelette. My personal favourite, though, has to be Go-Kart Mozart's *On the Hot Dog Streets*.

By 2015, Lawrence knew how to write hits for a modern age. The only problem was, that modern age was when Ted Heath was fighting to keep the lights on and Lieutenant Pigeon got to number one with a music-hall number featuring their mum on piano called

'Mouldy Old Dough'. *On the Hot Dog Streets* was Lawrence's attempt to make sense of his Birmingham upbringing, his complex attitude to sex, relationships and the society he was a part of, wrapping it all up in the colourful clothes of '70s novelty and '80s synth-pop. Beginning with the clarion call of 'Lawrence Takes Over', poignant because the chances of his taking over were by then as likely as his getting stuck into a cheese fondue, the album goes on to include scenes straight from an Andrea Dunbar play.

'White Stiletttos in the Sand' captured package-holiday gaudiness in a similar way to 'Girls & Boys' by Blur, the difference being that when Lawrence sang about girls in too-tight skirts downing flaming sambucas in the Nags Head in Lloret de Mar, he was referring to the kind of people he grew up with. And the bitterness that simmers below the surface of Lawrence's lovable eccentricity came out on 'Retro-Glancing', on which he imagined leaving an old girlfriend with nothing but a screaming-ass kid, her former glory a 'distant pawn shop haze'; a Midlands version of 'Play With Fire' by the Rolling Stones. But could staying with him ever have been an option? As he announced in metallic tones on 'I Talk With Robot Voice', he had by then cut himself off from emotional and sexual attachment in order to never get hurt again. Or at least he tried to. Becoming a robot in sunglasses like Lou Reed was never going to happen to someone so much of the blood and flesh as Lawrence. As he confessed at the end of the chorus, 'I admit I'm still susceptible to vagina's allure.'

Driven along by a crazy panoply of cosmic keyboard sounds from Go-Kart Mozart's resident synth wizard and co-songwriter Terry Miles, the album came with a reading list. *Sanitary Ramblings: Women With Their Knickers Down* by Dr Ono Powers was one I had so far failed to find a second-hand copy of.

Amid these unwholesome songs our children used to sing along to on car journeys down to Cornwall was a moment of innocence. 'Ollie Ollie Get Your Collie' was an exhortation for someone, namely Ollie, to come and get his collie. Given Lawrence's history with dogs, I assumed the song was about a border collie. I should have listened to the words more carefully.

'When I was eleven,' said Lawrence, as we sat on a train heading towards the London/Hertfordshire border suburb of Waltham Cross, opposite a woman with a child who kept staring at us in unblinking fascination until the woman moved herself and the child down to the other end of the carriage, 'my dad got a pitch in a brand-new market in Birmingham called Corporation Square. Our stall was in the centre, right next to a big one selling nighties, and then you had the vegetable stall. This tiny kid with the funniest voice you ever heard stood there from morning to night, going, "Ollie, Ollie, get your collie!" He was a strange little guy. Could have been anywhere from eight to fifteen. Shouting away, nonstop, all day . . .'

Staring out the window at the neat rows of houses, Lawrence's brown eyes sank deep into the well of memory as he reflected, I imagined, on times past, the camaraderie of youth, the touching sincerity of the Ollie boy's task at hand.

'Come to think of it, he might have had a dinner break.'

We came to Waltham Cross – a place where the Orthodox Jewish community Lawrence had attempted to befriend in Temple Fortune communed with the boisterousness of the East End and the placidity of suburbia – because it had one of Lawrence's favourite markets. And I wanted to understand, before Corin Johnson's giant bust of Lawrence and his yet-to-be-completed new single turned him into a superstar, the childhood forces that brought him to where he was today, psychologically speaking. Why wouldn't he eat an olive? Why couldn't he be with a wife and kids, or at least a girlfriend? Why was he so obsessed with wealth and fame and yet so resistant to it? Where did the hygiene mania come from? Why did he love liquorice so much?

Perhaps Waltham Cross would hold the answers. 'Look at those local girls, all made up and off somewhere,' he said as we came out of the station and passed a couple of gum-chewing teens with tight ponytails, giant eyelashes and enhanced lips walking the other way. 'I wonder where they're going? To a shopping centre, probably, in a more exciting location than this.'

We, on the other hand, were heading straight to a market occupying a good chunk of the town centre. It was a bright day and people seemed happy to be out – and happy even to see a pair like us walking about. 'It's the market at the end of the world,' said Lawrence as we passed an empty fish stall where the guy shouted, 'At my other market, I've got them fifteen deep!'

We came upon a mountain of giant underpants, three for a fiver. 'Look at the size of these,' said Lawrence, holding up some vast pale-blue Y-fronts, which for some reason were flat-packed to show their girth to maximum advantage. 'I like them massive, but these are too big even for me. Perhaps they could work for some of the larger fans. I don't know why, but people who buy my records are quite often on the large side. Especially up north.'

At a stall selling non-branded sweets in clear polythene packets, a plaster- and tattoo-encrusted builder was going through the wares.

'Have you got beer bottles?' he asked the thin woman in plastic-framed glasses in charge of the stall.

'I do have beer bottles, but have you tried them recently, sir?' she asked, in a way that sounded like an imitation of a sales assistant at a smart department store. 'They *have* become gelatine-free.'

'Oh no!' cried the builder.

'Don't blame me – I don't make 'em!' she squawked, her voice plummeting a few notches down the poshometer. 'One-fifty a packet. The flavour's the same.'

Lawrence got going on his liquorice negotiations. 'Give me two of them. No, three,' he commanded, pointing to what used to be known as liquorice pipes. 'I'll have a packet of that hard liquorice, and some of them bobbly aniseed ones for my friend here.'

'Since you like liquorice so much,' said the lady, 'you can have a packet of red liquorice for free. Have a lovely weekend.'

'What about that, then?' said Lawrence, button eyes shining. 'Thanks very much.'

This was how it was at Waltham Cross market: no suspicious glances, no sniggering schoolkids, just a friendly acceptance of another regular doing his best to get by on whatever he had. Perhaps because it was such a mixed area, not wealthy, not totally run down, there was a feeling that everyone was in it together and your background didn't matter.

I wondered if there had been a similar atmosphere at the places that held Lawrence's happiest memories: the markets of the Midlands in the late '60s to the early '70s. I also wanted to find a stall similar to the one his dad ran, which Lawrence helped out at from the ages of six to twelve, the one that sold chemists' goods: Nivea soap in a packet of two, Cuticura talc, Sunsilk hairspray, Radox bath salts (a popular seller) and Elnett hairspray, which was expensive, the gold standard. 'We also had unmarked soap in a cardboard box, which you could buy one bar at a time. We had the cheap stuff, the quality stuff, myriad goods. And the star of the show, as it were, the big name of the stall, was a thing called Oil of Ulay. I think they stopped the oil. It is known as Olay these days.'

Lawrence's father's stall travelled all over the Black Country: Walsall on a Tuesday, Bilston on a Friday, Brierley Hill on a Saturday. Around once a month, father and son would get in the estate car and drive down to London to pick up stock, passing through the smart suburbs of High Barnet and Golders Green to arrive at the Holloway Road, not far from where Lawrence would spend a year and a half in a hostel four decades later. Lawrence worked with his father on the markets every weekend and on Tuesdays during school holidays, getting up amid the frosty black of winter nights and the misty haze of summer dawns to clamber into the car and take off in the silence of the morning, driving through foggy industrial landscapes and soot-clogged streets to set up and start the day.

'He would rock me awake at about five in the morning,' Lawrence said as we walked through the market. 'He would be driving and not talking, but it wasn't a problem with my dad at that point. I would be looking out of the window, staring at the houses . . . always houses. If they had a light on, I thought, *What's going on in there? What is the family like?* And when we came back to our house after a day at the market, we put the football scores on. I never went, "Cor, Man United's won again," because I liked Man United. He never went, "What do you like them for?" because he supported Aston Villa. That was him: didn't say much.'

There is a scene in *Slade in Flame*, a grimy classic from 1975 that fictionalises Slade's journey from Black Country yobbos to glam superstars, in which Noddy Holder's would-be singer Stoker is selling crockery from the back of a lorry: flirting with the crowd, offering unbelievable deals, demonstrating his wares by smashing a cup and calling it a tea break. Apart from the fact that Stoker is wearing a shirt by the ultra-fashionable designer Ossie Clark, the whole thing feels highly authentic. I imagined Lawrence and his dad, whose name was Josh, occupying a similar world; a world with characters like Bill from Bilston, who also sold crockery and who Lawrence helped out every now and then.

'He was a ball of fire, a proper hawker, was Bill. He would be going, "I've got one over there, two over there," and I'd be running with cups and plates, delivering them to the women as fast as I could. I was only six.'

Lawrence's brother Sam was too young to get involved and his sister Beverly wasn't interested, so it was Josh and Lawrence, manning the stall, plugging the Elnett, charming the customers.

'The girls on the other stalls looked out for me, and everyone liked me because I wasn't naughty. I didn't argue with my dad. I was there, helping him, and everything was cool. The old ladies of the Black Country came along and said, "Isn't he a lovely bab? Ooh, 'e's good as gold. He never gives me the wrong change, your boy." We had no till, no calculator, just a metal box to keep the money in, and I could do it all in my head even though I wasn't very good at maths at school. I never stole off my dad, ever. I would wait until the end of the day when he said, "Go and get yourself some sweets."'

We stopped to root around a stall selling old mobile phone chargers and other bits of redundant technology.

'I liked working on the market.'

Josh was an orphan. The family had only one black-and-white picture of him in the orphanage, aged eleven, a tiny, unsmiling boy sitting crossed-legged in a row at the front of a formation with all the other kids. Josh had a handful of stories that in rare moments of verbosity he imparted to his children. He had a trial for Aston Villa. His own father walked out of the family home in a pair of white pumps, never to return, when he was very young. He liked his mother and kept a photograph of her, but for reasons never divulged, she couldn't look after him and he spent early years in a fish and chip shop run by his aunt and uncle, in a run-down part of Birmingham, where he slept under the counter.

As we sat down outside a Costa Coffee shop, where Lawrence had his extremely milky tea and millionaire shortbread, he told me the story of his father. 'I don't know what happened exactly. He didn't get on with his aunt and uncle, and he played up, probably because he was sleeping under the counter of a fish and chip shop on Gooch Street, so they put him in the orphanage. It was in north London, strangely.'

After that, Josh was in the war, stationed as ground crew for the RAF in north Africa, but he never talked about it, which was not unusual for the war generation: my grandmother told me she had a perfectly nice time as a teenager in the East End of London during the war, Blitz spirit and all that, and it was only after she died that I discovered she came home from school one day to find her house bombed and her father killed. Where the silent Josh and the tiny Lawrence did share an interest was in clothes. An old photograph captured a young Josh in a trilby hat, wide-brimmed trousers and finely cut checked jacket.

'My dad was a walking anachronism,' said Lawrence. 'He looked like Ernest Borgnine. Have you seen *The Poseidon Adventure*, the one about the ship? Ernest Borgnine had a big part in that. The sad thing is that by the time we came along, all the style and pizzaz had been beaten out of him and he would settle for an old man's cap and shapeless trousers. I think he regretted that side of things because, in his glory days, he dressed like he was from one of them old gangster movies. I've still got a hanger from his tailor's. He took me there once – Chut the Tailor.'

There were real-life gangsters in Birmingham and Lawrence's family brushed against them. *Crumpet All the Way* by Patsy Manning is a self-published memoir by the heavy of a well-known Midlands gangster family who owned nightclubs, ran gambling rings, and had a hand in the markets. You have to wonder if Josh had some kind of connection with Patsy Manning, who even Reggie Kray, in an endorsement of *Crumpet All the Way,* described as 'a bit of a rogue'.

When Lawrence's sister Beverly split up with her first husband, she got together with Patsy Manning's nephew, a gambler just like Josh; this was the man Beverly was with when Lawrence and Michaela visited her in Birmingham. Michaela had been wondering how a man who worked on a market stall lived in such a big house.

'My sister was working in a tatty jewellery store in the Bull Ring and this guy who had a stall there used to come in all the time,' said Lawrence. 'She ended up with him and they had a child together, and it turned out this guy's uncle wrote a book and she gave it to me. It describes how Patsy takes a trip to Thailand and keeps ending up with girls who are not what they at first seem. "Would you believe it, it's only another boy!" is his favourite line. The guy is not a writer and *Crumpet All the Way* is all the better for it.'

Back in the early '60s, Josh met Lawrence's mother when she was working at a petrol station with a difference: all the attendants were on roller stakes. Something about the way she glided up in a skirt, stuck the nozzle in, and skated back to the booth with the money must have done it for him because he kept coming back, more and more, until they got together. He was twenty-two years older than Lawrence's mother. Her name was Doreen.

'Doreen!' Lawrence exclaimed. 'Can you believe it? She was a war baby, from the Beatles era. She wore the fashions of the day, same as my sister, and maybe the attraction was that he was an older guy, smartly dressed in tailored suits, although playing cards all night and doing the horses every day did him in quickly enough. I once said to her, "Why did you get married?" She replied, "Well, he wanted to. I didn't make him." He was trying to be a dad by then. Didn't work, but he tried. He couldn't even say my name properly. It always came out as Larrr or Larrence.'

Then there was Doreen's family. Her parents had twelve children and all of them – apart from Uncle John, who looked like Gene Kelly, and Auntie Janet, who lived with her friend Janet – shared a semi-derelict house in Perry Bar. Lawrence described the suburb as 'just awful. You get off the bus and you smell Perry Bar: industry, petrol, fumes.' There was Uncle David, a dead ringer for David Bailey, had he never used moisturiser. He loved the Beatles and played guitar for hours on end. There was Uncle Geoffrey, only a year older than Lawrence. He stole a car and drove it to Paignton for a day trip. Uncle Geoffrey ended up in reform school.

'He was a wrong 'un, Uncle Geoffrey was,' remembered Lawrence. 'My mom was always down on him because he was such a handful for my nan, but I liked him. And Janet and Janet were great. Janet – not Auntie Janet, but the other Janet – turned up one day with a full-page advert for T. Rex because she knew I liked them. She looked just like Mickey Finn, T. Rex's conga player, with long black hair and a pale, pretty face.'

Wouldn't it be great, I suggested, if Auntie Janet looked like Marc Bolan?

'It would have been, but sadly she didn't. She did have corkscrew hair, but apart from that she looked like a man, which Marc Bolan didn't. Worked on the dogs at Perry Bar. It was her job to bring the greyhounds to the track. The great thing was that nobody commented on Janet and Janet: no jokes behind their backs, no sniggering about lesbians. It was completely normal as far as our family were concerned.'

None of the family were particularly interested in Lawrence's musical endeavours, apart from one person: his grandmother. 'My dad was still around when I started in music and he was completely aghast, couldn't comprehend it at all. My mom thought I was mad. She didn't understand that there is a world away from *Top of the Pops*, which you can exist in if you want to: the *NME* world, the John Peel world, the underground music world. She thought people in bands stood on tables and made everyone notice them and I wasn't like that at all. Even my sister would look at my new clothes and go "What are you wearing that for? You look like Rigsby from *Rising Damp*." And when I made "Index", that was the end of it. They wanted to hear it and, of course, I didn't want to play it to them. Then my nan came round and asked about it and I couldn't say no.'

I pictured the scene. Lawrence and his family, sitting on the frayed three-piece suite in the living room in Water Orton, Father resembling an angry walnut, Mother clutching her set and wave in shame, Nan lightly tapping arthritic fingers on a bony knee, bobbing her head from side to side as four minutes and eleven seconds of poorly recorded strums and incomprehensible murmurs seeped out of the record player.

'Those were four of the most excruciating minutes of my life,' said Lawrence, taking a mini towel from his bag to wipe the beads of sweat forming on his brow. 'The idea of "Index" was to make the worst record of all time and there was my nan, listening intently as if it were a normal song. At the end of it she went, "Isn't 'e clever? Well done, Lawrence." After that, me and my parents had the biggest row ever.'

Lawrence's unswervingly loving grandparents were among the first of their generation to go to Spain, thanks to a holiday club into which they made monthly contributions. Each summer, they took off on package holidays to Benidorm, returning with deep tans, straw donkeys and tales of an exotic land where you can't drink water out of a tap, only out of a bottle. But problems were brewing. Lawrence's grandfather was only in his mid-fifties when he died, leaving his grandmother to cope with their many children on her own. And Josh increasingly didn't want to engage with the family at all.

'Nan would try to talk to him because she was such a sweet woman, but when we made our yearly visit to her house on Boxing Day he would walk in, say hello, and go off to the bookies. One time, I caught him. Vicky was the good-looking auntie. She was trying to better herself, didn't talk in a Brummie accent, was the most fashionable of the lot and was just coming out of her teenage years, so she was a bit of a catch. I saw him pinch her backside. I told my mom when we got home and that's when all hell broke loose. It was the '70s, wasn't it? That kind of thing went on all the time. My mom was having affairs anyway. It was when we moved to Water Orton that I noticed.'

The big one happened when Lawrence was thirteen and it was with someone rather too close to home. Roger, the family friend and neighbour from two doors down who introduced Lawrence to *A Clockwork Orange*, had been taking Doreen out for driving lessons, and at some point, she put her foot on the accelerator. 'It probably carried on for a bit without anyone knowing until one day Roger got drunk and broke into our house. For some reason, he laid out all of my mom's underclothes on the bed . . . the marital bed. Naturally, my dad saw it and went mad, went round there to sort him out, and that was it: we weren't allowed to talk to Roger from then on. I didn't speak to him again until my parents divorced, and it really hurt me because I liked Roger. I didn't even care that he had an affair with my mom; he introduced me to *A Clockwork Orange*, which turned out to be more significant as far as the rest of my life was concerned. We were thirteen when the affair happened and had to wait years for my dad to leave. Can you imagine? Every time Roger came up the drive, we had to look the other way and pretend he wasn't there.'

The first serious fission between Lawrence and Josh came a year before Doreen's affair with Roger, when Lawrence was twelve. 'These two girls from my class came to the stall and I remember thinking, *I don't like this now*. Markets were for poor people and I was embarrassed, just like I was embarrassed to be living in a slum railway cottage in Water Orton when my friends lived in spotlessly clean new houses, so I would walk past my house and pretend I didn't live there. I turned to my dad and said I wasn't doing it any more.'

Lawrence took out a cigarette – every time he bought a new packet, he moved the cigarettes into his old one which featured a horrific image of rotting, diseased teeth because it was his favourite government health warning – lit it, and sent a plume of smoke high into the sky. 'It was a terrible thing to do. I dropped into adolescent self-consciousness and didn't want to work on the markets any more. It is a big regret.'

We went on down the market at Waltham Cross, trying to find that elusive stall selling chemists' goods. We came across one offering lipsticks and other cosmetics, but that was the closest it got. The only consolation came in Lawrence finding a pair of socks for diabetics. They were unusually loose on the ankle.

'I wear them all the time. Not that I'm diabetic, but if I wear a tight sock, I'll get indentations on my leg.'

Lawrence didn't think *On the Hot Dog Streets* was about his childhood. 'The hot dog streets are everywhere, but maybe you're right. Maybe Birmingham is the template. When writing songs, your past will creep in whether you like it or not.'

We walked along in silence.

There was one song about Lawrence's past that I had been plucking up the courage to ask about. 'Budgie Jacket' is on the final Felt album and it concerns an incident that happened when he was thirteen. 'When I was a little boy, an old man, he touched me,' Lawrence announced in his gentle way. 'He thought that I was a little girl because I looked so pretty.'

Maybe this would be a probe into the past too far. Maybe the old man was a close family friend, even a relative, and Lawrence had been dealing with the psychic fallout ever since. I had asked Michaela about it and although she wasn't familiar with the song, she advised against mentioning it. 'Who knows what skeletons lie in Lawrence's closet?' said his former girlfriend. 'Whatever they are, they are best left in there.' But, finally, with a fair bit of preamble, prevarication and general skirting about the issue, I asked if 'Budgie Jacket' related to the one defining trauma of his life.

'Nah,' he said with a shrug, before wandering off to inspect a pale blue towelling vest and matching Y-fronts, a fiver all in, which he was considering purchasing for his next photo shoot. 'I was waiting for my friend when this old man appeared and said, "Do you want to come in the house? I've got some pop bottles and you can take them back to the shop to get a refund on them." I knew he was funny and, yes, he did touch me up, and, yes, he did think I was a girl. You can't blame him. I was really pretty back then, with lovely long hair. But I could handle it. I wasn't going to the police. I waited until he finished, then I got the bag of pop bottles and thought, *What a sad old man.* No, the significant event in my childhood was my sister being chased over the fields by a maniac. I was so angry with my mom for making us leave the council estate and move to Water Orton and what happens? My sister is almost killed.'

That wasn't the only reason Lawrence was angry with Doreen. Paul Kelly recalled Lawrence saying the reason he didn't go to his mother's funeral was because she refused to buy Lurpak butter and would only get the supermarket's own brand, but that was typical of Lawrence's tendency to focus on an insignificant detail as a way of processing a wider emotional story. We wandered further up the high street and came across a huge furniture shop called Fishpools. Among the beds and carpets, the leather sofas and standing lamps were some unusual decorative items. There were giant chess pieces, oversized indoor gnomes, and the one that really caught our eye: a three-foot-high naked woman in repose, carved from black-and-white marble, called Dancing Mariana. She was reduced from £600 to £249.

'I'd love to be able to buy her,' he said, staring transfixed at the figure, even though her womanly curves were most definitely not his thing. 'Can you imagine people coming round the flat and seeing her when they open the door?'

There was no way he could afford Dancing Mariana in his current circumstances, but I noticed a sign announcing Fishpools was looking for a warehouse assistant.

'That's me!' he yelped. 'If it all goes wrong, I'm coming to Fishpools and becoming their warehouse assistant. I could join one of them employers' clubs and put in a pound a week to get that statue. My mom always went, "Why don't you get a job during the week, and do your music at weekends?" She even gave me the forms to apply to be a dental technician, but I threw them away. Her main thing was that I shouldn't work in dead-end jobs in factories and I shouldn't be a musician. Turns out she was right. Should have listened to my mom.'

After 'Index', Lawrence never told either of his parents about making records with Felt, partly because tensions concerning his new direction ramped up when he was seventeen and starting to take day trips to London to visit Rough Trade. For some reason, his father was furious about it. 'But I never found out why, because at fifteen he stopped talking to me entirely. He simply stopped. When you're young you go: "Well, I won't speak to him, then."'

What was the cause of sending his own son to Coventry – the state of silence, not the city only thirty minutes away by car? The only holiday the family ever went on had something to do with it.

It was to Paignton in Devon, scene of Uncle Geoffrey's car-stealing escapades. Josh stayed at home while Doreen, Lawrence, Sam and their grandmother headed off to the English Riviera, with its rows of brightly coloured beach huts and its grand department store, rumoured to have been the inspiration for the '70s sitcom *Are You Being Served?* They returned to discover that Josh had wallpapered the living room.

'They were still together at that point, just about. He had decorated the living room, thinking she would be happy, but she went mental,' said Lawrence as we passed through the rug department of Fishpools, unimpeded by security guards or overzealous sales assistants. 'I suppose she went ballistic because he had done a terrible job, and that was it: he never spoke to me ever again. It was me he wouldn't talk to, not my brother or sister. I could have nipped it in the bud, but why bother? There is something wrong with men. Men are crazy.'

Perhaps men have been taught to be crazy. Or maybe they act on some hardly understood but deeply felt ancient resentment, some flickering light of a historic grudge, passed down through the ages from father to son with bitter resilience against all forces of reason. I couldn't compare Lawrence's situation with my own because my father was a gentle soul who always appeared to be pleased when I called him, even if he never called me, but it did sound similar to something that happened with my mother's late boyfriend. We had spent a nice evening together at their house in Worthing, drinking wine and sharing stories. The following morning, he buried his face in a newspaper and wouldn't even say hello, and carried on with the stonewalling until he died, five years later. For some reason, his pride was hurt, but even my mother couldn't work out why because he wouldn't tell her beyond the made-up excuse that he didn't think I was treating her with sufficient respect. It was pride, I suppose. Men will destroy their relationships and themselves in the name of pride. Lawrence went on holiday with his mother and left the father at home. For years, they had been a team, on the market stalls, flogging Elnett hairspray, rolling out the Oil of Ulay, listening to a strange young boy shout 'Ollie, Ollie, get your collie' from morning to night, and then they went home and listened to the football scores. Talking was unnecessary: they were together. Until they weren't.

'Does he think I'm gay and he doesn't like it? Does he not like it that I looked a bit like a girl, with nice shoulder-length hair? What have I done? Why is he ignoring me?'

Assuming the hyper-sensitivity I witnessed in Lawrence was inherited, I imagined there was another reason and it had nothing to do with long hair or perceived sexuality. It had to do with an orphaned boy who grew up to have a son of his own and loved him very much.

We wandered out of Fishpools, headed back along the market, and Lawrence told me what happened in the years following his dad leaving the house, never to talk to him ever again. Doreen had a whirlwind affair with a travelling salesman in a suit from Burtons who lived in a three-bedroomed house in Water Orton with bay windows and a privet hedge. She moved in with him, taking Sam with her, and since Beverly was already married with kids, Lawrence was left in the Water Orton house on his own. He was eighteen.

'She came up to me one day and said, "I'm leaving. Keep the house if you want." I was working at the theatre as the cellar man and I found out the rent was about £7 a week, cheaper than council rent, so I said, "Yeah, I will." People came to stay, friends dropped round, me and Maurice practised all day and watched TV all night, and it was great. Then, all of a sudden, Mother and her salesman had a row and she walked back in. I said, "What are you doing? I've taken it on. I've been paying the bills, paying the rent, doing the cleaning." She took no notice. It was really awful, the way she did it.'

It got worse. Doreen had not actually split up with the travelling salesman, merely argued with him, probably about money, because then she announced that he had to sell the three-bedroom house with the bay windows and the privet hedge after a bad run and now *both* of them were moving into the railway cottage.

'Well, that was it. We completely fell out at that point. I didn't like this guy anyway, so I said, "If you're moving back in, you're paying the bills and rent." She wouldn't have it. The culmination of it was this guy standing over me, holding my guitar, going, "I'm going to smash it over your head!" He chased me up the stairs and dragged me back down, and it was the end of me and Water Orton. Pulling each other up and down the stairs . . . That's how I moved out and got my own flat.'

Many years later, Lawrence tried to reach out to Josh. Lawrence was in his forties by then, living in the flat in Belgravia, and he found out from Beverly that his now elderly, unwell father was living in an old people's home in Birmingham. He got the address from her and wrote Josh a letter.

'I said, "I want to know, when we were fifteen and came back from that holiday, what happened?" I wrote some nice things, like "Can't you tell me something about the war? There were some good

dishes you used to cook. Maybe you could give me the recipes."
To me, that was a fucking amazing letter, a letter from a boy opening up to his dad. I've got to find out what happened because he was
ill, in a home, time was running out. He was going to die.'

A letter did come back, which Josh had given to Lawrence's sister to pass on. It read: 'Don't be a misanthrope. Forget the past. It
doesn't matter. Just go forward.'

That was it.

'It answered none of my questions,' said Lawrence disconso-
lately as we passed the sweets and the giant pants and took a left
turn into an indoor market, having given up on finding the stall
selling chemists' goods. 'Not even a recipe, nothing. He must have
been furious about his wife's affairs, but you don't bring it to your
children's table, do you? *I* didn't do anything. All of a sudden, it
was like there was another guy in the house, plus he never came
to the school to watch me play football. He wasn't like my friend's
dads. He wasn't my dad, really.'

A few months after Lawrence sent the letter, Josh died. He did
not go to the funeral.

Within the indoor market was a branch of Holland & Barrett.
While Lawrence fell once again into silence, I suggested we go in
there to see if they had any RJ's Choco Logs Liquorice.

'They won't,' said Lawrence gloomily. 'None left. The pirates
have got them all.'

'We may as well look on the off-chance.'

'Alright, then, but I'm telling you, it's a lost cause.'

A smiling youth with large glasses and the air of someone
who liked to spend his evenings wearing a cape and being the
Dungeon Master was behind the counter. He offered a bright hello

and told us to ask if we need help, but not in a way that suggested he thought we were up to no good. Lawrence explained how he was searching desperately for RJ's Choco Logs Liquorice, but they had become incredibly hard to find because the last few boxes were somewhere in the Malacan Straits, being feasted on by the bandits of the Seven Seas.

'Do you know what? We haven't had a delivery in months,' said the youth. 'I have been led to believe they are discontinued . . .'

'I knew it,' said Lawrence with disconsolate acceptance. 'Oh well, it was always going to be a slim chance.'

The youth, whose name tag said Ian, raised a finger. '. . . And yet . . . I think we might have a few left.'

Ian bounced out from behind the counter and rummaged through the racks. Buried behind bountiful stacks of Panda Natural Liquorice were four bars of RJ's Choco Logs. Ian bowed his head, went down on one knee, and presented them with both hands as if bequeathing to Lawrence the sword of Excalibur.

'Behold, sir. Four of our very finest Choco-Logs.'

Lawrence stared at them in wonder.

'I don't believe it. Not thinking there were any left anywhere, we came here on the off-chance. For once in my life, I have found the pot of gold at the end of the rainbow. These are the last four in the Western world and I've got 'em.'

Ian scratched his goatee thoughtfully.

'You could try our Chesham branch.'

CHAPTER ELEVEN

ITCHY TEETH IN MARGATE

It was September, Corin Johnson's massive marble bust of Lawrence still had no home, and Lawrence's year of activity was running down the clock with remarkable rapidity. The Gallery of Everything rejected the head. The woman with a gallery on Soho Square disappeared. Holding a private view in Corin's Camberwell studio was out of the question on account of the fact that Lawrence imagined Corin would arrive on a woolly mammoth before attacking the guests with a spear carved from a mastodon bone. The situation was looking increasingly desperate. Then, out of the blue, came a glimpse of hope.

One morning, while he was having his usual cup of milky tea in a disposable cup at the café on his street, Lawrence got chatting to an artist called Philippa Horan. Incredibly, Philippa had her own studio in Mayfair; not just a studio, in fact, but an entire gallery. How she could afford to pay the rent was something of a mystery, but the staggeringly expensive business rates were waived on the agreement that she used the building as a community arts space. For that reason, she was open to supporting people in the community who might need a bit of care – like Lawrence.

'Can you believe it?' he said as Corin and I walked alongside him on our way to Philippa's studio, passing one smart gallery after another. 'My head is going to the heart of high society.'

Philippa's studio was on the second floor of a building, up a creaking, clanking lift that opened out onto a wide and airy space filled with scratchy expressionist paintings of men in their various forms. There was one on the floor of Douglas Hart, naked from the waist up and fishlike from the waist down; a mermaid, or, at the very least, a merman. There were phallic cacti sticking out of glazed pink ceramic pots, and feet and busts made of mycelium; fungal threads that were, Philippa informed us, very much alive.

Lawrence looked at them with widened eyes and backed away.

Philippa seemed supremely relaxed about it all, wandering around with a large bulldog called Marley and announcing that Lawrence and Corin could use the space for the grand unveiling of the head any time they wanted.

'Would you like something to eat?' asked Philippa, as Lawrence froze entirely at the sight of a fly buzzing out of the mycelium head and towards the kitchen. 'I could make some pasta.'

'No, thank you,' he replied, once he had regained his composure enough to talk once more.

'Yes, please,' said Corin and me.

'How about a pork pie, Lawrence?'

'I'd rather not.'

'Have a pork pie.'

Philippa produced an enormous pork pie of a golden hue, of the type that looked like it came from an extremely expensive Mayfair butchers called something like Block & Flock, and insisted on wrapping it in paper so Lawrence could take it home and eat it later.

Corin and I finished the pasta and we all took the lift to the street, where Lawrence rushed about the entrance to Green Park Underground with his gigantic pork pie, holding it before him like it were a bomb about to explode. He hopped across a street of beeping cars towards a bin, before thinking better of it. He placed the pork pie on a metal stand containing copies of the *Evening Standard,* then picked it up again.

'What will I do if she comes down and sees the pork pie in the rubbish?' he fretted, the offending item hovering before him. 'I'll feel bad about that.'

'Why don't you just leave it on the pavement for someone to find?' I suggested. 'That's a high-quality pork pie.'

'Have you gone mad? The rats will get it.'

Eventually, he settled on putting it on the bonnet of a silver Mercedes parked down a side street, reasoning not only that Philippa was unlikely to walk down the street, but also that the rats were unlikely to be so brazen as to jump onto a flash car in broad daylight.

'Well, what do you think of the place?' asked Corin.

'The moment that fly crawled out of the giant mushroom,' Lawrence quavered, 'I knew it was over.'

It was time to head to Margate, the coastal town that had been a traditional working-class holiday resort since Victorian times, but which for the last decade or so had become home to an uneasy mix of Thanet locals, Down From London escapees and Eastern European workers. This led to an ensuing blend of old-fashioned pubs with St George crosses, antiques shops in the old town bestowing the tainted patina of architectural salvage, and Polish supermarkets proffering cans of Krakus goulash and Knoppers nut bars. Margate was home to 60 per cent of Mozart Estate, which Lawrence named to reflect the tougher times Britain was now facing. At least we would be heading to Margate, had the train journey not been afflicted by the kind of disaster that always seemed to happen to us.

'Good morning,' said the voice coming over the Tannoy, which had in its strains that uniquely British ability to sound apologetic, bossy and defensive all at once. 'We have an important announcement.'

Lawrence sighed. 'Here we go.'

'Due to a lineside fire at Whitstable, this service will terminate at Faversham. Everyone for stations beyond Faversham will have to detrain and use alternative sources.'

'Detrain?' I repeated, wondering if this was a real word.

'I have been on to our control centre. They are currently trying to source buses from Faversham,' the voice, which I was interested to note had a West Country burr to it, continued. 'Alternatively, if you want to go to Ramsgate, Margate or Broadstairs . . .'

He stopped for a while, as if wondering where he was going with this.

'. . . You can get off at Faversham and take a train on the Dover service to Canterbury East, then walk to the town centre for Canterbury West. Please listen to station and platform staff. Once again, there has been a lineside fire. This incident only happened in the last twenty minutes.'

'Pathetic, innit?' Lawrence sniffed. 'Throw a bucket of water on it and let's go.'

That didn't appear to be an option for the train operators, so we were forced to 'detrain' and wander the streets of Faversham in the hope of either catching a bus to Margate or convincing Xav or Charlie, with Tom being otherwise engaged, to come and pick us up. 'He's got a car. Give him a ring,' commanded Lawrence, referring to the genial Xav. Once again, I found myself doing as I was told before wondering why Lawrence couldn't perform this basic task himself. 'He won't do it, but we can certainly ask.'

As it happened, Xav was more than happy to pick us up. But it was a forty-minute drive, he had a few things to do beforehand, and if we could fill our time for a couple of hours, he would be there by lunchtime. So we went down the high street and took in such sights as a branch of Wetherspoons called the Leading Light, which occupied a glass-fronted building with an art deco facade and was an enormous space filled with sturdy wooden tables and chairs neatly dispersed over a swirly red carpet.

The Leading Light appeared to serve as a low-budget, one-stop refreshment centre: it opened at 8 a.m., offered a full English breakfast in the morning to bangers and mash in the evening, and had unbelievably cheap pints: lager started from a little over the one-pound mark. You could spend the entire day in there and, from the looks of it, a lot of people did. I had the impression that, rather like those pubs in the airport where it is perfectly acceptable to have a pint at 6 a.m., morning drinking went unremarked upon in the giant Wetherspoons. From the wizened, angular man on crutches guarding the door with a pint and a cigarette, like a track-suited version of the gargoyles perched on Notre Dame, to the table of large women stabbing at rubbery fried eggs with insufficiently sturdy forks, nobody seemed particularly bothered about what anyone else did or who they were – and that included us.

'What an amazing pub,' said Lawrence, taking in the scene before him.

'I thought you didn't like pubs.'

'That goes back to Water Orton,' he said as we carried on down the high street. 'From the age of thirteen, all the kids could think about was the ultimate challenge of entering a pub. "Let's go to the Dog Inn and try to get beer." Water Orton was a suburb where everyone knew everyone, everyone commented on everything, everyone was so small-minded that you had to do the same thing as everyone else did. I came from a place, the city centre, where nobody was small-minded, where the kids on the estate accepted you for who you were, so I refused to be a part of it. I liked music, but if I tried to talk to them about it they went, "What you on about?"'

Lawrence's pale face stared hard at the pavement, as he appeared to undergo a bout of mental suffering at the injustice of the situation. Or perhaps he was reflecting on the concrete utopia of his early childhood. It was hard to tell.

'I was single-minded.'

* * *

I witnessed that single-mindedness a few days previously. Malcolm Doherty and Daphne Guinness were hiring a small studio in Abbey Road and Lawrence wanted to finish off his soon-to-be-number-one smash hit there, if only to say he did. The deal was simple. Malcolm's studio engineer, a youth of capacious patience called Ali, would take the analogue tapes recorded by Lawrence and Terry Miles, and turn them into digital information via an interface and sequencer, after which they could be edited, produced and mastered by Malcolm. For this, Lawrence would pay them a grand total of nothing.

'Classic Larry,' said Malcolm, looking the model of a suave record producer in his wide-lapelled jacket, opaque shades and silver rings, as he sat on a swivel chair and manned the controls. A giant computer screen was before him, alongside a mixing desk with so many dials, buttons and faders, you had to wonder if a few were just for show. 'He gets you to do this stuff and somehow you find yourself doing it. Ultimately, it is because he's an artist and artists need supporting.'

'Yeah, I am,' Lawrence piped up from a shadowy corner of the room.

'As an example of his behaviour, look at those keyboards I've got there,' said Malcolm, pointing to a wall of Moogs, Korgs, DX7s and other vintage synths. 'These are some of the most iconic keyboards of the late 20th century. None of them were right for Lawrence. No, he made me hire some other keyboard at £260 a day to get the sound he wanted. Annoyingly, he was right.'

'Yeah, I was.'

As Malcolm fiddled with the levels, Lawrence offered comments on the future hit as it went along. The keyboard melody had an '80s television theme tune feel; the vibrancy of *Match of the Day*, the hopefulness of *Tomorrow's World*, combined with the brittle energy of clever punk bands like Subway Sect and Wire, fused into a contemporary pop structure.

'Intro,' said Lawrence, raising an index finger as the song began – a single keyboard note onto which was added a beat from a Linn drum machine. 'I'm not going to say anything,' he added, before shouting, 'first chorus . . . get ready . . . First verse! Second chorus!'

Lawrence stopped his commentary to peer out of the window, where the usual array of tourists were either recreating the famous cover photograph of the Beatles on the zebra crossing or pointing their phones and cameras at the building itself.

'They're taking pictures of us,' he said. 'Someone must have leaked it to the papers. Ooh, second verse . . . middle eight . . .' A bubbling keyboard became the focus as everything else fell away. 'Break! This song has it all. It sounds like a hit, doesn't it? It is the best pop song I've ever done.'

'What is very interesting for me is the middle eight,' said Malcolm in a scholarly fashion. 'It goes from 4/4 time into 5/4 time, like Dave Brubeck.'

'Does it?' asked Lawrence, before adding, 'I mean, yeah, it does.'

'What we've ended up with here is the character of all these analogue machines interacting with each other,' Malcolm continued. 'It is retro to a point, simply because the synths were made in the early '80s, but it also has a deeper quality as a result of that. Most modern pop is made in the box, within programs in which nothing really happens. The benefit of these keyboards is that we can layer them to create a unique sound, but we're contextualising it in a modern way.'

Malcolm isolated a bassline to illustrate his point. It sounded like it came from a bass guitar, but it was entirely machine-made.

'We've got a keyboard called a U20, which is a really naff instrument nobody wanted at the time,' Lawrence explained. 'But it had one amazing sound, which is this bass thump. We used it on the

Denim records. Terry Miles and I were talking about how it made the best bass sound we ever had, so he bought another one just to make this. They're really cheap these days. Now we're thinking of the video. What I'd like is to have a bloke on a keyboard, with a girl dancing around.'

Malcolm asked with hushed, conspiratorial reverence: 'Why don't we ask the girl at Daphne's?'

He was talking about the will-o'-the-wisp from Daphne's launch in Belgravia. Her name was Nikki Kahr and she was a womenswear student at Central Saint Martins school of art. There was a moment of contemplating the possibility.

'Oh, wow. Imagine that. My video, starring the beautiful girl from Daphne's party we all fell in love with.'

'*You* fell in love with,' I corrected.

'She's a top model. She's been on the cover of *Vogue*.'

Perhaps this blue-eyed, blonde-haired, eyebrow-free beauty with the air of a homo sapiens from another dimension would indeed be the right person to encapsulate the song's words, which were about science, religion and the possibility that the human race arrived on Earth from a distant planet, although the title did not reflect this particularly: 'Deliveroo Delivery'.

'Are we from outer space or are we from God?' Lawrence asked. 'Did God make us, or did aliens come to Earth and plant the seed? That's what "Deliveroo Delivery" is asking. I've never had one myself and I doubt I ever will, but life is like a Deliveroo delivery because it comes and goes without a great deal of substance. And I've given it that title so it will appeal to kids who get Deliveroo deliveries all the time. Sometimes you have to think about the wider audience.'

The other thing about life and Deliveroo, I pointed out, is that both always end up costing more than you expect.

'I like that. And because the synths in the '80s sounded so modern, the lyrics to the songs would be modern too and they would always get visions of the future completely wrong in a really sweet way. I'm aiming for something similar. I'm also trying to get the word trilobites in there, because they were the beginning of the human race. Thermal vents are holes in the ocean bed that let out water at the same temperature as a kettle, which turns out to be ideal for life. This created tiny creatures that eventually crawled onto the beach, and here we are today.'

Lawrence's lecture on the theory of evolution inspired me to come up with a solution to the trilobite problem. 'How about, "When they crawled out of the sea / Trilobites gave rise to you and me?"'

He pondered on this.

'Trilobites have crept into the song, but they might need to creep out again because if this is going to be a hit record, I'll have to say goodbye to trilobites. They don't scan good enough for the top ten.'

Lawrence thought he had already come up with the catchiest song of all time, more than once in fact. He thought 'Relative Poverty' was a guaranteed smash. He was convinced that 'When You're Depressed' would resonate with millions. What stopped them from taking over? Perhaps the realism of the lyrics proved a problem in pop, which deals in fantasy, or at best in shallow visions of reality. For that reason, 'Deliveroo Delivery' was intended as an electronic fantasia, but as is so typical with Lawrence's songs, profound questions could not help but find their way in there.

'Originally I wanted it to be without meaning entirely. Then I got the idea: are we constructed or are we divine?'

'You're addressing an idea that keeps coming around,' Malcolm observed. 'It is happening right now with AI.'

'It might actually be a hit, then.'

* * *

Before Mozart Estate got to be playing their smash hit in arenas the world over, it was time to get to know them a little better. Xav did come to meet us in his little red car, driving us back to the pretty seafront cottage in Margate he shared with his girlfriend. It had an upstairs room, filled with musical instruments, where he and Charlie cooked ideas for Itchy Teeth, the harmony-laden sunshine pop trio they had been running since their early twenties. Xav also composed soundtracks for children's television, while Charlie worked, as Lawrence put it, 'with maladjusted children'. As Lawrence disappeared to wander the streets of Margate, I got their story.

Xav and Charlie met in halls on their first day at Southampton University, and although both were there to study English literature, they made a pact: they would form a band and become famous. They did just enough work to pass their degrees, then moved to London to play as many gigs as possible. Both were thirty-four and had a healthy glow about them, a product not only of a cheerful temperament but also of going swimming in the sea every day. They seemed far too young and breezy, in fact, to be recovering substance abusers.

'When we started, the people in music that we really liked got wasted all the time,' explained Xav of their downfall. 'The Libertines, the Strokes . . . We thought that was what you were meant to do.'

'It only became a problem when I realised I was drinking every day, just to feel normal,' Charlie elaborated. 'It was 2011, Amy Winehouse had died, and half of my body had gone numb. I went to a doctor and was told that if I carried on like this, I'd be dead before thirty. I thought, *That's me done*. When I came out of hospital and told Xav he said, *That's me done too*. We were twenty-two.'

'It was fun but it got out of control very quickly,' said Xav. 'Tom stopped last year and Rusty has been sober for decades. That's how Lawrence finally got his dream of having a band who don't drink.'

After four years of touring through Europe, Itchy Teeth got what looked set to be a major break: being cast as the band in *Yesterday*, Danny Boyle's preposterous feel-good movie about a struggling busker who wakes up one day to discover that the entire world has forgotten the Beatles songs apart from him. Itchy Teeth did make the final cut, but you need to hit pause at the right moment to get a good look. They met Paul Kelly through one of the people working at the film's production office.

'Paul had this idea for an Itchy Teeth sitcom, which never happened, but that led us to *Lawrence of Belgravia* and we got obsessed with Lawrence's music, Go-Kart Mozart in particular,' said Charlie. 'Then Xav bumped into Lawrence in Fopp on Shaftesbury Avenue.'

'I introduced myself and he went, "Itchy Teeth, you guys are famous,"' said Xav. 'We're not, but it is interesting that fame was mentioned in the first conversation.'

Charlie and Xav got to grips with the person they were working with. They learned that he didn't use the internet or anything associated with it, he was never without cash, his bags and his books, and although he talked about wanting to be an international superstar, they decided there was a more manageable level of fame within his reach if Mozart Estate got it right.

'He could definitely be a cult figure with a big resurgence,' suggested Xav. 'That's where it would be nice to help him get to.'

Charlie said something that reminded me of the Felt song 'I Don't Know Which Way to Turn': that Lawrence hated playing gigs, chiefly because an awareness of his limitations made him terribly nervous each time he was about to hit the stage.

'Singing in tune is an issue, but he's got enough competent musicians around him that he can just be Lawrence so who cares if he goes off pitch? He told me once that the three worst singers in Britain are Ian Brown, Shaun Ryder and himself.'

Charlie and Xav knew that with the help of the unflappable Tom Pitts, who had given up his job as a postman to more fully dedicate himself to the Mozart Estate cause, and Rusty Stone, whose rhythmic sensibility was as rock-solid as his name suggested, they could give Lawrence the best backing band he ever had. Their health and vitality would be a bonus: Lawrence was the dark and mysterious figure at the centre, so surrounding him with benevolence and light would bring that alive. But there were challenges, a big one being having to travel back from a gig, wherever it was, after the concert ended rather than stay in a hotel.

'I don't expect to be paid well from a Lawrence gig,' said Xav. 'We do it for the love of it. But I want it to be safe. I want to have a bed at the end of the night.'

'He made us drive to Glasgow and back in a day,' said Charlie. 'He has to be back home because of his OCD or whatever, and we can't even have a reasonable conversation about it because he'll say something like, "We're not that kind of a band." He can wear you down, talking about travel logistics.'

Xav nodded with gentle acceptance. 'His boyish charm means you find yourself accepting his demands against your better judgement, and we do like this man who made so many amazing records with Felt and Denim. One of the things I've noticed about Lawrence is that he'll be as interested in talking to the guy doing the door as he will the head of the label. You can't help but respect him for that.'

Lawrence could be generous in his own way too. That afternoon, he gave Charlie the Felt sweatshirt featuring a double image of the '60s superstar model Penelope Tree on it. 'He is not the typical lead singer type,' said Charlie. 'Rather than tell you about the last thing he's done, he'll ask you questions about what you've been up to. He really is interested in people, which is extremely rare in this world.'

Charlie, Xav, Tom and Rusty had all been playing their instruments for a long time, and all had a pretty good grounding in music theory, but Lawrence wasn't of the mind to take their word against his. 'All four of us will agree on something and then Lawrence will go, "No, it has to be like this",' said Charlie, imitating that petulant tone I knew so well. 'He'll describe what he wants in a way none of us understand. Or sometimes he'll insist on labouring on one tiny note for an hour until we all go, "We just want this to be over." That's how he ends up getting his way.'

'Do you remember when we were in that horrible crack den of a rehearsal space?' Xav asked Charlie. 'It was forty degrees, the hottest day of the year, and we were in this awful studio owned by a drug addict who sleeps in there when it isn't being used by bands. We had been doing "When You're Depressed" for hours on end when, for some reason, Lawrence decided the ending was terrible. It was exactly the same as on the record, the same way we had been doing for the past seven gigs, but that's him all over: getting completely obsessed about some micro detail and being horrible to everyone as a result of it.'

Lawrence was also, Charlie and Xav couldn't help but notice, pretty ruthless with the kind of fans who went out of their way to put on Mozart Estate gigs in Britain and Europe. The problem with the cult artist/alternative world is that it is so frequently run by enthusiasts on a semi-professional level, which is why it was not uncommon for Lawrence to blow up during a soundcheck after a live engineer, working on not much money, failed to meet his exacting standards. Not that kowtowing was the answer. They recalled a time in Denmark when a promoter had done everything he could to please Lawrence, right down to finding a decent brand of liquorice.

'And he'd be going, "You've got the wrong one,"' said Charlie. 'Now and again, he turns. Once, backstage in Margate, a mate of mine sat near Lawrence's sheets of lyric papers – not on them, near them – and Lawrence screamed, "What the fuck are you doing?"'

'It is an S&M dynamic,' said Xav. 'At every festival in France, there will be someone running around, doing anything for him, and he'll be as difficult as possible. There was one in Paris where he demanded the guy order a taxi and then he wasn't there when it arrived. And this is the same person who wrote a hand-written letter to a record label in Germany telling them to sign Itchy Teeth. Most people don't go above and beyond like that, least of all lead singers. He also told us he wanted us to do co-writes.'

Lawrence, doing co-writes? That came as a surprise. My general impression of his creative process was of one similar to Miles Davis:

the musicians could go off on their own tangents, but it would always be Miles Davis's name on the title. Likewise, it didn't matter if it was Felt, Denim, Go-Kart Mozart or Mozart Estate: no matter what contributions countless band members made over the years, it was Lawrence's vision.

'He's like Michael Jackson,' said Charlie, using the comparison in the musical sense, thankfully. 'He likes working with musicians who do their thing, then he'll put a hook line on top of it. He takes on a directorial role.'

Charlie and Xav felt the force of that role on a song they thought they had written together. Lawrence said he wanted something with edgy, punky energy, so they came up with a riff, got the rhythm, and Lawrence started chanting, 'Four brown men in a black car . . .'

Lawrence claimed it was an observational piece on young Bengali men driving up and down Whitechapel Road in east London in souped-up cars, not drinking, and frequenting fried chicken outlets. When Charlie and Xav pointed out that it sounded like the beginning of a racist anthem, he claimed: 'I just think they're really cool.'

'We explained how we didn't feel his message was coming across,' said Xav of the song that ended up on *Pop-Up! Ker-Ching!* as 'Four White Men in a Black Car'. 'Meanwhile, he hadn't given us any other direction beyond saying he wanted edgy, punky energy, so we wrote the music. When the album was about to come out, I asked Lawrence if we were getting a co-writing split. He said no.'

After being pushed to expand on his terse reply, Lawrence said he subscribed to the Bob Dylan method in which all the music was written by Bob Dylan, even if it wasn't. 'He said that Bob Dylan will come in with a song and someone else might write a guitar line,' Charlie elaborated. 'But that is called an arrangement. Lawrence had only the words, we had the chords.'

Xav leaned back on the sofa and put his hands behind his head. 'We pushed him on it and he claimed the lyrics, the feeling . . . that *was* the song, and the music isn't anything. But the music *was* something. Because it is Lawrence, we ended up saying we could live with it, but next time . . .'

Charlie and Xav were normal guys. They went to the gym, they cleaned their teeth, they washed their clothes. Charlie had his day job to think about, not working with maladjusted children as Lawrence thought, but with normal children and maladjusted adults: he did music therapy in schools and for old people with dementia. Xav had his children's soundtracks. Both had solo projects, on top of Itchy Teeth. It all meant it was easier for them to contribute to Lawrence's vision without getting too worked up about it and accept that his obsessing over details was part of the deal. When Lawrence made one of his regular visits to the factory that manufactures most of the UK's album sleeves in order to inspect the cardboard used on the Mozart Estate album, he got chatting to a foreman who had been working there for three decades. He said to the man that he must have met a lot of pop stars in his time, coming to the factory to do quality-control checks.

'You're the only one to have turned up in all the years I've been doing this,' the foreman replied. 'Come to think of it, there was one other bloke who came once, about twenty years ago. Strange fellow, kind of quiet.'

After a bit of detective work, Lawrence worked out who the foreman was talking about: Kevin Shields of My Bloody Valentine, who got so obsessed with achieving a certain timbre of distortion on his 1991 classic *Loveless* that he bankrupted Creation Records and drove Alan McGee to a nervous breakdown in the process.

It was a terrible thing to do. If anyone was going to give Alan McGee a nervous breakdown, it should have been Lawrence.

'There are a million things you can do with your life,' Xav concluded. 'Most people feel the need to do the accepted thing, but Lawrence has the guts to live life his way, according to his rules. These days, a lot of artists spend a lot of time trying to work out who they are. That isn't the case with Lawrence. He knows who he is. He is committed to the vision of Lawrence.'

* * *

I found the emaciated visionary in a bookshop on the sea front, peering into *Earthly Powers* by Anthony Burgess. The boys suggested going for a swim in the sea, but it was extremely cold, it was raining, the only thing I had eaten all day was a vegetable samosa bought from a market stall in Faversham for three quid when Lawrence wasn't looking, and it was time to go home. Lawrence and I walked along the front, where the multi-coloured arcades were filled with elderly men and women feeding coins into slot machines and the wind shelters housed lines of teenagers who shouted out various alternative terms for male and female reproductive organs as we walked past.

'Bloody depressing, Margate, isn't it?' said Lawrence as the teenagers delivered a parting message; the first word got blown away by the wind, but the second was definitely 'off'. 'The Itchy Teeth boys love it. Can't see why myself.'

In the railway station café, a sixteen-year-old girl tried to follow Lawrence's specifications concerning the tea-to-hot water-to milk ratio in a disposable cup. I told him about Xav and Charlie's comments, praises and gripes, and the first to come up was the travel arrangements.

'Number one, we don't have enough money to stay in a hotel,' Lawrence declaimed, with enough laissez-faire attitude to be able to stir his tea in an unchanging revolving motion without breaking the rhythm. 'Number two, I like to come back home. They may not realise this, but when you come back from Glasgow after a gig, there is nothing on the road and it is lovely. The last time we went up there, I was in the café by the morning, drinking tea at my usual table. We had a wonderful journey, we did.'

On that Glasgow jaunt, Kiko the driver was playing music as Mozart Estate soared down the M1. They hit the verdant climes of the Lake District as dawn broke, setting the fields and forests in a brilliant shimmering orange. From then on, the sun was out for the rest of the journey and they sailed through London like a schooner riding a gentle breeze all the way to the shore. Kiko, said Lawrence, loved every minute of it.

'What a driver,' Lawrence sighed.

'Two weeks later, he was dead.'

You wonder what would occur if Mozart Estate got a proper tour of the US, bouncing from city to city and hotel to hotel. How would Lawrence cope? 'It is not a question we have to answer because it is never going to happen,' he proclaimed. 'I'd love to tour America. Well, I'd hate to tour America, but I'd do it. Anyway, we did go to Japan once. The Japanese are fanatical about making sure you get over jet lag, so they book you in for two days before you even do a gig, with the idea that you will be fully rested before blowing their minds with the concert of the century. I refused, of course. I told Jack, our booking agent, to tell them that Lawrence doesn't get jet lag. I got off the plane, drove into the city, did the soundcheck, did the gig, the next day the drummer took me around the clothes shops of Japan, we went back, did the soundcheck in the afternoon, did another gig, signed loads of things, got up in the morning, went home. I don't want to hang around in foreign countries any more, because all the excitement was punched out of me the moment the rest of Felt refused to do the museum trips with me. I don't even know what jet lag is. Do you know what jet lag is? Is it real?'

Rather than bother to answer that question, I asked Lawrence about his attitude to fans. He seemed to think they were everywhere, furtive creatures hiding under rocks, watching his every move, ready to pounce with their albums to sign, their questions on whether he remembered having a chat with them at the Wrexham Miners Shed in 1987, their demands that he make their life complete and get Felt back on the road for one last triumphant tour of the world's stadia. He wouldn't, for example, reveal the name of the brand that made his ever-present white-and-blue baseball cap with the clear plastic visor, because he didn't want to turn up on stage to see a load of fans in the front row wearing it. He was always telling me what I could and couldn't put into the book on the reasoning that the fans wouldn't like it. He seemed to truly love these multitudinous acolytes, yet fear and resent them too. I recounted to him Xav and Charlie's tales of his treatment of various fan promoters in Europe, in particular the time he made one order him a taxi only to disappear when it arrived.

'They're talking about that guy in Paris,' said Lawrence, after we succeeded in not only getting on the right train back to London, but also in finding a carriage where nobody was interested in staring at us – a major achievement. 'We got there expecting to be met and taken to the hotel, but I went off to do something and when I got back, I found out that the guy didn't look after Itchy Teeth properly at all. He told them where the hotel was and they had to find it themselves. It took Itchy Teeth half an hour to walk to the hotel because he didn't give them any money for a taxi and, when they got to the hotel, no one was there to book them in. Eventually, someone came and they were told the wrong room to go to, so they walked in and a woman was standing there – completely naked! She was getting ready to go out and now she was faced with Itchy Teeth, at the doorway, staring at her. None of that would have happened if they had the promoter with them, taking them up the stairs, depositing Itchy Teeth into the correct room, ensuring there were no embarrassing encounters with naked women at the end of it. It was unprofessional. That's why I was angry with the guy and that's why I went off in a mood when the taxi arrived. I was in a mood with everyone all night, actually. It was terrible.'

As the train shunted through the slate-grey wastelands on the edges of the Thames, sometimes, inexplicably, with a horse on them – shadowed by the blank impenetrability of factories at the end of weed-strewn roads with high gates embellished with curling rows of barbed wire, I thought about how much was yet to be achieved in Lawrence's year of activity. 'Deliveroo Delivery' had to be a hit. Corin's bust had to find a home. Mozart Estate had to play a triumphant hometown concert before an adoring crowd of fans, ideally ones not wearing blue-and-white baseball caps. So much had to change. My fear was that Lawrence, for all his dreams of glory, would do everything he could, consciously or not, to stop those changes from happening.

Who could we turn to for advice and inspiration?

CHAPTER TWELVE

UNTIL THE LIFE DRAINS OUT OF ME

Vic Godard lived in a bungalow in Kew, a pretty south-west London suburb, wealthy but discreetly so, where the cosy coffee shops, tasteful boutiques, world-famous botanical gardens and row upon row of houses with well-tended rose bushes and crunchy gravel drives with large shiny cars suggested a place where nothing truly terrible could ever happen. In theory, a mad axe murderer could turn up here and wreak untold havoc, just like anywhere else. But it seemed unlikely.

'I've got a really good idea for an album,' said Lawrence, shuffling along the quiet street from Kew Underground station towards the home of the man who, in 1976, formed Subway Sect and in doing so became the guiding light for Lawrence's own immersion into the world of music as a conduit for whatever idea happened to be dominating you. 'It will be short, with ten three-minute songs leading up to thirty-one minutes, and it will be called *Minimax*. That's a good pop name, isn't it? A mini record with maximum impact. I'm going to include a song by Vic on it called "Hey, What's Your Name?", because he's the best songwriter who ever lived. I'm on a lifelong quest to write great songs and Vic is the master, so hopefully today we will convince him to teach me how to play "Hey, What's Your Name?". Along the way, I'll get general advice on how to write a song as good as Vic Godard's.'

Vic grew up in Barnes, a mile or two down the road, and has stayed in the area ever since. He moved into the bungalow with his dad in 2006, and since his wife died in 2016, it had been the two of them, Vic and Harry, living together, quietly getting on with it. Harry was 102.

'I remember you,' croaked Harry, when Lawrence and I went to see him in his bedroom. Vic, a figure as slight as Lawrence but with tufts of grey hair shooting upwards on a flinty head that brought to mind French philosophers and Nouvelle Vague film-makers, brought in a custard cream and a cup of tea for his dad. Harry was entirely bald, propped up in a hospital-style bed in checked blue pyjamas. His reddened eye sockets seemed to pull backwards into a hinterland between life and death, although his toothless grin spoke of mischief and curiosity and belonged very much to the world of old jokes and hidden strengths. Harry raised a hand, long bony fingers like knotty roots of an ancient oak, and pointed at Lawrence. 'You're in that terrible band.'

Seven years previously, Vic had taken retirement after thirty years as a postman and now, here he was, a mere sixty-seven, still writing songs that Lawrence considered better than anyone else's alive or dead, but finding his career as a touring artist curtailed because of a dedication to his very, very old father.

'I can't do gigs any more because I'm here the whole time, looking after him,' he said in a rusty, elongated moan, firing a thumb back in the direction of Harry's bedroom as we walked into the kitchen, where Formica cabinets above a blue-and-grey carpet gave way to yellow, red and blue linoleum before opening onto a garden with a bright green lawn and a bougainvillea in a stone urn. It was all very neat, normal, suburban, somehow reassuring.

To the left of the lawn was a garage that, Vic told us, contained at least 400 copies of a forty-four-track compilation he put together in 2014 called *30 Odd Years*. He put the kettle on and made us a cup of tea. It was the first time I had ever witnessed Lawrence accept a cup of tea in someone's else's home. Vic brought out fondant fancies. Lawrence passed. I accepted. We sat down at a small wooden table, where an old laptop with a speaker attached provided Vic with his current musical set-up, and Lawrence began his tale.

'I started looking at punk in 1977, but there was not much on Subway Sect until I went into WH Smith and I saw this.'

From his multi-use vintage WH Smith bag, Lawrence unsheathed an August 1977 copy of *ZigZag*, a British music magazine that, by then, devoted itself almost entirely to punk. Subway Sect's name was on the cover, but there was nothing inside.

'On the contents page, there was a line that said something like, "Oh, sorry about Subway Sect. They were meant to be in the magazine but we couldn't find a photo."'

The second issue of *ZigZag* Lawrence presented was from September 1977. Inside was a black-and-white photograph of Subway Sect outside a hairdresser's that offered a midweek 'Jubilee Cut & Blow' for £2.75. With their short, tousled hair, three-buttoned shirts, black jackets and grey trousers, they didn't look like punks at all; more like adolescent versions of Antoine, the naughty but philosophical boy hero of Truffaut's *The 400 Blows*. It was the image of the band, before he got acquainted with Vic Godard's scratchy take on the classic pop song, which did it for Lawrence.

'Bernie made us do that,' said Vic of the picture. He was referring to Bernie Rhodes, the nominally communist manager of the Clash and Subway Sect, who sacked all of the band members apart from Vic just before what should have been the release of their debut album in 1978. In the end, it didn't come out until 1980, several lifetimes in the lightning-flash world of punk.

'I loved all the details of that photograph,' Lawrence continued. 'The way you wore a T-shirt underneath the three-button shirt, the looping of your belt . . . I couldn't imagine what the music could be like because Birmingham was very behind London as far as punk was concerned, but I knew it had to be brilliant.'

'I did that with Television,' said Vic, who didn't seem to be affected by Lawrence's praise in any way whatsoever. Was he ignoring it? Was he embarrassed by it? There was no way of knowing. 'I saw a photo of Richard Hell and Tom Verlaine in *Interview* magazine, sitting on a settee. Tom Verlaine is wearing a budgie jacket and Richard Hell has a ripped jumper. I hadn't heard a note of their music.'

After the image came the lyrics. *ZigZag* published the words to 'A Different Story', an early Subway Sect song containing the line, 'We oppose all rock 'n' roll / It's held for you for so long you can't refuse'. Lawrence took the lines to mean that rock 'n' roll was finished, that it had been replaced by punk, that this was the new way. And when he finally got to see Subway Sect live, playing with the Damned at the Top Rank beneath Corporation Square market in December 1977, it was the greatest concert he had ever seen. Vic was wearing an orange mohair jumper, similar to the ones

Vivienne Westwood and Malcolm McLaren were selling for extortionate prices in their King's Road shop SEX, but knitted by his auntie.

'It was everything to me,' said Lawrence, now so excited he couldn't let his hero get through a sentence without interrupting him. 'You were wearing school-like grey trousers, but with a really flash jumper. I still do that combination to this day.'

For one song at the Top Rank, Vic read from a piece of paper because he hadn't memorised the words yet. It would be a major influence on Lawrence's own performance style. And he wasn't playing guitar at the concert because he hadn't learned how to do it: an equation of intention and knowledge balanced heavily towards the former. There were so many more aspects of Vic Godard's approach that reminded me of Lawrence. His friendship with the band's original guitarist Rob Symmons was cemented after he discovered that the caretaker of the block of flats where Symmons lived in Putney was Marc Bolan's dad. He chose the band's third drummer, Bob Ward, because of the length of his hair.

'It was not far above his waist. Bernie Rhodes said, before we found a new drummer: "Just make sure he has short hair." So we went for the bloke with the longest hair we could find.'

What became clear, as Vic Godard sat at the kitchen table and spoke in slow, clear tones about his way of doing things, was that he was as much of a contradiction as Lawrence. He was defined by punk rock, yet his musical heroes were Hoagy Carmichael, Johnny Mercer, Irving Berlin, Cole Porter . . . 'All the old ones,' as he called them. He had cult status as the ultimate outsider, but he saw himself as an establishment figure: he told us he had once been asked to recite Allen Ginsberg's 'Howl' for a recording and couldn't see why. 'Howl' came from the countercultural underworld and Vic was a regular guy, a suburban kid, the son of an engineer and a cleaner, not a bohemian dropout.

'I went to see Frank Sinatra in '77, right in the middle of punk,' Vic continued. 'Me mum used to give me and me sister some money each month to buy half a dozen singles and there were plenty of family favourites: Thunderclap Newman's "Something in the Air" was a big one. "Somethin' Stupid" by Frank and Nancy Sinatra was another. Rod Stewart's *Every Picture Tells a Story* was the first album I bought. I loved Rod Stewart . . . until he went really shit.'

Lawrence asked Vic about the inspiration for his early songs. 'I got it all from school,' he said, going on to explain how his favourite class at Sheen Grammar was French, so he took it from there. 'I got into Guy de Maupassant because our teacher used to read us these short stories. Our local library had all the scripts of the Jean-Luc Godard movies and I used to copy them for the songs. I wrote them in the free periods at school.'

Vic and Lawrence both grew up as working-class boys with broadened horizons. Vic discovered French romantic literary classics like Molière's *Le Misanthrope*, Lawrence went on a day trip to Boulogne and was introduced to *The Lord of the Rings* by Sue the Librarian and *A Clockwork Orange* by Roger the Neighbour. Both loved school; Lawrence for the rough and tumble, Vic for the education.

'I didn't want to leave,' said Vic. 'I would have stayed there forever if I had the chance.'

There was one major difference between the two men: family. It helped explain why Vic was living with his father, getting him meals and helping him to go to the toilet, which is something Lawrence, who had never forgiven his mother for slights perceived or real and whose bond with his father was shattered forever at fifteen, would have never, ever done for Josh – nor would Josh, claimed Lawrence, have wanted him to. Lawrence asked Vic what his parents thought about the whole punk rock thing, given it became a tabloid bête noire very quickly indeed.

'Jonesy and Cook came round for tea,' he said, referring to Steve Jones and Paul Cook, the guitarist and the drummer of the Sex Pistols. 'I did my A levels – economics, French and geography – so my parents didn't mind about the group at all. By the time Malcolm McLaren met us, he made us rehearse in a youth club for seven days a week from 9 a.m. in the morning, which made us good enough to be allowed to play at the 100 Club. Sid Vicious played our drum kit because none of the other lot would let him use it.'

There was another difference, actually. Lawrence thought everything he did, however bad, was fantastic. Vic thought that everything he did, however good, was awful. 'I only felt I could write songs recently,' said Vic, who had a new one called 'Until the Life Drains Out of Me'. It was about how he was trying to get back to where he used to be; how he would keep on chasing four-leaf clovers and let others – other bands, other people, other worlds – get on with the show as he continued to perfect his craft. 'I was never in control. I've been working with this producer and he said the other day, "You're bloody good at this, aren't you?" Nobody ever says that to me, probably because they don't think I am. I suppose I did think I was quite good at melodies. Even the Clash's roadies, back when we were rubbish, used to say: "Your melodies stick in the head."'

'Ambition', Subway Sect's second single, revealed Vic's attitude. 'It's really sad,' he said of the song, with its wobbling but dynamic organ melody and words about being a dried-up seed that cannot be restored. 'I sound like an old man who has given up on life, but I was only nineteen. I suppose it had a lot to do with not getting anywhere. All these other groups were taking off and we hadn't even made a record.'

Vic went on to write for a soul group called the Black Arabs, who did a fantastically funky rendition of 'Anarchy in the UK' for the soundtrack to *The Great Rock 'n' Roll Swindle*. In February 1980, Vic did a gig with the Black Arabs at the Music Machine in Camden, supporting Siouxsie and the Banshees, but they got so much racist abuse from white audiences that they fell apart. Lawrence told Vic that 'Split Up the Money', released as Vic Godard and Subway Sect with backing from the Black Arabs, should have gone to number one. It went nowhere.

'You were always the influence,' said Lawrence. 'I mean, how do you write a song like "Split Up the Money"?'

'Don't forget, after the band split, Bernie Rhodes was paying me £50 to write ten songs a week,' said Vic by way of answer. 'I'm a songwriter for his supposed label, but the whole thing fizzled out and hardly anything got released. Meanwhile, I wanted to get as far away from punk as possible, so I went towards jazz and swing on *Songs For Sale*. My upbringing allowed me to do that.'

That album, which came out in 1982, was one of Lawrence's all-time favourites: a collection of '40s-style crooner music, not something many former punks were doing at the time, which he backed up with a series of performances at a swing night called Club Left at the Wag Club in Soho. Lawrence quizzed Vic on the meaning of countless lyrical lines, on the kind of bass guitars used by Subway Sect, on trying to write material for Tony Bennett's television show. There was a song called 'Moving Bed', which

Lawrence was particularly fascinated with, partly because he couldn't make sense of the words.

'There's a line here that goes, "I may fall asleep while compiling a verse, I may set myself alight again . . ." I never understood what it was about.'

'It's about gear,' said Vic, who spent much of the 1980s on heroin, cleaning up in 1989 after becoming a postman, although he had a relapse in the late '90s after his mother died. 'I used to smoke it in bed and I put all the burnt bits of foil in the drawer of my bedside table. One time my mum came in to clean my room and went, "What's all this?" "Oh, I've been asked to make an artwork using tinfoil . . ."'

Before we left, Vic taught Lawrence the chords to 'Hey, What's Your Name?', which he wrote after reading the 1860 novel *The Romance of the Mummy* by the French writer Théophile Gautier. Finally, he wanted to make sure that, as a student to Vic's master, he had paid his respects sufficiently.

'To me,' said Lawrence, '*Songs For Sale* is unquestionably the best album of the 1980s. It has it all: the best songs, the best music, the best ideas, the tightest band. It was on London Records, which is great, because that's the label Denim signed to.'

'Yeah, it is good,' conceded Vic without a great deal of enthusiasm, before getting up from the little wooden table. It was time to change his dad's commode.

CHAPTER THIRTEEN

NO POOR PEOPLE ALLOWED

As the leaves turned from green to brown, as pavement corners filled with those damp pulpy clumps so redolent of the English autumn, Lawrence's fortunes began to change, finally. 'Vanilla Gorilla', an upbeat imaginary children's television theme of a song by Mozart Estate, was coming out as a picture disc single, backed by what he believed to be a revolutionary new promotional form: the lyric video.

'I don't think anybody has ever thought of it before,' said Lawrence as the train rumbled past the conifers of south-east London and a grey blur of rain splashed against the windows. 'It is the most unusual lyric video you will see, completely different to any others. The words flash up on the screen at the same time as the music. It is based on Lora Findlay's artwork for the album and it didn't cost any money to make because we didn't have any.'

I didn't have the heart to tell him that this was not exactly a new phenomenon, so I let him move on to enthusing about a new video for 'Primitive Painters', finally completing the proper visual accompaniment to Felt's greatest song, which was curtailed first time round.

'We've unearthed Super 8 footage from the mid-'80s. We've got Felt in Spain, Felt in Italy, on the road, all from Vikki's camera. At one point, she gave it to Phil King and he did some filming, and there is also footage of Vikki and me in Kew Gardens. Finally, after all these years, "Primitive Painters" will have the fantastic video it deserves.'

On top of this, the designer Rick Owens cast Lawrence to model in his new campaign alongside the communist fashion victim Ian Svenious, Saul Adamczewski from the South London grots the Fat White Family, and Peter Perrett of the punk-era band the Only Ones, a man to match Lawrence with his apparent inde-structibility in the face of a less-than-healthy lifestyle. Lawrence wore a Dracula cape, oversized black sunglasses, giant boots and a black baseball cap. The shoot took place over a day in Paris and Lawrence got paid . . . a lot. Certainly more than he ever did from the music industry.

'Everything was tip-top,' said Lawrence of the experience. 'Fantastic people, great money, and I'd like to do more modelling because it was an entry into another world. Rick Owens wanted craggy-faced rock characters only. It was the Mount Rushmore of ageing rock.'

Lawrence's life was turning a corner and maybe the year would not end in the way we had expected it to: with bitter disappointment. To celebrate, we were going to the place where he first glimpsed the possibility of a glorious future: Orpington, Kent.

'It's a secret world of rich people, no poor people allowed,' he whispered. 'I've never seen anything like it. You know when you come out of the wardrobe in Narnia? It is like that. On one side of the train, the normal people get off. But there is another, secret exit leading to rolling countryside and huge houses, all of them encircled and arranged in cul-de-sacs, so there is no way of getting into the place if you didn't know about it already. I need to show you the house I'm planning on buying and living in once the millions roll in.'

It was on the train, heading towards his new imaginary life, when Lawrence got a phone call from Cherry Red about the latest stage in an affair that could stop everything. Five years previously, Cherry Red had reissued all ten Felt albums in new gatefold editions, and shortly before the albums came out, the label received a legal letter from former members of Felt. They were taking Lawrence to court unless they received what they saw as unpaid royalties from the band's time together.

'Nobody came to me and talked about it,' said Lawrence. 'The letter came through when I was still working on the artwork and hadn't even thought about who got what. We didn't know how many we were pressing, how many we were going to sell, it was all so early. And what these people probably didn't realise is that we never made any money from the Felt albums first time round anyway. Whenever I asked Alan McGee about how many copies an album sold, he would say "Ten thousand". I believed him at the time, but as it turned out, he was just trying to make me feel good. Felt were selling two to three thousand copies at the most. Maybe *Forever Breathes the Lonely Word* sold five thousand, maximum.'

According to Lawrence, Gary Ainge got together with Marco Thomas, a bassist from 1985 to 1987, alongside, surprisingly, Maurice Deebank and the late Martin Duffy. 'Marco said to me, when I accused him of starting all this trouble, that Gary actually started it, which really shocked me because Gary was my friend.

They thought there was going to be all this money, so let's get the paperwork in place because otherwise Lawrence will steal it all.'

Why hadn't he mentioned this to me before? Why had he waited until now when the year was almost out?

'Because I have spent the last two, maybe three years in a constant state of fear about going to court. I couldn't mention it to you. That would make it real.'

Did Lawrence really have other people's money? Through the year I spent with him, from lugging sacks of pennies to the bank to watching him subsist on a Costa Coffee milky tea and a bit of liquorice a day, my conclusion was that he didn't even have his own. Yes, a tour came about, a record got made, a fashion shoot took place, an inappropriately expensive item of clothing got bought. But wealth, money, comfort? Perhaps he had talked about his fantasy lifestyle so much that old bandmates, no doubt resentful of his unquestionably controlling ways and tendency to push and push until they could take it no more and resolved never to have anything to do with him ever again, actually thought it was real.

'"He bought a flat with our money." That was one of the arguments. I did buy a flat in Birmingham in the mid-'80s, after getting a publishing deal for songwriting worth £5,000, but that went on the mortgage. "All those gigs we did that we didn't get paid for, he put the money into his back pocket." That was another of their lines. There was no money for gigs. Nobody got paid a wage and any money went into paying for the next gig. It might have helped if Felt had a manager, but I was unmanageable, like Morrissey. The truth of it is that if there had been loads of money hanging around, there would be loads of managers hanging around. But there wasn't and there weren't.'

We loped off the train and went first into the unattractive part of Orpington, where the bright yellow Walnuts shopping centre dominated the high street. 'It hurt me so much that they would think of me that way,' said Lawrence as we walked along the pavement in search of a Costa Coffee. 'Especially Gary Ainge. We met up in Soho, in the Coach & Horses, and I said, "What's this all about? Let's sort it out." I told him that if any royalties come in from the reissues, we'll share them. He said it was nothing to do with him, it was all Marco, and I believed him. Then this Marco guy calls me and I told him that Gary didn't want to be involved, and he said, "Well, that's a lie. He's the one who instigated it."'

Gary Ainge was the one Felt member who stayed the course, who was amenable enough to deal with whatever Lawrence threw at him. Felt's original drummer Tony Race had an apprenticeship, he liked football and, to cap it all, he had curly hair. It was never going to work and by 1981 he was out. Then, one day in Virgin Records, Lawrence saw a bit of ripped cardboard pinned to a noticeboard bearing the words: 'Drummer wants to join band, into Tyrannosaurus Rex, Cream and Brian Jones-period Rolling Stones'.

'I thought, *That sounds interesting. Who would write on a tatty piece of card and pin it to the wall?* Gary came to a rehearsal room in Balsall Heath, which we had because a cool guy from our village was in a heavy metal band called Money and they let us use their space. Instantly I wanted Gary in.'

Maurice Deebank wasn't keen, chiefly because Gary Ainge wasn't as good a drummer as Tony Race, but Gary liked Vic Godard and that was good enough for Lawrence. 'I didn't even know what drumming was and I didn't care. All I knew is that I didn't want any hi-hats or cymbals and he was accepting of my ban on metalwork, so he was ideal as far as I was concerned. I only found out, years later, that if it hadn't been for his girlfriend, a real full-on Black Country girl from Cannock, he wouldn't even have turned up for practice in the first place. She would force him to go because she thought we were going places, and when she finished with him, all he did was drink beer and play pool in his mother's pub. He liked photo sessions and he looked good, so I was imagining we could be like Marc Bolan and Mickey Finn in T. Rex. I was thinking about external things as usual, living in my head instead of seeing reality.'

Once the legal threat got serious, Lawrence refused to provide paperwork about the royalties before the album reissues came out and he refused to talk to Marco Thomas unless it was in court. There was a get-together in Birmingham for Martin Duffy's family, which according to his cousin, the fellow keyboard ace Terry Miles, Duffy spent complaining to the whole table about the situation. 'It got to the point where Terry's dad had to say, "Nobody else here knows who this guy Lawrence is, so can you shut up about it?" Martin was drunk and he was talking about me the whole time, so that proves he was involved as well.'

Lawrence believed, despite the bassist's insistence on how Gary Ainge was behind it all, that Marco Thomas fired the others up after reading *Autobiography* by Morrissey, in which the former singer of the Smiths goes into lengthy, bitter detail about the court case brought about in 1996 by the band's bassist and drummer, Andy Rourke and Mike Joyce, for a bigger share of the royalties. There was a difference, though. The Smiths were the biggest alternative band of the '80s. Felt were not.

'We were culturally big, influentially big, but we never sold many records,' fretted Lawrence, after we went into the Costa Coffee and he instructed another Costa girl on how much water to pour out of his tea to let the milk in. 'This bassist didn't take that into consideration. He was thinking, *Well, there must have been money, and it went into Lawrence's pocket.* The crazy thing is, he was the only person in the history of Felt who ever got paid anyway, because he came in as a session guy and we gave him £300 to play on *Ignite the Seven Cannons*. At one period, it all went quiet and I was thinking, *They're getting their case together. They have a big lawyer. What will they do to me?* Marco was not answering the emails sent by Cherry Red. I was waiting for the lawyer's letter, announcing, "You will be appearing in court, you will explain yourself, and you will lose all your copyrights."'

Perhaps, I thought, the old band members had a point, Maurice Deebank and Martin Duffy in particular. They were creative members of Felt, they contributed to the sound of the albums, and Lawrence, knowing him as I did, may well have not credited them properly. In this, it turns out I was wrong. In the music business, there are recording and publishing royalties, the latter relating to songwriting, and Lawrence shared songwriting credits where it was due. If 'Primitive Painters' got used in the new film by Martin Scorsese, Lawrence and Maurice Deebank would get paid. If one of those bossa nova-tinged tracks from *Train Above the City* made it onto an advert for Disney World, the money would go to Gary Ainge and the estate of Martin Duffy because they wrote them.

'These people are talking about the recording, not the publishing,' Lawrence explained. 'They're talking about albums, CDs, online platforms, but that's not where the money is. Maurice is still annoyed with me, probably because I tried to tell him what to wear back in the early '80s, so I wrote a letter to him explaining that he had never been denied his money and, what's more, we're getting old, so let me come to where you live and sort this out once and for all. He lived in a monastery for a while. I think he might have been working there as the cleaner. But I can't be sure because he never replied.'

Lawrence claimed it was never his intention not to share any royalties due, but because the four Felt alumni ganged up behind his back, he put his foot down and refused to talk to them. 'And this lot want equal payment for all members of Felt! Maurice was on the first four records, Martin came in for the second half, and Marco Thomas was only on a few. There are other people who came and went in Felt, who are my friends, who would never sue me. There was never paperwork for Felt anyway and I'm not going to start now.'

The call received on the train to Orpington made it clear that burying his head in the sand was no longer an option. We sat in silence outside the Costa Coffee as Lawrence contemplated his fate. What would happen if he went to court and lost?

He stared glassily at a gaggle of girls, tight ponytails flapping in the wind, pushing prams down the high street.

'It will be the end. The end of me, for sure.'

His big fear was that a judge would rule his Felt royalties were to be taken away forever and divided up between the band members. 'The judge might think, *Yeah, this guy ripped them off and now he deserves to never have any royalties again.* If that happens, I imagine I will spiral down into a cycle of doom, which will lead to the ultimate Wagnerian end. I won't see anyone ever again. I will seek out sustenance in another capacity, as I did before. I will lose the flat. All that will be left is to die a terrible death.'

An icepick to the head from an irate former girlfriend seemed like a suitable way to go. But who would deliver the fatal blow?

Michaela didn't care enough to murder him. Vikki was in New Zealand and still loved him, sort of. Rose McDowall moved on decades ago. What about The French Girl?

Lawrence considered the possibility.

'It did end pretty badly between me and her,' he mused. 'I didn't tell you the real reason why either. She would get really cross with me and say things like, "Why won't you touch me any more? Don't you find me attractive?" I *did* find her attractive. She was my type completely: slight and slender. But there was a major problem.'

He paused a while, as if wondering whether he should reveal it or not.

'It was as if Dracula and Beelzebub were having sex inside her mouth – constantly.'

What did he mean?

'There is a stereotype of French people having bad breath, and I can't tell you if it is true or not. Whether it is down to too much coffee, garlic and cigarettes, whether there are cultural reasons for the French keeping the use of toothpaste to a minimum, it may or may not be real. All I know is that I suffer from a terrible fear of nasty smells and it is a serious problem. It meant I couldn't even bring myself to say, "Hey, let's go and clean our teeth," or "Do you think it is time we started flossing?" But I can't think about The French Girl now. I've got to work out what to do.'

From his WH Smiths vintage multi-use carrier bag, he pulled out a piece of paper and a pencil, and started plotting, in block capitals, a complex graph involving names of Felt albums, songs, and band members. Lines went back and forth, Venn diagrams interlocked with family trees, question marks were scored against names. An hour later, he had the solution.

The graph marked out who played on what throughout the history of Felt and what percentage they would be paid accordingly. It was the fairest way, the only solution to Lawrence being sued and facing even more penury than he currently suffered through.

'I'll send this paperwork to Cherry Red and leave it with them,' said Lawrence, standing up and putting the graph into his bag. 'We're not talking Smiths money here, but this way they'll receive any royalties owed. Seems fair, doesn't it? They'll get royalties for as long as the albums are made, and once they've banked the first cheque it becomes legal and they can't go back.'

It might just work. If it did, it meant Lawrence had a reason to keep living. We left the Costa Coffee, walked back to the station and crossed over a bridge to walk up a narrow tarmac path decorated by the odd discarded Walkers crisp packet or nitrous oxide canister. Could this alleyway really be leading to paradise? Quite often, you did have to go through something unpleasant to arrive at a new Eden, like a dusty wardrobe, or a nuclear apocalypse. As we turned the corner, just as the rain stopped and a brilliant ray of sun beamed down, a heavenly suburbia revealed itself before us: Chelsfield.

It was a suburbia of mock-Tudor houses and picket fences, of colourful bunting strung across the roads, of postmistresses and parish churches, homemade lemonade on the village green and picnics by the old oak tree. Edith Nesbit used the train station as inspiration for her children's book, *The Railway Children*, and you could see why. Discreet wealth and comfort made this a place, as the chalkboard outside the local red-bricked pub had it, to unwind and relax. It was also a silent land. There was nobody around apart from the occasional builder, driving past in his van.

'This is the kind of place where you can guarantee at least four people are peering out from between the curtains, looking at me and going: "Who is he and what is he doing here?",' said Lawrence as we walked up the empty street. 'But the great thing is that in the UK we are free to roam. I'm allowed to walk around here, and in doing so, I'll come up with all the best song ideas. *Pop-Up! Ker-Ching!* was written entirely in my head, wandering around places like this.'

We came to the south London home that Lawrence was planning to buy when he won £72m on the Euro lottery, which would go alongside his other homes in the north, east and west of the city. It was a four-bedroom house from the 1930s with bay windows, a green door and a green garage. A patch of lawn set it apart from the road, and hedges and trees enclosed it on all sides. It wasn't flash, more a picture of old-fashioned familial respectability; the kind of house Rupert the Bear might live in. Incredibly, it was on the market – for £1.2m.

'I would gut it, take everything out, do the walls and the floors, and in the living room I would have beautiful speakers and a record player,' said Lawrence of his plans for renovation as we stood on the front of the lawn and peered in. 'I would come in, play a few records and go home. Maybe, in one of the bedrooms, I would have a guitar and an amplifier, but there would be nothing in the kitchen whatsoever and nothing in the bedrooms because I have always dreamed of having an empty house. There would be a Super Hoover in the cupboard, which I would buy from Terry in Welling. You know, the guy with the penguins.'

What about guest bedrooms?

'Nah, nobody's coming in my houses. Perhaps one day I'd have a party . . . but I don't know about that. I wouldn't like the floor to get scuffed. Obviously, I would need a gardener for a place like this, but I'm actually scared of hiring one because I would be easy prey. They might get someone to take over my house and then I'd never get them out. More likely I'll hire someone I know to come over and tend to the garden, someone who could do with the work while being guaranteed to leave at the end of the day . . . Bobby Gillespie, maybe.'

Lawrence also wanted to inaugurate in Chelsfield a Bungalow Protection Society, because the few remaining ones were being pulled down and replaced by hideously vulgar mansions with Roman urns on turrets and giant cars in the gravel drives. 'The thing is, it's going to be hard to find the time, simply because I've got four houses to go to,' said Lawrence, explaining how his new life would take shape. 'On top of this, there is my altruistic mission to think about. There was a period in life where I had to go round and borrow ten pounds from various people, so I would like to go up to them and give them a hundred grand. Or at least buy them a drink. Paul Kelly, I'd buy him a pint. Pete Astor, I'd buy him a bottle of wine. I always daydream when I come to places like this and I've been daydreaming since I was a tot. I used to run down the drive and imagine I was Georgie Best.'

Countless times through the year, Lawrence had complained of being lonely, of never having the buddy he thought he would have, of never meeting his one true love. I couldn't help but wonder who would be with him in his new dream life.

'I would like to pay a woman to accompany me for nights out,' he announced, as we went up the hill to a road fringed with high trees, huge houses hidden behind them: modernist white cubes, appropriations of gabled mansions, weathered family affairs. 'Let's say I've got this bloody thing I've got to go to, an awards ceremony for Greatest Pop Star of All Time or something. I could hire a girl to stand with me. Or maybe she'll come to Reading to see a band I've heard about so she gets a free night out and a bit of cash. If I need a drink, she'll get me a Coca-Cola. We'll be driving back home and I'll be in a bad mood because someone gave me The Look, and she'll agree to not talk for the rest of the journey.'

A girl on your arm, you mean?

'I don't want to touch her. I wouldn't go that far.'

He went on to explain how, after Mozart Estate do a show and he gets the front seat because he's the singer and the others are in the back, he doesn't like talking. He's exhausted, spent, nothing to offer, and if he were rich, he could pay the band not to talk to him. I wondered if he might also pay his female companion to be in one his four houses every now and then.

He took a few pensive steps down the suburban street.

'She would walk around and dust the table, or do the ironing, perhaps without any clothes on?'

He scratched his hairless chin. 'I hadn't thought of that. Now you mention it I will be investigating the possibility, once I win my £72m.'

Even if the fantasy didn't pan out, perhaps reality wouldn't be so bad. If the former members of Felt agreed to Lawrence's suggestion of paying for the tracks they played on, if the head found a home, if he could get on with making Mozart Estate a going concern, maybe it would be okay after all.

'We'll play with anybody,' he claimed, as we started down a public footpath between two fields but had to turn back because he was worried about getting his shoes muddy. 'Anybody who fills a big hall. If all goes well, the new album, *Minimax*, will be ready to come out next year, and people will identify with "Deliveroo Delivery" and get it into the charts. We want to go to Europe and the rest of the world, apart from the Philippines or Africa. Too many bugs and lizards. With any luck, we'll be promoted by Glastonbury onto one of their big stages, because someone of my standing has put up with a lot already by playing the Bimble Inn.'

He stared at one of the vast houses poking out from behind the trees.

'We deserve a shot at the big time.'

CHAPTER FOURTEEN

WAVE OF ADULATION

Martin Green found a home for the head. It was an ornate chapel in Fitzrovia which, with its gothic revival-style vaulted ceiling, zig-zag wall mosaic, golden fresco and baptismal font carved from solid green marble, looked like a spiritually inclined corner of Lawrence's brain. He had been to an exhibition based around the performance artist Leigh Bowery, another one-time Smashing regular, and realised it was the perfect place for the head: exhibited by itself, at the end of the nave, worshipfully placed on the altar. Martin imagined something similar to the scene in Ken Russell's *Tommy*, where Eric Clapton leads the faithful in the worship of Marilyn Monroe as a cure for all ills; the ultimate false idol and, like Lawrence, not the most saintly person in the world but still an enigma, glittering in the patina of fame. In the meantime, there were homecoming concerts to round the year out with: the first in Birmingham, the second in London.

Finally, things were looking up.

We were slapping along the rain-soaked Walthamstow streets, towards Rusty Stone's flat on a council estate where the van would come to pick us up, the band's new driver having agreed to go up to Birmingham and back in one go. 'Our new guy is called Dave Evans. He used to be in Biff Bang Pow! and he's really good,' said Lawrence, shoulders hunched, clutching his WH Smith multi-use vintage carrier bag, which was stuffed with pieces of cardboard and a copy of the Mozart Estate album, alongside a few other things I thought best not to inspect too closely. 'Kiko was great, but he was on drugs a lot of the time, which I didn't mind but it did make the other band members a bit nervous. Dave is a very straight guy and he'll do the long drives without complaining. After coming back to London tonight, he'll drive the Itchy Teeth boys to Margate, then he'll end up back at his house in Portsmouth. You can't ask for more than that.'

When I asked Dave about the arrangement that evening, he said in a quiet and unassuming tone: 'It is a bloody long way.'

The night before, Mozart Estate played a massive six-song session for Marc Riley, the former guitarist of the Fall who had since become one of the most popular DJs on the BBC radio station 6 Music. This was major news: new Mozart Estate songs, celebrated on the nation's home for alternative music broadcasting. I listened to the show as it went out. 'Poundland', 'Vanilla Gorilla' and the rest already sounded like classics, established highlights from the novelty pop underground. Lawrence, however, was yet to hear the session, so once we got to Rusty Stone's cosy flat, with its leather sofa in the living room and various guitars about the place, Rusty played the show back to us. Lawrence sat and listened with silent intensity, standing up, leaning forward, a question mark in a baseball cap. Having gigged extensively over the past year, the band sounded super-tight and ultra-sharp. The backing harmonies from the Itchy Teeth boys complimented Lawrence's reedy snarl, defeated yet defiant on 'I'm Gonna Wiggle', evoking punk aliena-tion on 'Lawrence Takes Over', capturing the indomitable spirit of gloomy people the world over on 'When You're Depressed'. A triumph, in other words.

Lawrence crumpled onto the sofa and sank his head into his hands.

'It's a disaster.'

'Whassa matter now, Lawrence?' asked Rusty, a pugnaciously solid, wire-haired sixty-one-year-old, in a bright but distracted way as he put pedals and guitars in cases.

'The snare drum,' he lamented. 'The snare drum sound is hor-rible. I did my best to get rid of it, but the guy didn't understand. Either he didn't know or he didn't care . . . about the importance of a dead snare.'

The guy, it turned out, was the BBC engineer in charge of the session. Knowing that, for him, a rattling snare was worse than a fork striking a porcelain plate or fingernails down a blackboard, Lawrence had taped dusters and J-cloths to Tom Pitts' snare drum, and then Tom had done his best to tune the snare up tight, but to no avail.

'To make matters worse,' Lawrence continued, 'the rest of it is great. I was even singing in tune. The whole thing is ruined now, of course.'

At least I had something to cheer him up with. A friend of mine called Matt Sullivan ran an American reissue label called Light in the Attic, which specialised in pulling out of obscurity great records that had fallen by the wayside first time round. A year previously, he asked if Lawrence would contribute to an album he was putting together called *Light in the Attic and Friends*. The idea was for artists friendly to Light in the Attic's vision to record cover versions of songs from albums the label had reissued, leading to Iggy Pop doing a menacing version of Betty Davis's hooker anthem 'If I'm in Luck I Might Just Get Picked Up' and the Hollywood father-daughter duo Ethan and Maya Hawke harmonising on a sweet version of Willie Nelson's outlaw country classic 'We Don't Run'. Lawrence agreed and opted for 'Low Life' by Public Image Limited, turning John Lydon's caustic eulogy to Sid Vicious into a punk singalong with added easy-listening pizzazz.

Light in the Attic always did a great job on the presentation of their records, so I handed over to Lawrence a finished copy of the album, with its kaleidoscopic cover artwork evoking psychedelic innocence, its red, blue and yellow marbled vinyl, its extensive liner notes.

'Oh, wow,' said Lawrence in a gentle monotone. 'It looks great, doesn't it?'

It seemed to have worked. We helped Rusty carry a load of gear out of the estate and around the corner where Dave the driver was waiting with a six-seater van. 'I take the front seat because I'm the singer,' Lawrence declared, hopping up beside Dave. As we passed the grey slabs of factories on the city's edges and the little houses between them, with their hopeful caravans in the drive and pampas grass beside the crazy paving, Rusty explained how he came to be one of Lawrence's most loyal companions. He grew up in Canning Town, earned a black belt in karate and went on to run the local karate club as a way to defend himself against the brutalities of life in the '70s East End. Then he ended up in the clink after stealing some shirts.

'It sounds a bit harsh,' I suggested, 'to be sent down for stealing a few shirts.'

'To be fair, it was an entire lorry load of them. We nicked the lorry and all.'

Resolving to go straight and dedicate himself to bass guitar, Rusty Stone came prepared for the challenges of life in Mozart Estate, but sometimes it got to him. After one concert, his bass pedals were stolen, setting him back to the tune of £600.

'Instead of saying, "Sorry about that", Lawrence went, "That's a pity, I was getting used to those sounds." There was me thinking, *Shall I hit him?*'

He did come close a few times and it's a good thing he held back: an upper cut from Rusty could have made Lawrence disintegrate entirely. A disastrous return journey from a concert in Denmark saw Mozart Estate end up at Heathrow Airport at three in the morning, by which point no trains or buses were running and the only option was to order an Uber. To drop Lawrence off at his flat in Old Street, and then Rusty in Walthamstow, came to a cool £160.

'I get Uber on my phone, the car turns up, and he refuses to get in,' Rusty recalled as Lawrence busied himself with the liner notes to the Light in the Attic album in the front seat. 'He was wandering around Heathrow with his head in his hands and I fucking lost it. I had tried to get him home, he didn't want to pay, the Uber got fed up and left, and it was the final straw as far as I was concerned.'

Instead of employing his well-honed karate skills, Rusty screamed 'Fuck off!' and told Lawrence, after anger turned to upset, that he couldn't do it any more, that he was pushed to his limit. 'Eventually I calmed down and ordered another Uber, which turned out to be the original one. We got in, not talking all the way. Dropped him home, but the final kick in the teeth came when I got in. Uber fined me for cancelling the first one – even though it was the same guy.'

Touring with Lawrence involved no small degree of sacrifice. Terry Miles opted to stick to co-songwriting after a concert where the promoter handed each band member a tenner to go and get themselves something to eat, only for Lawrence to snatch the money back and shout, 'You've come here to play a gig, not to eat.'

'It's awful,' cried Lawrence from the front seat. At first, I thought he was reflecting on the shame of that incident, but no. He was talking about the liner notes on the Light in the Attic album.

'They describe Mozart Estate as indie-pop,' Lawrence fretted. 'It is official: you can't win.'

'You are indie-pop, ya dickhead,' said Rusty Stone.

'Indie-pop is lily-livered music for puny weaklings,' he complained, in a feeble whine.

'What are Mozart Estate, then?'

'We're underground. Although I'd like to be overground.'

'There's always a fly in the ointment with you,' I said, jabbing a finger in his direction. 'Nothing is ever good enough. You only see the bad, never the good.'

'I'm going to prove you wrong,' Lawrence claimed. 'Before the year is out, I'll find something that will not be bad.'

'Good!'

We picked Itchy Teeth up at the house they were staying at in Ealing in west London, and after an impressive feat of engineering by Dave that got all of their equipment into the ungenerous space in the back of the van, we were off. Tom sat in the front next to Lawrence, chosen as a travelling companion for his willingness to stay silent on the long ride home. Somewhere around Milton Keynes, Charlie recalled a gig in the north of England where Lawrence went off on a mission to find individually wrapped mini Wispa chocolate bars.

On a stretch of the M6 not too far from Rugby, Tom detailed a concert in Manchester where Lawrence wandered off in search of Mark E. Smith's house, got lost, and had to be directed back to the venue by the promoter over a lengthy phone call, only making it to the stage in time with minutes to spare. A few miles south of Coventry, Rusty remembered Lawrence announcing that he wasn't allowed to use the open A string on the bass guitar any more.

'I didn't take any notice of him,' said Rusty, as he beheaded a pale-yellow jelly baby. 'I don't think he knows where the A string is.'

The venue was an upstairs room of the Hare & Hounds, a huge corner pub with a mock-Tudor exterior and an art nouveau interior in Kings Heath, a Birmingham suburb around 4 miles from the centre where Lawrence's early literary hero J.R.R. Tolkien once lived with his grandparents. These days, it was a home to an emerging coffee shop-frequenting, sourdough loaf-munching demographic that extended from Moseley down the road. As Lawrence put it, you were not going to get killed in Kings Heath. You had to head 10 miles up the road to Chelmsley Wood for that. There was a little room at the top of the Hare & Hounds with a couple of sofas, a fridge filled with no-alcohol beer, packets of Haribo sweets, Dairy Milk chocolate and some cashews and pistachios, while in the empty concert hall stood a youth from Wolverhampton who turned out to be Lawrence's biggest fan. His name was Charlie and he travelled from gig to gig with his girlfriend, always at the front, shouting along to the words of every song. Now they had formed a band called Me And Thee and they were on the bill.

'I offered Charlie a support gig. That's my altruism, man,' said Lawrence, after kicking Charlie out of the hall because he didn't want anybody watching Mozart Estate as they did their soundcheck.

'I wanted to do it for him because that's what the Fall did for Felt. At first, Mark E. Smith was very nice to us, telling a story in the back of the van about how Stan Ogden from *Coronation Street* came to give a talk at his school, but as it went on, he would walk right past me without saying anything. It's not nice, is it? I made a point of thinking that I would never do that to people when I got famous.'

They ran through the soundcheck. There were certain requirements: no white lights, nothing too bright, Xav and Charlie's vocals were to be at the same level as Lawrence's. His monitor must be placed up high on a chair otherwise he couldn't hear his own voice. Afterwards I went for a curry with the band, which was part of the pre-gig routine: Mozart Estate went to a restaurant without Lawrence who would never, ever come in, although occasionally he might stand outside and peer through the glass. Terry Miles had remembered a particularly generous concert promoter in Sweden who treated the band to lobster and champagne. Lawrence took one look at the delicacies proffered and announced he wanted to go home.

'His real genius is getting us to do this for next to nothing,' said Rusty as Dave the Driver handed out the per diems – ten quid per person – while the pilau rice and Peshwari naans piled up and everyone got stuck into the curry, just like any other hard-working band on the road. 'We'll sit there, listening to him talk about his favourite fabric softener, and for some crazy reason, we come back for more.'

Nonetheless, the punishing all-night drives, the lack of hotels, the to-and-from-Glasgow-in-one-go journeys were taking their toll. 'We're done with it,' said Charlie, stabbing his fork into a fiery hot chicken Naga. 'We've all got lives. Why can't we do two or three gigs in a row like a normal band, rather than going all the way there, all the way back, dropping everyone off . . .'

I told them that Lawrence said the band didn't realise how lovely it was to arrive back in London at the break of dawn.

'No, we don't actually,' said Tom, to the crack of a poppadum. 'That's what I don't like: the gaslighting. We stayed in this really fucking weird house in Rochdale . . .'

'Oh God, that place,' said Xav. 'It looked like a paedophile's hellhole.'

'. . . And Lawrence was going, "Just think of it as a funny story to tell your grandchildren."'

Birmingham was particularly significant, not just because it was Lawrence's childhood/teenage/young adult home, but also because he had set himself a goal with Felt to never play there until coming back as a returning hero. 'You have to *not* play your home-town. That shows ambition,' he said when we met after the curry to wander down Kings Heath and towards Moseley, location of his businessman's flat with the beds that came out of the walls. 'The goal was to play Birmingham Odeon, because that's where I saw T. Rex, Cockney Rebel and Television. When we were famous, we would come back and triumph at the Odeon.'

Unfortunately, it didn't work out that way and, instead, Felt's first and last concert in Birmingham, on 19 December 1989, was at a little nightclub called Burberries. It cost a fiver and 'Budgie Jacket', 'Ballad of the Band' and 'Primitive Painters' were on the setlist, alongside a cover of Lou Reed's 'Bottoming Out'. They split up afterwards. A few years prior to that, Dave the Driver and Creation Records' co-founder Dick Green came to Birmingham because Felt were touring Germany and the pair, acting as tour manager and roadie, drove the van to pick up Lawrence and the other Felt members from their homes. Naturally, they suggested staying at his businessman's flat, but Lawrence had other plans. As we crossed the threshold into Moseley, he pointed to an unloved building on Alcester Road; a large, shadowy, ominous hall of emptiness set back from the pavement.

'This place used to be a homeless hostel,' he said. 'I tried to put Dave the Driver and Dick Green up in it, simply because I wanted to see inside. I've always been into transients and derelict people in general, and I saw this as my one opportunity to go in there as a prospective room booker and have a good poke around. I brought Dave and Dick here, telling them it was a normal hotel and a very nice one at that, but it became pretty obvious something was up as soon as we got there because all the transients were outside, drunk and wobbling.'

Dave the Driver and Dick Green walked up to the entrance of the hostel, surveyed their proposed accommodation and told Lawrence to fuck off.

'See that road up there?' said Lawrence, pointing into the black of night. 'That's where my executive pad was, where I had to install the girl from Cockermouth into a separate bed, and where Vikki went into the bathroom one evening and came out dressed as Pat Nevin.'

We passed a mock-Tudor building, once home to the Moseley branch of WH Smiths, which impressed Lawrence greatly in his pre-school years for its wooden lattice facade interspersed with tiny panes of glass. 'When I came back to live in Moseley, they had replaced the original windows with plastic-framed ones and it was one of the biggest crushes of my life. It made me realise that, as a young child, I was a tiny aesthete. I must have been because even then I cared about what I wore. We always went to the seaside, once a year, for one day only, and I wouldn't take my shoes and socks off. My mom and sister would be going: "Get in here! We're paddling! What's wrong with you?" But I couldn't take my sandals off because they were leather with a crepe sole and on top of that, I didn't want to get wet. I wouldn't go in the sea because it was so messy and, besides, I couldn't swim. Still can't.'

Further up the road was King David Infant and Junior School, which Lawrence attended with his sister until the fateful move to Water Orton. When he was five and Beverly was six, they went to King David's on a bus without adult supervision. 'Can you imagine that now? I was dying to go to the big school because you would get a bus home from the city centre outside Rackhams, the Harrods of Birmingham. Every day in town you saw the schoolkids in their uniforms outside this amazing department store, grown up, respon-sible, and I would think, *I can't wait to be one of them kids*. But the dream was snatched away from me.'

As we spoke, vast swathes of kids and their parents were pouring out of a bigger school nearby, seemingly after an end-of-term pag-eant, or maybe a school play. Lawrence watched them disappear into the darkness.

'For me,' he said, as the children headed down side streets and clambered into the back seats of cars, 'it was all about the city centre.'

* * *

We only got back to the venue twenty minutes before Mozart Estate were due to go on, which meant Lawrence had just enough time to spin off into a vortex of panic. As the promoter arrived in the little room to announce it was stage time, the rest of the band duly trooped off while Lawrence, after performing the obligatory pre-gig ablution of cleaning his teeth, commanded me to tie the over-sized postage label containing lyrics and between-song banter onto his wrist. His fingers made a little flutter of dismay as I attempted to untie the knot in the string and inadvertently touched his skin in the process, before he announced that he had forgotten every single word, why had the band left without him, he didn't know where to go, he didn't know what to do, the whole thing was a nightmare. Then we went down the wrong corridor and ended up not by the stage but at the back of the packed and expectant venue, just as the band were chugging their way through a singer-free version of 'Lawrence Takes Over'. There was no choice but to grab Lawrence's hand and pull him through the crowd. I put on my sunglasses in an attempt to look like a big scary bouncer, but my authority was weakened somewhat by the fact that I managed to somehow end up with Lawrence at the opposite side of the stage to where the stairs onto it were, which meant we had to fight our way through the people at the front to get to the other side of the room. I guided Lawrence up onto the wooden boards, placed some sheets of lyrics and his copy of the album on a music stand, and scarpered off.

From there, it all made sense: this papery little fellow really was a star. 'How's it going, Birmingham?' he asked, before announcing that he spent his early years in Edgbaston and once worked on the market at Corporation Square. The Mozart Estate favourites sounded great: dynamic, cheerful, engaging, funny. Then, disaster. Tom Pitts' bass drum pedal broke; with no cymbals or other forms of metalwork to rely on, he really needed it. I assumed Lawrence would have a meltdown, but no. While Tom went off to borrow a drum pedal from the support band, Lawrence and the lads performed a drums-free rendition of 'Pink and the Purple', his tribute to the ultimate fizzy can drink from *Pop-Up! Ker-Ching!*. And when that finished, and Tom still hadn't returned, Lawrence used the opportunity to do a bit of selling. Explaining that the album was not available at the merchandise stand because he wanted fans to go to their local record shop to buy it, he pointed out that T-shirts and the picture disc version of 'Vanilla Gorilla' were on offer at very reasonable prices. Not to mention the cheap posters, which Mozart Estate still had an annoyingly large number of.

'I know in Birmingham you haven't got any money,' he pointed out. 'That's why we made posters for £2.50.' Everybody cheered.

After the concert, Lawrence went to have a cigarette on the street outside and an overexcited Black Country teen, who turned out to be the cousin of number-one fan Charlie, got down on his knees and proclaimed Lawrence as his new Messiah. 'It's the best thing I've ever seen!' announced the boy. 'I'd never heard of you before, but that's my life you're singing about . . . You're the best lyric writer in the world today!'

'Yeah, I know,' said Lawrence quietly. He pulled on his cigarette, puffing a cloud of smoke into a black night illuminated only by the cold neon of a kebab shop over the road, before adding: 'Tell your friends.'

* * *

A few days later came the London date at a pub called the Lexington. For this, Lawrence envisioned a revolutionary concept: both a matinee and an evening performance. It happened in theatre all the time but not, funnily enough, in the world of gigs, so Lawrence saw the matinee as a way for mums and dads to bring their children and introduce them to a real band, as opposed to the kind of sparkly pop stars who mimed along to backing tracks as their junior audience gorged on overpriced jumbo Coca-Colas in vast arenas on the edge of town. Lawrence announced the concept on Marc Riley's radio show, telling the 6 Music audience to bring their kids.

Unfortunately, the Lexington was not down with an underage show at all. 'Somebody must have heard me on the radio, telling everyone about the matinee performance and saying if any parents out there wanted to bring their kids, it's fine,' said Lawrence. 'Because they called up Cherry Red and said, "No! Don't bring your kids! It is not fine!" I thought it might offer a nice opportunity for the moms to drop their kids off for a couple of hours while they went to do the shopping, but apparently not.'

Lawrence had done a matinee concert once before, during one of the most disastrous episodes of his career. It was 2006 and Go-Kart Mozart were invited to do an afternoon and an evening gig in Paris. Lawrence got a live band together, featuring Terry Miles on keyboards and his old friend Johnny Male on bass, and although the matinee went off without a hitch, it meant there were a few hours to kill before the evening concert. That proved almost fatal.

'I got back to the dressing room about twenty minutes before we were due to go on stage and everyone was sitting around, looking a bit, you know, sorry for themselves,' remembered Terry Miles. 'Johnny Male was lying on a makeshift bed in the corner, and I thought he was just having a little rest. Then Lawrence said, "We're not doing it."'

Terry only found out later that Johnny Male had helped himself to some of Lawrence's methadone and it flattened him.

'Lawrence was refusing to go on stage because he couldn't face the idea of doing the gig without a bass player,' Terry continued. 'There were 400 people out there, waiting for us, so I told him I could play the bass parts on the keyboard. When he still refused, I said I would go on without him. That scared him enough to do it.'

It wasn't the end of the night's troubles. Celebrating the sort-of success of the gig, with Johnny Male safely ensconced back at the hotel, Terry and the band's roadie got through a bottle of vodka between them. Sometime in the middle of the night, the roadie, whose name was Patrick, duly mistook his hotel window for the bathroom door and plummeted to the street, four floors below.

'He broke every bone in his body and spent the next six months in hospital,' said Terry. 'Funnily enough, Patrick must have liked it in hospital because he fell in love with a nurse, forgot all about England and lives in Paris to this day.'

At least Lawrence could retain the plans he had for the Lexington's evening concert. At a London show earlier that year, he spotted three girls and a boy wearing Mozart Estate T-shirts, singing along to the words. Impressed by their combination of youth and fandom, he hired them to do their stuff at the Lexington.

'My core fanbase tend to be men and women of a certain age who shuffle around a bit but don't let go,' Lawrence explained. 'With any luck, these youngsters will encourage more movement in the place.'

I couldn't make it to the concert. Lawrence got it into his head that I had been sent off on an urgent mission to Belgium and it seemed easier to let him believe this than reveal I was actually celebrating my birthday with old friends. But over our year together, I learned something about Lawrence: he was the 'You should have been there' kid, to be found in every school. If he went to some event without you, everybody was there. If he went to a concert and you didn't, it was the best concert of all time. Even if he had a bag of chips without you, they were chips the likes of which nobody before had ever tasted. So it was that the Lexington turned out, inevitably, to be the greatest Mozart Estate concert in the history of humanity.

'Song after song, the place took off,' he claimed when I met him a few days later to hand over his Christmas present: a box-set of Bob Dylan's 1978 concerts at the Budokan in Tokyo. 'The Mozart Estate girls I hired had the required effect because there were outbreaks of shuffling in more than one place. More significant was something different to any other concert I have performed, something I have only ever previously read about in books: a wave of adulation. The audience moves you with their warmth and love and it engulfs you totally. They clap and they make these noises like "Hooray!" or "Yeah!", and it is overwhelming. It wasn't just, "Ooh, they like us." Oh, no. It was something bigger. Now I understand, after all these years, why performers cry at the end of a show.'

A couple of years previously, Lawrence, my teenaged daughter Pearl and myself made a highly unlikely group outing to a concert by the overarching pop star Charli XCX at Alexandra Palace in north London. After recovering from the shock of not having our own special VIP area, after asking why we couldn't be on a raised platform to the side and after I had to explain that it was reserved for people in wheelchairs, Lawrence did his best to get into the swing of it, having announced to anyone who would listen over the past five years that Charli XCX was his favourite pop star of the modern age. He certainly liked it when she commanded her fans to 'fucking dance, you bitches'. 'She's bossy, isn't she?' he said, sounding impressed. Then Charli XCX got overwhelmed by the love coming her way and started crying. 'She's lost me now,' Lawrence sniffed, dismayed at the display of actual, non-confected emotion cracking through the facade. He announced that he wanted to go home.

Now it had happened to him.

'Everything I said went down a storm, every quip I made was greeted with howls of laughter,' he boasted. 'It is a cliché, but it is impossible to describe: like heat, hitting you from the audience as 300 people hang on your every word. Usually, some people go to the loo. Some people go to the bar. At this gig, nobody left the room. *Nobody*. I was watching them.'

I asked Lawrence what he would prefer: love from friends and family or love from people he had never met before.

'Unconditional love from strangers is so much better than unconditional love from friends and family,' he announced as he stared into the distance, as if stunned into reflection by his own profundity. 'It means so much more. It is great to go to a town where you don't know anybody and get that kind of adulation, which is what Bowie and all those people found. He talked in interviews about it and I never really knew what he was on about. Now, finally, after all these years, I know what Bowie meant.'

CHAPTER FIFTEEN

COMING TO A HEAD

At Terry Miles's large, ramshackle family house in Hackney, as his wife and daughter crouched on the floorboards of the front room and put the baubles on the Christmas tree, we headed down to Terry's basement, stuffed with vintage keyboards, and listened to 'Deliveroo Delivery'. Terry's electronic melodies bubbled along with futuristic hopefulness, words about a cross on the hillside and a vapour trail of rocket fuel brought God and science together in a most unusual fashion, and I thought, *'Deliveroo Delivery' is too weird to be a hit and Lawrence surely knows it.* But in expressing something within him – in this case, the question of whether or not there was a higher force out there – and in containing the blend of good cheer, obscure thinking and bleak reality the fans came to him for, the song served its purpose.

'The thing about Lawrence,' said Terry, in a Midlands accent not so different from his subject's own, a mop of jet-black hair topping a round face that, framed by aviator glasses with shaded red lenses, suggested an amusing approach to life, 'is that he thrives on failure. I have a feeling he only wants to be a success once he's departed.'

Terry ran through the various ways in which Lawrence had over the past three decades annoyed him to the point of insanity. 'There are the times I've set all the gear up in the studio and he doesn't turn up. Or he disappears for six months and everyone is wondering if he's dead, only for him to reappear and act like he's been away for a day. He's a bloody control freak. He said once: "You're not allowed to play the black keys on the piano." I said okay, carried on playing them, and he was perfectly happy. He'll do interviews about songs we wrote together and forget to mention my name. There have been issues with money.

'You can say we have had our ups and downs, in other words, but on the first Go-Kart Mozart album, there is a song called "We're Selfish and Lazy and Greedy", so it's not like he ever pretended otherwise. And over the years I've learned to appreciate Lawrence. When I met him, I was playing in wedding bands. He taught me about the cool music world, the creative world. He taught me about the rules of songwriting, the way it works and that you can do it yourself. He changed my life for the better.'

As our year together ended, people were dying while Lawrence, against our understanding of medical science, lived on. Terry's cousin Martin Duffy, whose organ skills gave the later Felt records that swirling baroque richness, was gone. WH Smiffy, who played synthesisers on the Denim records and contributed to the melodic abandon of 'Before and After the Barcode' from Mozart Estate's *Pop-Up! Ker-Ching!*, died shortly before the year was out. Mick Lloyd, a Felt bass player who featured on their magical realist masterpiece *The Splendour of Fear*, died in 2016.

'He came home drunk one night,' said Lawrence. 'He forgot his keys, so he shimmied up the drainpipe. It broke, he came crashing down, he lay on the front lawn all night and by the time they found him in the morning, he was dead.'

How about those disgruntled former members of Felt, whose threat of legal action could have sent Lawrence over the edge entirely? The case was dropped. Maybe they realised it was a lost cause after he used the Mozart Estate Instagram site – run by an accommodating fellow called Marc, who had also taken it upon himself to flog the merchandise at gigs – to part with some of his beloved rare books to raise a bit of cash. Each one came with Post-it note descriptions courtesy of the owner. *You will not have read anything like this before – Ian Curtis knew and kept his copy underneath the floorboards!* went one to accompany a first edition of J.G. Ballard's *The Atrocity Exhibition*, on sale for £150. *The best English fiction book of the 60s – so beautiful – so simple – so honest – so revealing*, wrote Lawrence of Nell Dunn's *Up the Junction*, before quoting a few lines about a woman pushing a pram piled high with dirty clothes for proof. That was going for £60.

A life where you became hysterical at the prospect of a former girlfriend's innocuous anecdote about a cheese omelette being exposed to the world meant a life on your own, and there were few people who stood the course with Lawrence. His parents were dead. It was decades since he had spoken to his once-beloved sister Beverly, or his younger brother Sam. He had fallen out with most of his former bandmates. There would never be another girlfriend. There were people who *did* things for him, myself included, but were there any pure friends, companions without purpose?

'I've always wanted a special friend,' he lamented, 'and I've never had one. Someone to check up on me. Someone to knock on my door and say it is time to go to the appointment. Someone to pick up my clothes from the launderette.'

'That isn't a friend,' I pointed out. 'That is a servant.'

Maybe he did have his life the way he wanted it: going for a milky tea at Fix each morning, saying hello to the people he met in the street, getting by on not much at all, living with the freedom that comes with anonymity, having enough fans to give purpose to his latest band, losing himself in cult books and records, and, perhaps most importantly, keeping the myth of Lawrence going for more than forty years. He drove you mad with his selfishness and then surprised you with his generosity: over the year, he had presented to me, out of the blue, books he felt I needed to read including *Ice* by Anna Kavan, *The Duke in His Domain* by Truman Capote and that rare classic, *Crumpet All the Way* by Patsy Manning.

This was a man who screamed at his bandmates if they played the wrong (or right) note, then gave them a friendly pat on the back as they left the stage. His sympathies lay with the mad, the addicted, the penniless, yet some lingering vestige of deference meant he worshipped uncritically at the altar of the rich and famous. He was a celibate who went to bed at night dreaming of Kate Moss, an ascetic whose indulgences almost killed him, a man so controlling he wouldn't allow me to use the word 'just' but whose literary contribution to a book about himself was a misspelt text about reality TV stars on the streets of Brentwood. The world was one way and Lawrence was another and that, I couldn't help but suspect, was how it was and how it would always be.

I hadn't seen Lawrence for a couple of weeks. Like the tortoise he once eulogised in poetic form, in winter he hibernated. He rarely answered his phone. He wasn't spotted on the streets of Soho, passing by like brightly coloured smoke. If he did leave his flat, he headed to ever-more-distant suburbs, to places where he was guaranteed not to bump into anyone and have to talk to them about how his life's mission was unfolding. And before we knew it, the day came of the unveiling of the marble bust at Fitzrovia Chapel. Between Corin, Martin Green, myself and presumably Lawrence, we invited pretty much everyone who entered into his world over the past year. Among the people on my list was Terry from Welling, who appreciated the gesture but was not able to leave his beloved penguins; I would have liked to invite Ian from Holland & Barrett, that Dungeons & Dragons enthusiast who found the last few RJ's Choco Logs not feasted upon by the pirates of the Malacan Straits, if only I had a number for him. The people who definitely couldn't make it were the old girlfriends. Vikki was in New Zealand. The French Girl was in France. As for Michaela, she made her thoughts on the whole affair very clear indeed.

'I have no desire to see that sculpture,' she said by way of RSVP. 'I'm astounded it's been made. I'm amazed Lawrence still gets this much attention. I can't fathom it at all. Why does Corin want to make a giant marble bust? Why are you writing the book? Why does Daphne Guinness want to make music with Lawrence? Why did I go out with him for four years?'

I could only answer one of those questions: because he made you think about the world in a different way. I was under no illusions about Lawrence. His was not a life for any sane person to aspire to. But the year spent with him had taught me that he was someone you couldn't second-guess; you could never tell how he was going to react to something and that was inspiring in itself. Actually, there was a very simple reason why I wanted to write a book about him, and why, after twelve months of so many tears and joys, I came back for more. Because he was interesting.

In the meantime, there was a massive head to unveil. Martin Green wanted Jarvis Cocker to do the honours, but he couldn't make it and I was pleased – not that Jarvis couldn't come to the party, but there was only one person who should pull the shroud off and it was the slight fellow in whose likeness the image was made. An event of this magnitude needed a suitable outfit, so I wore a wide-lapelled suit in grey Merino wool with flared trousers and Chelsea boots: I was thinking Yves St Laurent, the streets of Paris, 1970. Unfortunately, the moment I stepped out of Tottenham Court Road station, a wild-eyed street person pointed a finger and screamed, 'The Sweeney!' – which was annoying, if perceptive. Nonetheless, I arrived at the Fitzrovia Chapel late afternoon to find the head in place, raised high on the altar, surrounded by hundreds of flickering white candles and covered by a black sheet. It had taken four men of Corin's brutal strength to raise it aloft, and now there wasn't a great deal to do but wait for everyone – including Lawrence, with any luck – to turn up.

Corin had also made ten miniature heads, ideal for the mantle-piece, on sale for £300. 'I can't believe it,' Lawrence had grumbled when I finally managed to get through to him on the phone the day before. 'The last thing I wanted was hand-made heads. I told Corin they had to be mass produced and made of plastic – something the fans can afford.'

'Like a "free-inside" gift in a box of Shreddies, you mean?'

'More like one of them superhero toys.'

I wasn't sure there was enough of a demand for Lawrence stunt-action figures to make the numbers work, but in the event there were Lawrence head postcards and posters, which even the most penury-stricken fan could afford. As Terry Miles played the theme tune to *Grange Hill* on the church organ, and Corin chatted to various dishevelled, straw-haired and, as it turned out, quite famous artist friends of his in the courtyard, I found a quiet corner of the chapel to talk to Martin Green, the curator of an exhibition named, with suitable inevitability, Lawrence of Fitzrovia, on why he helped us in our quest to put the bust on show in the first place.

'When Lawrence and I became friends in the '90s, you couldn't find rare music from the past easily. You had to hunt for it,' said Martin, a bear-like fellow with booming tones reminiscent of Bernard Bresslaw, the good-natured lunk of *Carry On* fame. 'Now you can get anything at the press of a button and anyone can become famous, which means everything from music to fame has been devalued and nothing is special any more. The idea with the head, and the limited-edition miniature heads, is that they are one-offs, rare and beautiful pieces, just like Lawrence is a one-off in a world of commercial pop and the Fitzrovia Chapel is a remarkable byzantine building surrounded by bland, faceless modern developments. I knew the head needed to be displayed on its own to bring a sense of devotion but also isolation, which is a state that performers inhabit. That, and the church scene in *Tommy,* was the inspiration.'

Lawrence arrived, ready for his close-up in a Gap Kids rainbow stripe balaclava over a baseball cap with a plastic visor and oversized shades, a Burberry duffle coat, white shirt and a blue Vivienne Westwood tie. He seemed strangely relaxed about the whole thing, like he had resigned himself to not being able to control the situation and now he was going to let it wash over him. There was no rushing around, no telling people what to do, no hopping up and down because the head didn't have, say, the right arrangement of candles around it. Instead, he greeted everyone with a little 'hi' and a slight nod of the head before going outside for a cigarette. And, before we knew it, people started arriving, more and more of them, an unending stream until the place was so packed you couldn't move. There was Martin Kelly and his brother Paul, whose wife Debsey talked about the purgatory her husband went through as he spent seven years trying to get *Lawrence of Belgravia* made in the face of his leading man's lack of reliability. There was Lora Findlay, who designed all those Go-Kart Mozart and Mozart Estate covers, however much Lawrence took the credit for them; a Frenchman called Fabrice Couillerot, who put together a book on Felt and designed those album reissues that had caused Lawrence so much legal pain; Rusty Stone, looking like an East End gangster from the '70s in his flat cap, shades and leather jacket; Dave the Driver, who revealed, uncomplainingly, that he had not got home until 5 a.m. after that gig in Birmingham; Caroline Catz, actress, director and unofficial parking monitor for Mozart Estate; Bobby Gillespie, moving about in his big black leather coat; Pete Astor, in whose house Lawrence had developed such a special relationship with Bill the Affenpinscher, and Miki Berenyi, who recovered sufficiently from the shock of seeing Lawrence at Glastonbury to make it to the unveiling.

I suspected the Lawrence Thief was also somewhere in our midst, but there was no way of knowing. And I realised, as Terry Miles pumped out the melody to 'I Wanna Murder You' on the church organ, these people were his friends. For all his claims of being a lonely guy, for all his dreams of being worshipped by strangers, the people who turned out to witness the unveiling of the marble bust were people who knew him, who liked him, perhaps even loved him.

I gave a short speech on the main thing I learned about Lawrence over the year: that he had a vision, and everything else had to fall into place around that. Then, without saying anything, Lawrence pulled off the black shroud to reveal the solemn figure underneath.

The next hour or so resembled nothing so much as the honouring of the sacred relic of a martyred saint. The faithful paid their respects with appropriate solemnity by coming up to the altar and circling the marble bust, albeit clutching a glass of cheap prosecco and nattering away to each other, which probably didn't happen in the veneration of Thomas Becket. It was, as one person after another took photographs of him standing unsmiling beside his marble counterpart, like Lawrence was attending his own funeral.

I watched him and thought. If Lawrence really did achieve the goal he had been announcing to anyone who would listen since his late teens, what would he become? Just another famous person, and who needs another one of them?

Lawrence was something else entirely.

Lawrence was a street-level superstar.

EPILOGUE

Down a narrow path, around the corner from the train station, near a stretch of shops with a Tesco Express, the Lavish Look beauty salon and the Water Orton Fish Bar, stood a row of sweet little cottages. Low picket fences separated the dark green lawns at the front of the cottages, which had been rendered and painted in complementing shades of magnolia, eggshell and tallow. The one at the end of the row had bay trees in terracotta pots, flanking a door painted in Farrow & Ball Purbeck Stone. The honeysuckle over the window on the cottage next door crept over and climbed up the drainpipe.

'My bedroom was the one up there,' said Lawrence, pointing to the far window of the cottage with the grey door. He gestured to the window next to it, the one closest to the honeysuckle. 'That was my sister's bedroom, and the walls were so flimsy that she could put her hand through and into Pat Potts' daughter's room. There, on the other side of Pat Potts' cottage, was where Roger lived. None of these looked like they do now. They had exposed brick and flimsy front doors and they were poky and horrible.'

The lawns, said Lawrence, were not there when he was growing up back in the '70s, back when his mother inaugurated the defining crisis of his life by forcing the family to leave the city for the supposed safety of Water Orton, 9 miles from the centre of Birmingham.

'It was all waste ground, overgrown trees and bushes, like a jungle left to rot. That's where we had the big bonfire on Fireworks Night, when Jonathan Hodgson turned up and was excited to be in the presence of my sister. See that?'

He pointed to a grand house at the other end of the lawns.

'That was a slum. Two elderly sisters lived there and it was like a haunted mansion from a horror film. They would stand at the gate like gorgons, waiting, as we came home from school.'

We walked through the suburban roads, past a patch of land where the parents of a boy called Kevin McGee, aiming for the kind of '70s self-sufficiency later captured in the massively popular sitcom *The Good Life*, kept goats and a pig. We went down Church Avenue, past the church hall where Lawrence had to deliver the news to his tearful, platform-shooed girlfriend Jane that he could no longer be with her on account of the fact that she towered over him. We walked along a mulchy path where the old library once occupied a wooden shed, the smell of the wood and the books first impressing upon Lawrence the idea that the literary world could be an appealing place, and over to the new Water Orton Library and Community Centre, which Sue the Librarian made her domain. We headed down a cul-de-sac, at the end of which was a field on the other side of a wire-mesh fence.

'That's where my sister was chased by the maniac,' said Lawrence, peering through the fence. 'She ran across these fields, which we called the Stiles, all the way to our house, getting tangled up in the brambles along the way. If only I were older and capable of putting together a good argument, I would have said, "Look, Mother, at what you've done. You almost killed your daughter."'

On the village green, Lawrence pointed out the spot where the maniac's red car was parked, alongside the patch of grass where he and a girl called Karen pretended to lose their virginity. He asked me not to use her second name. I said I wouldn't, on account of the fact that she might be a headmistress by now.

'She won't be. She'll be a chip shop worker, and probably a granny, still living in Castle Bromwich, where the girls came from that night. This is also where the skinhead marauders from Chelmsley Wood congregated, ready to cause untold mayhem.'

'You know,' I said, as children played on the slide and the swings, 'Water Orton isn't half as bad as you made out.'

'I didn't say it was bad. I said it was boring, which is why my imagination went into overdrive and why the horror of the marauders, and the devil, was all in my head.'

At the far side of the green was the old Water Orton Primary School. There were metal sheets over the windows and a chain-link fence barring entry, alongside a warning sign announcing that twenty-four-hour CCTV cameras were in operation; a rather self-important declaration, I thought, given it was highly unlikely anyone could be bothered to break into this sad and forlorn building. Perhaps word got out that Water Orton's most famous son had returned and he might want to have a poke around, to see what kind of a state the classroom where Mr Blank once read excerpts from *The Great Gem of Rikkenberg* was in.

'See that window there?' asked Lawrence, pointing to a metal sheet to the left of the front door. 'That was Mr Beesley the headmaster's office. It was really warm, with a lovely lino floor, and he had tea on the go, when I went in there to get the cane. He would take it out of the cupboard, have a look at it, make you bend over, and give you a good whack. Not everyone got the cane, you had to deserve it.'

Lawrence got the cane twice.

'It wasn't squandered.'

The bridge that connected Water Orton with the massive Chelmsley Wood estate was gone, eaten up by a vast construction site for a motorway extension. As we walked through the little village, from the grand new builds of Vicarage Lane to the council houses of White City – actually a handful of silent streets – Lawrence pointed out the homes of old friends. That was where Maurice Deebank lived, where Lawrence first saw the possibility of his vision for Felt, and over there was where Gay Jon first tried to convince Lawrence that he was intimately acquainted with Rimbaud's *A Season in Hell*. That was Nick Gilbert's house, where the future Felt bassist's mother would make toasted buns in the afternoon, Nick had his own record player in the bedroom, and everything was clean and tidy. Over the railway bridge was the Dog Inn, where all the teenagers apart from Lawrence wanted to go as soon as they could. Here was the home of the first girl Lawrence loved, when he was nine. Here lived a four-teen-year-old girl who went after Lawrence when he was thirteen, shortly before he dropped into adolescence, before self-consciousness set in, and suddenly he was no longer the beautiful little kid he once was.

'She was called Julie. She was the only cool older girl who ever went after me and my God, she was beautiful,' said Lawrence as we passed a wide, sloping house on Vicarage Lane, where the odd person could be spotted washing their car or pruning their hedge. 'Then I hit puberty and nobody was interested in me any more. Imagine if we walked past these houses and someone shouted, "Lawrence!"'

Nobody did.

We hadn't actually come to Water Orton simply for nostalgic reasons. We came because, having spent a year with him, I still didn't feel I had got to the bottom of Lawrence. I still didn't know why he fell out with everyone, from friends to family members to bandmates, why he couldn't share his life with another person, why he had never eaten an olive, why he was so, to put it bluntly, mad.

'I don't know myself,' said Lawrence as he peered through the window of the Dog Inn in the hope, mixed with fear, of spotting someone he once knew. 'I want to go to a psychiatrist to find out, because I don't seem to be able to handle it when something happens that I don't like. I was never beaten. I was never abused. But when Nick Gilbert made me a cup of tea and did the washing-up himself, I saw what a family could be. He respected his parents, and I had no respect for mine. My dad was a gambler, my mom was having affairs, our house was filthy and terrible, Lucy the dog not only stank but also attacked everyone, and everything was dysfunctional and embarrassing. On top of that, I was a headbanger.'

'A heavy metal fan?' I asked, surprised at this previously unmentioned detail.

'I banged my head against the pillow, from when I was a baby right up until my early twenties. There must be something in it.'

After *Denim on Ice* in 1996, shortly before his life began its slide into the abyss, Lawrence did get back in touch with his mother. Doreen was living by herself in a flat in Coleshill, not far from Water Orton. 'She was happy, and I was glad she was happy, but we never had any meaningful discussions. We never talked about what happened in Water Orton. I never asked why she moved us away from that brilliant council estate in Birmingham, or why she threw me out of the house so her boyfriend could move in. We never got to the heart of anything.'

Doreen died a few years later, by which point Lawrence was, by his own description, in big trouble. 'We didn't talk about it, but she might have guessed, being a mother, and I got her to cash cheques for me because by then I wasn't allowed to have a bank account of my own. She could have said, "What's all this dirty money?". She knew something was up, but she didn't say anything and that was nice of her. Shortly before she died of cancer, we met in Harborne, near Edgbaston, after she had been in hospital and could hardly talk. We had a cup of tea, she got on the bus, and I said to myself, "That's the last time I'll ever see her." And it was.'

At the end of our day in Water Orton, I gave Lawrence the man-uscript of the book and waited, with no small degree of anxiety, for the expected letter of outrage at the way I had portrayed him; at my insurrection; at Michaela's less-than-celebratory summation of his character; at the inclusion not only of myriad anecdotes but also the word 'just'. A few days later, a letter in familiar block capitals carved out in marker pen did drop onto the cork tiles of the hall-way, but it contained no complaints, corrections or clarifications, just a handful of yellowed pages ripped from a Penguin paperback called *My Child Won't Sleep*.

'This could be a key component to understanding me,' he wrote on the first page, having underlined a handful of para-graphs including 'The effects of stress and the anxious child', which pointed out that children are very sensitive to their parents' mood and will frequently blame themselves for troubles in the family; and 'Head-banging, rocking and other habits', in which the authors claimed that head-banging is a product not only of anxiety but also boredom, misery and lack of stimulation . . . all the things Lawrence associated with Water Orton, in fact.

Also included in the envelope was a card of some water lilies, on which Lawrence had written the lyrics to a new song. During a recent trip to the Hertfordshire town of Potters Bar, he had suffered the twin indignities of not being able to get a decent cup of tea and finding himself dying for a pee without a public toilet in sight, so he turned the experience into potential smash-hit material:

You can't even get a decent cup of tea in Potters Bar
You can't even get a decent cup of tea in Potters Bar
When I got off the train there was nothing to do
I had to wee in a bush coz there ain't no **PUBLIC LOO!**
You can't even get a decent cup of tea in Potters Bar

'This is one of the choruses,' he pointed out, helpfully.

The year with Lawrence was over. That didn't mean he was going to stop writing songs, dreaming of stardom, instructing the Costa girls on how much water to pour out of his milky tea, and carry on with the routines and rituals by which he gave form to a life less average.

In Water Orton, when we were standing on the railway bridge, looking down the tracks stretching out onto the grey horizon, I put it to Lawrence that he fell out with family members, ended it with girl-friends, and burned through bandmates because the moment he got close to someone, he found a way of throwing a spanner in the works. He refuted the suggestion. He said he loved it when people liked him because so rarely did he get close to anyone, and then he imagined having a girlfriend, a partner, to show his childhood home to.

'I tell myself I haven't met the right person, but it must be more than that,' he accepted. 'I walk around here and think, *I'd love to be with a girl right now*. But it wouldn't work, because it would only be a matter of time before she wouldn't go down the path I wanted to go down.'

Lawrence looked out at the Dog Inn, over to the library, across to the little row of railway cottages once occupied by Roger, Pat Potts and his family, chimneys poking up into the sky, oblivious to the lives within, past, present and future.

'I've got to walk my own way.'

What is the price of a dream? On the face of it, Lawrence sacrificed his health, family, relationships and, arguably, his sanity for art, fame, pop, the pursuit of a singular vision. Maybe sacrifice is the wrong word, though.

It was dark by the time we arrived back at the outer edges of London after our day trip to Water Orton. As we sat in unmoving traffic on streets lined by mock-Tudor homes, Indian restaurants and carpet warehouses, I thought of something Xav had said, of how there are a million things you can do with your life, and Lawrence, whatever the consequences, had the bravery to live his in the way he saw fit. Actually, I don't think he had any choice. Whether it was down to leaving the city for the boredom of the suburbs, the impact of seeing the four members of Television looking cool on the cover of *Marquee Moon*, or never having a special friend to call his own, Lawrence was destined to walk a lonely road. That road could be in Beckenham, Welling, Waltham Cross or any number of places we passed through over the year we spent together, but it had no beginning and no end and Lawrence would be walking down it for the rest of his life.

PRODUCT AND PROMOTION OF THE LAWRENCE BRAND IN THE YEAR 2023

Mozart Estate – *Pop-Up! Ker-Ching! And the Possibilities of Modern Shopping*
West Midland Records
LP and CD

Mozart Estate – 'Vanilla Gorilla'
West Midland Records
Lyric video

Mozart Estate – 'Vanilla Gorilla'
West Midland Records
7" Picture disc

Lawrence – Mini marble bust by Corin Johnson
Limited edition in silver or blue
Aluminium resin

Mozart Estate – Blue logo on white
T-shirt

Mozart Estate – Pop-Up! design on white
T-shirt

Felt – Four squares logo on white
T-shirt

Felt – 'Primitive Painters' reissue
Cherry Red Recordings
10" clear vinyl with new artwork
Limited edition

Felt – 'Primitive Painters' reissue
Cherry Red Recordings
Video directed by Douglas Hart

Mozart Estate – 'Low Life' (P.I.L cover version)
Light in the Attic & Friends
LP
Light in the Attic Records

ACKNOWLEDGEMENTS

With thanks to Pete Selby, James Lilford and all at Nine Eight, Matthew Hamilton, N. J. Stevenson, Vic Godard, Caroline Catz, Paul Kelly, Bobby Gillespie, Martin Kelly, Teri Olins, Ben Olins, Tom Hodgkinson, Nige Tassell, Lora Findlay, Jonathan Hodgson, Miki Berenyi, Simon Benham, Siân Pattenden, Matt Sullivan, Corin Johnson, Malcolm Doherty, Daphne Guinness, Douglas Hart, Pete Astor, Justin Anderson, Fabrice Couillerot, Terry Miles, Martin Green, Jarvis Cocker, Charlie Hannah, Xav Clarke, Tom Pitts, Rusty Stone, Michaela, Vikki and, of course, Lawrence.

Nine Eight Books would like to thank Phil Sharp, Dave Harper, Paul Kelly, Corin Johnson, Bobby Gillespie, Marc Ollington and Marc Riley for their generosity and assistance with *Street-Level Superstar*.

For more information please visit:
mozartestaste.com

And follow:
Facebook: facebook.com/mozartestate
Instagram: instagram.com/mozart.estate
X: @mozart_estate

4

5

6

7

8

9

13

14

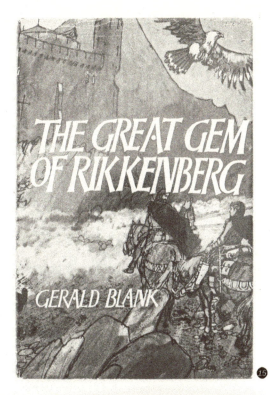

15

16

17

18

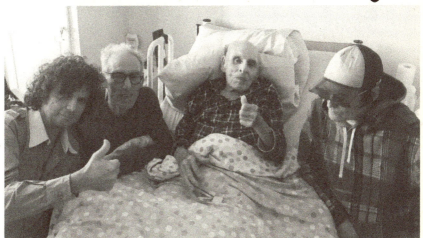

21

22

PHOTO CAPTIONS BY LAWRENCE, JULY 2024

1. On the bottom rung of the fame ladder. Before the Velvet Underground and Andy Warhol made their entrance into my life, I already looked like the coolest kid on the block. My sister's at the top. Photo via Boots
2. God damn – someone bought it! Photo by James Potter
3. My dream home in Chelsfield enclave. Will Bobby G. do the gardening? Photo by James Potter
4. Bitz of Glitz in Golders Green. Photo by James Potter
5. The broad-footed community of Welling buy their shoes here! Photo by James Potter
6. Terry proudly presents his electronics shop to two eager shoppers! Photo by James Potter
7. Terry's amazing emporium in Welling. Photo by James Potter
8. The beautiful Lawrence with the not-so-beautiful others. He tried but he could not crack the veneer of vanity – Felt, 1981. Mark E. Smith loved our curly haired tub-thumper. 'He's a good rock drummer,' he told me. But to my detriment I wouldn't listen. Photo by Paul Slattery
9. With Douglas Hart. The 'Primitive Painters' video is about to drop! Photo by Stefano Venturi
10. Vikki's in a photobooth with Martin Duffy! Photo via photobooth, Victoria Station
11. A Flower of Romance – Rose McDowall in 1987. Photo by Innes Reekie
12. Michaela – I guess you could say she didn't like me! Photo via Polaroid
13. At the House of Eve and Astor when I was in the Loft. Photo via Snappy Snaps
14. I love you Bill and I always will! Photo via Snappy Snaps
15. The hardback that laid a foundation for my interest in commerce and art at a young age. Photo by James Potter
16. Drop Fruit Duos – the best sweets in the world – ever! Photo by James Potter
17. Recording 'Deliveroo Delivery' at Abbey Road with Malcolm Powder at the controls. Photo via smartphone
18. Considering the great trilobite problem. Photo via smartphone
19. Vic Godard's dad. Mr Godard is 104 years old! He outlived the Queen who sent him a personal message. Photo by Paul Kelly
20. The writer – the singer – the father – and me. Photo by Will Hodgkinson
21. Tom Pitts at the traps. He says 'Yes boss' whenever I ask him to do something for me. With manners like that this boy will go far! Photo by Elspeth Moore
22. The great Rusty Stone. A real East-Ender. Once he'd done his bird he went straight! Photo by Elspeth Moore
23. A Hollywood pin-up? No, it's Charlie Teeth innit! Photo by Elspeth Moore
24. The Final Resting Place of Xav Clarke. Bringing the show to a mammoth crescendo! Photo by Elspeth Moore
25. About to unveil the marble head. The black shroud is lifted . . . Photo by James Potter
26. The sculptor and his muse. Photo by Paul Cox
27. . . . the audience gasp – then explode with delight! It's a Fellini scene on opening night. Photo by Stefano Venturi
28. The marble head by Corin Johnson at Fitzrovia Chapel. Photo by James Potter